Two-Stroke Motorcycle Engine Maintenance and Repair

Two-Stroke Motorcycle Engine Maintenance and Repair

Dave Boothroyd

THE CROWOOD PRESS

First published in 2016 by
The Crowood Press Ltd
Ramsbury, Marlborough
Wiltshire SN8 2HR

www.crowood.com

British Library Cataloguing-in-Publication Data
A catalogue record for this book is available from the British Library.

ISBN 978 1 78500 120 8

Disclaimer
Safety is of the utmost importance in every aspect of an automotive workshop. The practical
procedures and the tools and equipment used in automotive workshops are potentially
dangerous. Tools should be used in strict accordance with the manufacturer's recommended
procedures and current health and safety regulations. The author and publisher cannot accept
responsibility for any accident or injury caused by following the advice given in this book.

Frontispiece: Kawasaki KMX125 engine

Typeset by Jean Cussons Typesetting, Diss, Norfolk

Printed and bound in Malaysia by Times Offset (M) Sdn Bhd

contents

acknowledgements

This book would not have been possible without the help of the people who were good enough to lend me their bikes or engines to work on. Heartfelt thanks to the following:

For the Francis Barnett Seagull, my late cousin Bill Westwood of Wakefield.
For the Greeves Sportsman racer, BS Paints of Cobridge, Stoke-on-Trent.
For the Lambretta Li 125, Ken Rome of Biddulph, Staffs.
For the Vespa 90SS, Andrew Butler of the Vespa Club of Britain.
For the Yamaha FS1-E, Per Brandt of the FS1-E Owners Club.
For the RD350LC and RZ250, Norbo Lea of RD LC Crazy and UK 2 Strokes.
For the Kawasaki S2, DK Motorcycles of Newcastle-under-Lyme.
For the Kawasaki KMX, Anthony Goodwin of Stoke-on-Trent.
For the Honda RS125 and TZ350, Marcus Brown of Poynton, Cheshire.

Thanks for valuable advice and help from: Dave Rushton (Engines) of Burslem, Stoke-on-Trent; DK Motorcycles of Newcastle-under-Lyme; Niphos Chrome Plating of Crewe, Cheshire; The British Two Stroke Club (www.britishtwostrokeclub.org.uk); The Francis-Barnett Owners Club (www.francis-barnett.co.uk); The FS1-E Owners Club (www.fs1eoc.co.uk); Lambretta Club Great Britain (www.ilambretta.co.uk); RDLC Crazy (www.rdlccrazy.co.uk); The Scott Owners' Club (www.scottownersclub.org); The Vespa Club of Britain (www.vespaclubofbritain.co.uk); Villiers Services of Merry Hill, Brierley Hill, West Midlands.

Of course, the book would have been very plain without all the photographs that I was able to take of bikes belonging to exhibitors at the Stafford Classics Show. These include, among many others: Allen's Performance Ltd (RSW engine and Reverse Cylinder TZR engine); Excelsior Talisman Enthusiasts (Excelsior Talisman and engine parts); Fastline Motorcycles (NSR 250); Greeves Riders Association (various Greeves bikes); John Cook (Villiers 8E engine); Martin Plummer (Maicoletta); Stafford Motorcycles (Aprilia RS250); Steve Lawton Racing (125 Seel Racer); The Bike Specialists (Kawasaki H2 and Bimota V Due); BSA Bantam Club (various Bantams); The Scott Owners' Club; Triples Workshop (Kawasaki H1).

Also thanks to the many people who were happy to have pictures included without wanting any acknowledgement.

introduction

In his introduction to *The Two Stroke Engine* (1916 edition), Dr A.M. Low wrote:

> The object of this book is to write in an absolutely non-technical vein, and this should not be a disadvantage even to those who are experts, the idea being to touch upon the most interesting and practical points connected with two stroke engines.

Nearly a hundred years later, in the age of digital ignition and electronically controlled fuel injection systems, the same approach is still relevant, so that is what I have tried to do in this book. Sometimes, to provide an understanding of the reasons for certain procedures and processes, the underlying technical and mathematical basis must be explained. Equations are the most concise way of doing this, but they are accompanied by a simplified verbal description. You will not need a calculator or a computer spreadsheet to use this book, or anything beyond basic arithmetic and geometry. Anyone who seriously wants to become involved in engine development will find that the required level of scientific and mathematical knowledge and skill increases rapidly, and that a computer is as vital a tool as a socket set these days.

This is a step-by-step guide to working on two stroke motorcycle engines, so the mathematical complexity that lies behind these beautifully simple engines has no place here.

Although I have books in my two-stroke library that go back to the early years of the twentieth century, my own youthful fascination with two-strokes began in the very early 1960s, when I was taken to watch a sprint competition on the old airfield at Sherburn in Elmet, near Leeds. Top billing at the event went to George Brown riding the record-breaking Super Nero, an awe-inspiring 1500cc supercharged Vincent of utterly minimal chassis construction.

The memory that stood out from the meeting, though, was the sound of an Ariel Arrow, tuned by George and his brother, and ridden by his son Tony. The wail of the 250cc two-stroke twin, like ripping great sheets of cloth, has stayed with me to this day – it was definitely a case of love at first hearing.

There is no doubting the enthusiasm of two-stroke lovers. Evidence of this can be seen in the dozens of web-based groups all around the world. I suspect that the enthusiasm of the fans might come from the enthusiastic style with which a two-stroke delivers its power. For many years, during my racing days, it was the moment, often very early in the season, when the motor first came on to the power band for first practice that marked the end of winter and the start of a new year. The exhaust note would harden, the tachometer needle would swing and the bike would surge forward as if it too had been waiting for that moment. For many of us, two-stroke motorcycles are pure sensory pleasure. How could you fail to love that?

As we move into the second decade of the twenty-first century, there are far fewer opportunities to own a new two-stroke motorcycle. Personally, I am not convinced that there is any rational argument for this, but here is not the place to debate the political or technical issues. The fact remains that the majority of readers of this book will be seeking information and guidance on older machinery. That is not to say that two-stroke development is not continuing, for it can be seen in more specialized areas of the market, such as 50cc scooters and off-road bikes. Moreover, beyond the two-wheeled world, there are some signs of a revival of two-strokes.

A glance at the contents will indicate that this book attempts to cover a wide range of machines, from vintage to modern. While lecturing on motorcycle engineering to young apprentices about to enter the dealer chain, it soon became clear that many of the aspects of older machinery, which are familiar to me and people of my age, are a completely closed book to those whose experience is limited to much more modern bikes. I was fortunate to be a second-generation motorcyclist. So, thanks to my father, tales of Dunelts and Sunbeams and the bikes of the pre-war era were also a part of my experience. This book has been written from the viewpoint of those former students. Modern technology and techniques haven been taken as the norm, and the earlier ones assumed to be unfamiliar.

Clearly, a full description of every model from around the world and over a hundred years of history would require something along the lines of an encyclopedia, so this book concentrates on typical examples, or engines that an owner or restorer is likely to come across.

Conventions

Throughout this book, the conventions are as follows:

- A metric thread of 10mm diameter is referred to as 'M10'.
- A metric spanner measuring 10mm across flats is referred to as a '10mm spanner'.
- Imperial spanners are referred to by the thread size and pitch: for example, 3/8in BSF or 3/8in × 26tpi.
- British terms are used throughout: 'gudgeon pin' rather than 'wrist pin'. The origins of the word 'gudgeon' are so delightfully rude and Anglo Saxon that it would be a shame to lose it.
- Wherever possible, the use of colloquial or personal terms for items has been avoided: for example, 'cylinder', not 'barrel', 'pot' or 'jug'.
- Imperial units are only used for items that have been designed to those measurements, with the exception of torque wrench settings, since torque wrenches may not have Nm or lb ft markings.

pre-war two-strokes: transport for the working man
Francis-Barnett 250 Seagull (Villiers 14A)

Those who are familiar only with engines from the last few decades will find some very unfamiliar aspects to these early engines, so perhaps a brief introduction to their history will help explain why they are so different.

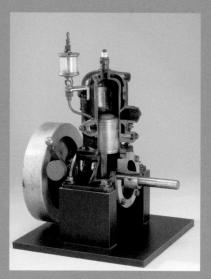

Fig. 1.1   Joseph Day's engine. (Copyright Science Museum)

TWO-STROKE ORIGINS

The very first two-stroke engines appeared in the early 1800s. They were mostly stationary gas engines based on steam engine practice. The most common design had two cylinders, one of which was needed to pump air and gas into the working cylinder, which contained the combustion process. In using the word 'gas', I am not employing the abbreviation for the American word 'gasoline'; I am referring to the town gas, or coal gas, that supplied the domestic lighting and streetlamps of the mid-1800s. The designers of the majority of these early engines have been largely forgotten, but it was on their work that memorable inventors based the designs that have become known as the Otto cycle, the Clerk cycle and the Day cycle.

Nikolaus Otto is regarded as the originator of the four-stroke engine, although at least two patents of the idea were registered a year before his own.

Two years after Otto's engine was produced, Dugald Clerk built and patented his two-stroke engine. Like the earlier engines, it employed a pumping cylinder to fill the working cylinder and had four-stroke-style poppet valves. Where motorcycling is concerned, the Clerk cycle engine seems like a blind alley, but with the addition of modern supercharging arrangements, Clerk cycle two-strokes represent the majority of big marine diesel engines in ships. Those who have worked with heavy construction plant will probably recall the Detroit diesels and similar designs of industrial diesel two-strokes, too.

In 1894, Joseph Day, of Bath, patented a two-stroke of the type we know from motorcycles. The fact that he was running a company producing the 'Valveless Air Compressor' gives a clue to where the idea may have origi-

nated. In fact, Day's very first design used a form of flap valve in the crown of the piston. It was his works foreman, Frederick Cock, who devised the three-port arrangement, adding the transfer port, which was the vital step to the two-stroke as we know it.

In *The Two-Stroke Engine* by Dr A.M. Low, subtitled 'A manual of the coming form of internal combustion engine' (Temple Press, 1916), the author describes a large number of odd variations of two-stroke design, many of which, I suspect, never went beyond the drawing board. By the end of the First World War, however, in practice two-stroke design had settled on the basic three-port layout.

There was an inlet port, low on the cylinder wall and controlled by the piston skirt; a single transfer port at the back of the cylinder; and a single, or sometimes double, exhaust port on the opposite, front wall of the cylinder. To prevent the incoming mixture from the transfer port from going straight down the exhaust, a deflector or baffle was cast into the crown of the piston.

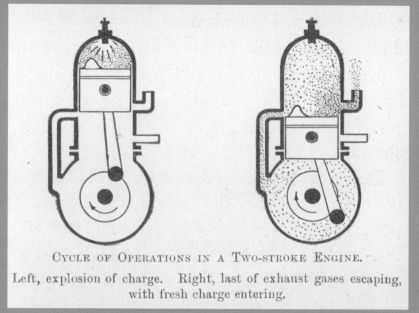

CYCLE OF OPERATIONS IN A TWO-STROKE ENGINE.
Left, explosion of charge.   Right, last of exhaust gases escaping, with fresh charge entering.

Fig. 1.2   Illustrations from A.M. Low's book, The Two Stroke Engine.

Fig. 1.3   Villiers 14A engine in the frame.

THE VILLIERS 14A

The motor studied in detail in this chapter is a Villiers XIVa (14A), made in 1936 and fitted to a Francis-Barnett Seagull Type 43. Examples were also fitted to the Francis-Barnett Cruiser and many other makes and models of the mid-1930s.

This bike has been in my family since new, but it has spent the last 25 years dismantled and stored in a sail bag. This was made possible because the frame is bolted together (*see* Fig.1.3).

The Villiers 14A is a typical two-stroke engine of the era, and it is remarkably similar in appearance to the most successful and prestigious Velocette GTP.

VILLIERS 14A STRIP AND REBUILD

The first point to mention is that the engine, gearbox and generator are completely separate units, although the ignition components – the points, capacitor and coil – were originally all inside the flywheel. Although this chapter concentrates on the engine itself, a brief description of the installation of the engine into the frame and its connection to the primary drive, clutch, gearbox and dynamo is included. This will be helpful to anyone wishing to inspect or restore any of the very many machines fitted with the Albion 3-speed gearbox. This one is the hand-change model, but the later foot-change models are the same, except for the presence of the positive-stop

mechanism fitted to the non-sprocket side.

Secondly, because the design of early two-strokes is so different from modern engines, there are some descriptions of basic procedures in this first chapter that will be useful for machines of subsequent eras.

Finally, it is worth pointing out that before you lay a spanner on a British bike of the pre-Second World War era, or the post-1945 period for that matter, you need the right sort of spanner. Imperial spanners can be a problem for people more used to working on modern machinery. Unified thread (UNF or UNC) or A/F spanners are referred to by the distance between the jaws of the spanner in inches, that is across the flats, hence A/F. A/F spanners are commonly used on some late-1960s Triumphs and cars built by companies based in America, such as Ford and General Motors (Vauxhall). Metric spanners are also measured across the

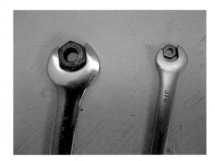

Fig. 1.4   A 3/8in Whitworth spanner and nut are shown on the left. The screw that fits this nut has a 3/8in-diameter shank and either a BSW or BSF thread. On the right are a 3/8in A/F spanner and nut. The screw that fits this nut has a 1/8in shank and either a UNC or UNF thread. This nut is just too small to be safely turned by a metric spanner measuring 10mm across the flats.

Fig. 1.5   Three different thread pitches, left to right: 3/8in BSCy (26tpi cycle thread); 3/8in BSF (British standard fine); and for comparison, the nearest metric equivalent, M10, thread diameter 10mm, which normally would have a 17mm nut.

VILLIERS 14A ENGINE SPECIFICATIONS

Bore and stroke: 63 × 80mm
Capacity: 249cc
Bearings: plain main bearings in bronze; plain small-end bearing; roller big-end bearing running on a bolted-up crank.
Cylinder head: detachable aluminium with 18mm plug and decompressor valve.
Piston: aluminium with deflector and two piston rings.
Lubrication: petroil, although a version was offered with automatic lubrication.
Cooling: air-cooled, though a rare water-cooled version was produced, too.
This was the last deflector-piston 250cc engine in the Villiers motorcycle range.

flats, but of course, their size is given in millimetres. Imperial spanners are sized by giving the outside diameter of the thread that accepts the nut turned by the spanner. And if that is not enough to make life difficult, the two common imperial standards for nuts and bolts, namely Whitworth (BSW) and BSF (British Standard Fine), have different size hexagons for the heads of bolts and nuts with the same size threads. This is why some imperial spanners show two sizes on the same spanner: '1/4, 3/16' for example. That refers to 1/4in BSW and/or 3/16in BSF.

Note that although A/F spanners are sized in inches, they will not fit Whitworth or BSF nuts and bolts without the risk of damaging the fixings.

Once you have a set of Whitworth/BSF imperial spanners, you will also be able to cope with the nuts and bolts of the very fine pitch Cycle thread fixings that are widely used on early and classic British bikes. The frame fittings on the Francis-Barnett, for example, have 26 threads per inch (tpi) Cycle thread.

DISMANTLING THE ENGINE

Removing the Flywheel

Out of the frame, and with the flywheel magneto in place, the engine will not be stable while standing on the bench. The flywheel is too big, so step one is to remove it.

Villiers' custom is to employ a flywheel design that is self-extracting. No puller is required, although you will need some means of holding the flywheel while you release the flywheel nut.

I prefer to use a strap wrench for this, since it ensures there is no risk of damaging the flywheel. A cheaper alternative is to use an old leather belt, or a tie-down strap, clamped tightly around the flywheel with a vice-grip wrench. The angle of the wrench will tighten the strap sufficiently to prevent the flywheel from turning as the nut is unscrewed.

Flywheel holders are also available. These have a Y-shape with a short peg on the upper end of each arm of the Y. The pegs fit in the inspection holes in the flywheel.

Do not attempt to use a screwdriver, or similar tool, pushed through an inspection hole and wedged against the coil carrier. The chances of destroying the coils or wiring inside are too great; you need a more positive holder.

If you are lucky enough to possess a genuine Villiers flywheel spanner, the process of removing the flywheel involves fitting the holder to the flywheel, then the special Hammer Tight spanner to the nut, followed by giving the spanner a sharp tap with a hammer. The thread is a standard right-hand type. A modern 1/2in BSW ring spanner does the job equally well and, being longer, may not need a blow from a hammer.

After a few turns, the nut will become difficult to turn again, but continue unscrewing it. It will have run up against a flange inside the flywheel, the resistance being caused by the nut forcing the flywheel off its tapered shaft. You will note that there is no key to locate the shaft in its correct position to give the right ignition timing, though there are permanent marks to

help you refit the flywheel in the correct place when the time comes.

After the flywheel has been loosened from the taper, undo the nut fully and lift off the flywheel, putting it aside for now. Do not drop it – especially not on your foot!

Removing the Stator Plate

Fig. 1.7   Remove the stator.

Two screws positioned in the cut-outs adjacent to the crankshaft secure the stator plate. You may need an impact driver to release them. Remove the stator plate, keeping it inside the flywheel until you are ready to refit it.

A magnet can lose power if left alone. Putting the stator plate back inside it creates a 'keeper', which minimizes the loss of magnetic field strength. After over seventy years, it is likely that the magnets will have lost power anyway. Both heat and vibration cause the magnetic domains within the material of the magnet to be jumbled up, instead of all being aligned along the direction of the flow of the magnetic field. Any description of a day in the life of a flywheel mag is bound to include both heat and vibration. So you need to preserve every Tesla of magnetic strength if you want an engine that is easy to start. We shall look at this problem again during reassembly.

The screws that fix the stator plate to the crankcase are unusual, and my standard procedure to avoid losing them or forgetting where they go is to put them back in the holes they came from in the crankcase.

Removing the Head

Before removing the head, it is best to take the spark plug out. In common with a lot of early engines, the 14A has an 18mm spark plug. This can present

Fig. 1.6   Hold the flywheel with a strap wrench.

Fig. 1.8   *A genuine Villiers plug spanner.*

a problem in that a deep-drive 26mm socket is needed – unless, that is, you have the original toolkit Villiers plug spanner, shown here.

The other item to consider removing is the decompressor valve. If there is any leakage from the decompressor, not only will the engine performance suffer, but also there will be a lot of oily residue over the cylinder head.

Fig. 1.9   *The decompressor valve.*

The 14A has an improved type of decompressor. Instead of just venting the cylinder contents to atmosphere, along with all the old oil, it vents into a copper tube that leads into the exhaust port, keeping the outside of the engine clean. The end of the copper tube stands a little proud of the head surface, and this provides the seal. Be careful not to damage or shorten the end of the copper pipe. The result will be a messy engine.

Fig. 1.10   *Three cylinder-head bolts.*

This engine has only three hexagon-headed screws securing the cylinder head, a 5/16in BSW ring spanner being needed to undo them. Loosen them gradually and evenly in turn. Do not completely remove one while the others are still fully tightened, otherwise there is a risk of distorting the head. The head should come off easily when the screws have been removed. Tap it around the edge lightly with a soft mallet if it seems to be stuck. There is no indication that there was ever a head gasket on this engine, so you must ensure that the mating surface of the head is not damaged while it is apart from the engine.

Removing the cylinder

With the head removed, you will see that the shapes of the cylinder head and the piston crown are very different from those of a modern machine.

Fig. 1.11   *The piston crown.*

It will be very obvious that the piston has a correct orientation; it is very important to make a note of this. Taking a quick photograph would be a good way of doing this.

Four studs and nuts fasten the cylinder flange to the crankcase. Remove the nuts, loosening all four gradually and in turn, as with the cylinder-head screws. Then the cylinder can be lifted from the crankcase.

A paper gasket seals the joint between the cylinder and the crankcase. Since gasket sets are hard to find for vintage engines, it is a good idea to preserve any gasket that can be reused later, if only as a template for making a new one. Gasket paper is readily available in a range of thicknesses, so this is not an impossible task.

The main jobs to be done on the cylinder are: first, to measure it to

discover whether it needs a rebore because of wear or damage; second, especially with a vintage engine, to decarbonize the exhaust ports. Old engines ran a very heavy dose of oil in the fuel, 16:1 being usual. The oil used was often a basic mineral oil, or for more highly stressed engines, a vegetable oil obtained from the castor oil plant – the famous and aromatic Castrol R. In either case, the burning of the oil produced ash and deposited carbon in a thick layer on the inside of the exhaust system. The carbon should be cleaned out of the ports using scrapers and a Dremel.

Fig. 1.12   *The 14A piston.*

Apart from the deflector, the piston has a number of features that are unusual from a modern point of view. There are no gudgeon-pin circlips. Instead, chrome-plated brass plugs are pressed into the ends of the pin. In place of the usual piston ring pins located in the ring grooves, a diagonal strip of copper is let into the piston, the ring ends being cut at the same angle. The photograph also shows signs of some blow-by, indicated by the carbon deposits below the rings.

Removing the piston

The gudgeon pin is a push-fit in the piston. Only the lightest tap with a soft mallet and suitably sized pin punch is needed to remove it; you can support

Fig. 1.13   *Measuring the piston with a vernier.*

the piston in your hand during the process. The next step is to measure the piston.

The standard bore size is 63mm, and there must be some running clearance between the piston and cylinder. Converting the difference between the nominal bore and the piston size, namely 0.21mm, to inches gives a piston clearance of 0.008in, which is within the acceptable range for an engine with a heavy, plain aluminium piston in an iron cylinder.

No rebore is contemplated at this stage. In fact, this is only an approximate method of determining piston clearance. It is far better to measure it directly with a feeler gauge placed between the piston and the cylinder. Even a digital vernier gauge is not really accurate enough for this job. One thing that can be done is to check the ovality of the piston by measuring from side to side as well as front to back.

Assuming that the piston is to be reused, the first task is to remove the piston rings. Those familiar with only modern two-strokes need to take extreme care in this task. Modern piston rings are made from springy steel and are difficult to break. Bikes manufactured before about 1970 often have piston rings made of cast iron. As a student, I had a holiday job at the Hepworth and Grandage factory in Leeds, where I was able to watch piston rings being machined from cast-iron tubes. Cast iron is durable and springy within

Fig. 1.15   Use shims to remove the rings.

limits, and it holds oil in the many tiny pores in the metal, but it is extremely brittle. When removing the rings from the piston, it is very easy to use too much force to lift them from the ring grooves and snap them.

The best and classic way to do this is to use three pieces of steel shim as shown. In the absence of steel shim, you can employ strips cut from an old 5ltr (1gal) oil can. An aluminium beer can might be too thin, though they do have other uses. Whatever you use, be careful – thin metal can inflict a bad cut.

Insert one shim between the end of the ring and the piston, sliding it around until it is on the opposite side of the piston to the ring gap. Then insert the other two shims between the two ends of the ring and the piston. Now you can slide off the piston rings easily, one at a time, taking care to keep them level. They will pass over the shims with no risk of breakage.

Next, clean the carbon and oil 'varnish' from the piston crown and skirt. Fine wire wool, ideally used in a parts washer, is the best way to do this. Examine the ring grooves. They should be clean and not clogged with carbon. The classic way of cleaning the bottom of each ring groove is to use the end of a broken piston ring – but what if you have not got one of those? A flattened piece of brazing rod filed to the width of the groove and sharpened like a screwdriver is ideal. Brass is less likely to remove metal from the piston and upset the ring clearance.

Splitting the crankcase

Four studs and nuts hold the two halves of the crankcase together. Removing these allows the case halves to be separated by holding the crankcase in your hand and tapping the flywheel side of the crankshaft with a soft mallet. The main bearings are long flanged bronze tubes, which act as both bearings and seals, so very little force is required to separate the crankcase halves. Once the crankcase is apart, the bolted-up design of the crank is obvious.

Fig. 1.16   The crank is bolted together.

CHECKING THE CONDITION

The real purpose of stripping down this engine was to check its condition before putting the bike back on the road. So the next step was to measure the cylinder for wear and taper, check for play in the bearings and ensure that the lubrication arrangements were in good condition.

To check the cylinder, you will need a specialized internal micrometer, a dial bore gauge or a relatively cheap set of telescopic bore gauges. To use the first

Fig. 1.14   Check ovality with a feeler gauge.

two methods, it is best to seek the help of an engineer who carries out rebores, who will certainly have that sort of equipment. A set of telescopic bore gauges will be useful for anyone who works on engines on a regular basis, so it is worth buying a set. Though many people have problems obtaining reliable readings with telescopic gauges, there is a technique that works.

Insert the bore gauge into the cylinder with the fixing screw on the end of the handle loose. Hold the gauge so that the handle is at an angle to the axis of the cylinder and tighten the screw lightly. Now straighten the handle of the gauge. As you do so, the plungers of the gauge will be pushed inwards and the fixing screw will drag sufficiently to prevent the springs from pushing them out again. When the handle is in line with the cylinder axis, it represents the greatest extent to which the plungers are pushed in, and you should tighten the screw a little more. If the gauge cannot now be moved from side to side, at right angles to the legs of the gauge, you have obtained the size of the cylinder bore at that point. Tilt the handle again so that the plungers are not pushed in any further, take the gauge out of the cylinder and measure its length with a digital vernier or outside micrometer.

The best way to discover the actual size of the bore is to use a feeler gauge between the end of the telescopic gauge and the cylinder wall, then add this measurement to the reading on the vernier. The 0.2mm feeler blade showed that the bore size was very close to the nominal 63mm, so no rebore was needed.

What the telescopic gauges are ideal for is checking the wear on the cylinder bore in different places. You can very easily determine whether the bore is oval or tapered from top to bottom.

Checking the big-end bearing is merely a matter of feeling for vertical play by hand.

Another process that was recommended at the time, if it was necessary to replace the main bearings, was to have them reamed to the correct size. Ideally, this should be achieved by assembling the cases without the crankshaft and reaming both bearings at the same time, using a long line-reamer running through both, thus ensuring that they are perfectly in line. This is a job for a specialized engineering company.

If it is necessary to replace the main bearings, they can simply be pressed out or tapped out with a hammer and drift, the new bearings being inserted in the same way. Note that aluminium and bronze have nearly the same expansion rate, so heating the case

Fig. 1.18   The oil channel in the crankcase.

does not make the bearings easier to remove. However, chilling new bearings in the freezer and warming the crankcase does make them easier to replace.

When replacing the bearings, it is important to fit them with the right orientation. The lubrication system for the main bearings is shown here.

The spinning flywheel throws the heavier oil droplets in the fuel to the outside of the crankcase. The recess at top right allows oil to collect there, where a passage leads down to a hole in the bearing. While the crankcases are apart, it is a good idea to check that these holes are clear. As a guitar player, I find that old guitar strings are ideal for this. A length of Bowden cable, such as an old throttle cable, would do the job, too.

REPLACING THE PISTON

Most two-stroke pistons have a correct orientation, but this is never more important than with a deflector-top piston. The general rule is that the short, steep slope of the deflector faces the transfer port and the long, gently curved side faces the exhaust port. The cylinder head is shaped to match the deflector, and the engine would not turn over if the piston were fitted incorrectly.

In this engine, the gudgeon pin can be pushed into place with thumb pressure only. Apart from the pads on its ends, the pin does not require any more elaborate method for retaining it in the piston, because the ends of the pin never pass over any of the cylinder ports in this engine. Note that there were many other arrangements for retaining the gudgeon pins in engines

Fig. 1.17   Checking the big end for play.

from other manufacturers, and some of these will be described at the end of this chapter.

REFITTING THE PISTON RINGS

This requires as much care as when removing them, and the steel shims that were used for that task will come in useful again. These rings do not have a specific top or bottom edge, though many types do. It may be that the rings are tapered or have a chamfer on the top edge to prevent them from hitting the wear ridge at the top of the cylinder. Sometimes the piston ring locating pin is offset towards the top or bottom of the ring groove. The diagonal ring gap and the inset copper strip of the Villiers 14A do not have a specific orientation, so the rings can be fitted either way up. It is vitally important to ensure that the rings are free to move in their grooves, however, and that the ring gap is correctly fitted around the copper strip.

REFITTING THE CYLINDER AND HEAD

I have always found that the keys to refitting a two-stroke cylinder without breaking the piston rings are to be careful and gentle, and to have the best possible view of the rings sliding into the cylinder. An iron cylinder is heavy, so to prevent the weight of the cylinder and the effort required to support it from complicating the task

---

COMPRESSING THE PISTON RINGS

I prefer to use my fingers to compress the rings. The expanding and contracting piston ring compressors used for fitting pistons to four-stroke engines are not really useful when working on a two-stroke, since two-stroke pistons are fitted from the bottom and you would end up having to untangle the ring compressor from the connecting rod. Sometimes the flat of a screwdriver blade can be used to settle a ring fully into its groove, but the main thing is to be completely sure at all times that the ring gaps are lying nicely beside the piston ring pins. That is why I like to be able to see what I am doing.

---

of getting the rings into the cylinder, I mounted the crankcase in the vice and fitted the cylinder in a horizontal position.

The weight of the cylinder is enough to break a ring. In addition, the nut that retains the drive sprocket should be clamped in the vice. This means that the piston will not move as the cylinder comes into contact with it, which is another difficulty overcome.

It is always a good idea to smear a little oil on the inside of the cylinder bore before fitting the piston. The first time that the assembled engine is turned over, this smear of oil will be the only lubrication that the engine has, so it is very worthwhile.

In this particular case, the cylinder base gasket was removed completely undamaged, so it was cleaned in the parts washer, dried off, given a light smear of grease and replaced.

It is important to stress that if there is any apparent resistance to

the piston sliding into the cylinder, stop and check to find out why – don't force it.

Never twist the cylinder while fitting it. Doing so makes it likely that the ends of the rings will catch in the ports and snap off.

The cylinder should fit easily on to its fixing studs. Once it is in place, the washers and nuts can be fitted. Tighten the nuts gradually and evenly in the usual diagonal pattern.

There is no head gasket on this model, so the cylinder head can be refitted at this stage. Insert the three hex-head screws, tightening them evenly and gradually.

THE FLYWHEEL

Only a couple of years before this model was introduced, Villiers engines featured two flywheels. There was a brass flywheel magneto on one end of the crank and a large iron external flywheel on the other. In fact, flywheel mass remains a very important aspect of two-stroke design to this day, as will be explained in Chapter 11.

The flywheel performs two tasks on this engine. By virtue of its high mass and large diameter, it smooths out the pulses in the engine output, but it also features magnets that generate the spark to fire the engine. Magnet technology has advanced massively since the 1930s, and the steel alloys used in those days do lose magnetism over time, and as a result of any heating, vibration or shock that they may have suffered in use. Remagnetizing a flywheel is not something that can be done at home, although I have read about a very simple method that, in theory, and maybe even in practice, can make some improvement to

Fig. 1.19 Fitting the cylinder.

a weary magnet. It involves spinning the engine for a minute or so using a power drill to turn the crank. The idea is that residual magnetism in the flywheel and stator will induce a current in the coil, which then will create its own magnetic field. This, in turn, will tend to remagnetize the flywheel magnets. If all else fails and you are far from anyone who can do the work, it may be worth a try.

On the other hand, flywheel magnets can be remagnetized by a proprietary remagnetizing machine. I have heard of these devices being called a 'Growler', but the one that I saw in operation in the workshops of Villiers Services in Merry Hill, near Birmingham, was an Italian machine with the wonderful name of Calamitatore.

Fig. 1.20   Il Calamitatore in action.

It sounds more dramatic than it is: *calamita* means a magnet in Italian, so the name merely describes the machine's purpose. You can see the two large coils, coloured red and black, that induce the magnetism in the poles of the flywheel. Only two are used in this case, but the supporting rods on the base plate allow the machine to remagnetize four- and six-pole flywheels. The bulbs gradually grow dimmer to indicate the current flowing through the coils, which falls as the flywheel becomes more and more saturated with magnetism.

The original intention was to fit a modern CDI ignition system to this bike, since the starting had not been very good the last time it had been running. I had made a small modification at that time, which allowed the ignition to be run from the battery for starting and then switched to the flywheel magneto once the engine was running. This employed an external HT coil, and it did solve the start-

Fig. 1.21   The points box.

ing problem. After some discussion with the people at Villiers Services, however, it was decided to have them carry out a total upgrade of the original system, replacing the points box, coil and capacitor with new or NOS (New, Old Stock) items and remagnetizing the flywheel. Thus the ignition would be completely to the original factory standard again.

The stator plate carries the contact points and the metal-covered rectangular capacitor inside a small cylindrical box. Originally, these boxes came with a round metal cover, held in place by a leaf spring pivoted on a post next to the box.

This lid serves no useful purpose, since there is an outer cover that fits over the whole flywheel/stator assembly and protects the ignition from the weather, while the post restricts access to the points. It is a good idea to remove it. Almost certainly, the little lid will have been lost anyway!

The stator (reconditioned or simply cleaned) can now be refitted to the crankcases. It should be positioned with the coil towards the upper front of the engine, giving the ignition lead

Fig. 1.22   Use a screwdriver to line up the stator.

a short simple run to the plug. The stator is quite a tight fit on the boss of the crankcase, and it helps to use a small screwdriver to line up the holes in the stator plate with those in the crankcase.

An impact driver is not necessary to tighten the screws. Originally, they were peened over to prevent them from vibrating loose, but we have thread sealants now, and this is recommended.

Fitting the flywheel is very easy. First, make sure that both the crankshaft taper and the tapered hole in the flywheel are clean and dry, and definitely not oily. Place the flywheel on the crankshaft end. The central nut will prevent the flywheel from dropping on to the tapered shaft.

Fig. 1.23   Align the marks on the flywheel and crank.

You will see the notch on the end of the shaft and a small arrow stamped on the flywheel. Line the two up. There is no keyway and Woodruff key to worry about. Tighten the nut fully.

In the absence of the Villiers Hammer Tight spanner, use a socket with a 450mm (18in) lever. A torque setting of around 80Nm (60lb ft) is a guideline. Of course the flywheel must be held firmly while this is done. A tie-down strap and vice-grip pliers can be used as an improvised strap wrench if you do not have one.

LOOSE FLYWHEEL

I have seen a backfire cause a flywheel of this type to come loose, knock off the aluminium cover, and go bounding down the road and through a hawthorn hedge into a field. I can give my word, though, that it was not on my bike!

Fig. 1.24   Vice grips can be used as a strap wrench.

Fig. 1.25   Setting the points gap.

Having tightened the flywheel, this is a good time to make a preliminary check to ensure that the points are opening just before Top Dead Centre, adjusting the gap as necessary. The points are secured by a screw with a brass washer underneath it. Next to the screw is the eccentric grub screw that can be turned to increase or decrease the points gap (*see* Fig. 1.21). To set the gap, turn the flywheel until the points gap is at its maximum, then use the adjusting grub screw to achieve the recommended gap of 1/64in. That is just over 0.015in or almost exactly 0.4mm. Incidentally, this setting seems to be universal for 'brass flywheel' Villiers engines, whether fitted to bikes, generators, lawnmowers or British Seagull outboard motors.

ASSEMBLING THE CLUTCH AND PRIMARY DRIVE

Fig. 1.26   The original cork clutch.

The original clutch friction plate (there is only one) was pierced with trapezium-shaped holes with sections of cork wedged into them as a friction material. The traditional way to reline the clutch was to push out the old corks and replace them, having given the sides of the new ones a coat of 'fish glue'. The corked plate would then have to be faced in a lathe to ensure that the corks were all level, with about 3mm (0.125in) of cork showing on each side of the plate.

The large corks used in the Villiers 14A are no longer available, but much better modern materials are, so Villiers Services were able to reline the clutch with a modern bonded material.

Fig. 1.27   Modern bonded clutch lining.

The clutch is assembled on the gearbox. The backplate is bolted to the input shaft of the gearbox, with the output sprocket fitting on the output shaft behind it. The input and output shafts are concentric, and in fact the two shafts are locked together when the gearbox is in top (third) gear.

There is a large ball race inside the friction plate (*see* Fig. 1.26). This runs on the central boss of the backplate.

The outer pressure plate fits over the three spring bosses, but do not forget the 'mushroom'. This is a separate extension of the clutch pushrod, which is pushed into the central hole in the drive end of the shaft and transmits the movement of the clutch pushrod to the outer pressure plate. You can see the head of the 'mushroom' in Fig. 1.27.

The next step is to fit the clutch springs and screws. The screws should be tightened fully to the end of the thread, and this takes quite a firm push to compress the spring. Be careful.

From this stage, the engine and gearbox must be assembled into the frame. Once this has been done, the dynamo drive chain is put on the inner sprocket on the drive end of the crankshaft first, followed by the primary chain. The boss at the bottom of the gearbox is a pivot point, while the boss at the top is slotted, allowing the gearbox to be moved forwards and backwards to set the primary chain tension. There is a little lever on the top of the gearbox that fits into a slot in the engine plate, which makes this easier. The lever can

AVOID INJURY

A slip of the screwdriver could injure your finger if it is in front of the blade, or the spring and nut could be launched into a dark forgotten corner of your workshop. I prevent the sprocket from turning with my arm while keeping my fingers behind the blade (*see* Fig. 1.28). My old woodwork teacher would be proud of me!

Fig. 1.28   Fitting the clutch-spring screws.

Fig. 1.29   The engine is back in the frame.

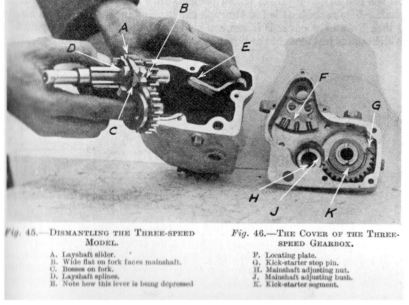

Fig. 45.—DISMANTLING THE THREE-SPEED
MODEL.

A. Layshaft slider.
B. Wide flat on fork faces mainshaft.
C. Bosses on fork.
D. Layshaft splines.
E. Note how this lever is being depressed

Fig. 46.—THE COVER OF THE THREE-
SPEED GEARBOX.

F. Locating plate.
G. Kick-starter stop pin.
H. Mainshaft adjusting nut.
J. Mainshaft adjusting bush.
K. Kick-starter segment.

Fig. 1.30   The Albion gearbox, from Motor Cycle Repair and Upkeep.

Fig. 1.32   The GTP Velocette.

be tightened to help keep the gearbox from moving under the load of the pull on the chain while riding.

THE ALBION 3-SPEED GEARBOX

The gearbox on my Francis-Barnett was in perfect running order, so it was not dismantled on this occasion. However, this will not always be the case.

Fig. 1.31   The Albion 3-speed gearbox.

Some time after the engine rebuild was completed, the restored bike was ready for the road.

OTHER ENGINES OF THE ERA

There were many other two-stroke engine manufacturers during the 1920s and 1930s, so I have included brief notes on a few examples.

In general, the cut-off date between the widely different, even quirky, veteran designs and the beginning of standardization on what was to become the basis for most engines of the vintage era is 1929. The next set of radical changes were brought in after 1945, following the capture of DKW models from Germany.

Fig. 1.33   The finished 1938 Francis-Barnett Seagull.

Fig. 1.34 Scott 600cc.

Scott

Possibly the greatest, most pioneering and successful two-stroke of the era, the Scott in its most usual form is a twin-cylinder, water-cooled engine. There were many radical variations, though. The 1913 TT bike featured not only rotary inlet valves, but also a rotary valve arrangement for the transfer ports, too. The example shown here is a much later road model. It has a number of very distinctive features. First, the items that appear to be the cylinder heads may actually only be the caps for the top of the water jacket. The cylinder heads were cast in one piece with the cylinders in the early engines. Cylinders with separate aluminium heads were first produced as an aftermarket accessory and only became standard after a major redesign. The need to work on the crankshaft bearings is unusual because, prior to 1929, Scotts came with overhung crankpins.

A central flywheel, incorporating the primary-drive sprocket, connected the two crank discs. Each had a pin, set 180 degrees apart, that formed the centre of the big-end bearing. The rollers of the big end could be inspected through windows on the ends of the crankcase.

In brief, a Scott engine is a very specialized design that changed radically over many years of development, and as a result of design changes and influences from at least four different manufacturers, beginning with Jowett and ending nearly fifty years later with George Silk.

A full description of all the procedures involved in rebuilding a Scott would merit a book of its own.

Velocette

Best known for their high-camshaft sporty four-stroke singles and their overhead-cam racers, Velocette also made two-strokes. The Model U, prior to 1929, had a 250 single-cylinder engine, which had an overhung crankpin. This was succeeded by the GTP engine, which had twin exhaust ports. I suspect that it was the success of this engine that lies behind the design of the Villiers 14A, because the Velocette GTP was a quality machine, which was held in more esteem than other, more workaday two-stroke bikes of the time.

Among other features, it had a remarkably modern oil injection system that adjusted the amount of oil delivered according to throttle opening.

There are many similarities between the GTP engine and the Villiers: the flywheel is self-extracting; the gudgeon pin is held in place by wire circlips, two in the case of the GTP; only one side of the piston has an extraction notch in the gudgeon-pin hole. Unlike the Villiers, the GTP's crank pin is pressed into the crank disc. Bronze main bearings support the crankshaft, but the oiling system requires care to be taken to ensure that the oil holes in the bearing bushes line up with the oilways in the crankcase. There is a small screw in each crankcase half to hold the bushes in place.

The earlier Model U originally came with a cast-iron piston. The gudgeon pin has an aluminium pad in one end, which must be fitted so that it runs on the opposite side of the cylinder wall from the inlet port. A circlip secures the inlet port side. Aluminium pistons have circlips on both sides of the piston. The official instructions on setting the oil pump say that the adjuster should be set so that there is 'a faint blue smoke at all times'.

The ignition timing procedure for the GTP is unusual. Mark the flywheel at TDC against a fixed mark on the stator. Measure 2.75in around the flywheel in the forward direction and make a second mark. Turn the engine back until the second mark aligns with the fixed TDC mark. Set the points so that they are just opening at this point. The Model U is timed in the same manner, only the measurement required is 2.7in.

Fig. 1.35 Scott single-sided 'overhung' crank.

Fig. 1.36 Dunelt 350cc.

Dunelt

The Dunelt 350 is very unusual. It employs a stepped piston so that the crankcase can pump more fuel/air mixture into the cylinder than with a normal piston, effectively supercharging the engine. My father owned one of these and always spoke very fondly of it.

Puch

The Puch 250 split single is actually a post-war, detuned development of the racing DKW split singles of the 1930s.

The carburettor is attached to the front cylinder, and as the pistons rise, the two connecting rods on the same crankpin pushing them up almost together, the mixture is drawn into the space under the front piston. Then it is compressed in the upper cylinder by both pistons and fired by two plugs in the joined combustion chamber.

As the pistons descend, the fresh charge is forced through the transfers into the rear cylinder, while the exhaust opens and lets the burned gases out of the front cylinder. Thus the fresh mixture does not mix with the exhaust gases. The result is a two-stroke that does not 'four-stroke'.

Fig. 1.37   The engine internals of the Dunelt. You can clearly see the oversize stepped piston skirt.

Fig. 1.38   Puch 250cc split single.

Fig. 1.39   EMC split-single crank and cylinder head.

Fig. 1.40 Early BSA Bantam.

BSA Bantam

When looking at the early BSA Bantam 125, the similarity to the DKW RT125 will be obvious. Development of the Bantam continued long after manufacture ceased in 1971.

Francis-Barnett

Francis-Barnetts moved with the times, too. The Fulmar of the mid-1960s showed the influence of the faired-in look that the Ariel Leader took to the limit.

Fig. 1.41 Water-cooled Bantam racer.

Fig. 1.42 Francis-Barnett Fulmar.

post-second world war: British two-stroke twins

Greeves Sportsman (Villiers 2T)

It seems to be a general rule in the history of technical progress that the seeds of the next development begin to grow just as the previous stage settles into a stable orthodoxy. So, just as the three-port, deflector-piston, two-stroke was becoming the standard approach, Dr Adolf Schnürle was developing a better idea.

In the mid-1920s, Dr Schnürle was working at the University of Stuttgart on the development of diesel engines for aircraft. The two main aims of his research were the improvement of power and the reduction of weight. A much lighter piston design was a step in the right direction towards both of these aims, and the heavy deflector on the piston crown was the obvious place to start the reduction in weight.

Schnürle's design divided the transfer port into two symmetrical ports on opposite sides of the cylinder. Both

Fig. 2.2   Demonstration of fluid flow.

ports were angled backwards, away from the exhaust port, and upwards. The idea was for the two streams of fuel/air mixture to meet and join, forming a coherent flow up into the cylinder head and pushing the spent gases ahead of it. Thus there would be no need for a deflector on the piston crown. The resulting piston was lighter and allowed a far better combustion chamber shape, higher compression and higher revs due to the piston being lighter. A simple experiment with two jugs of water shows how two fluid streams will unite and cling together.

Diesel engines for aircraft are a technology that never quite happened, but Schnürle's ideas were quickly taken up by DKW. The firm originally took its name from the fact that they produced steam-driven vehicles, *Dampf Kraft Wagen*. Later the initials were diverted to promote their subsequent products. The one that interests us here was *Das Kleine Wunder* (the Little Wonder), which also became known as the RT125. It is no exaggeration to say that this was the origin of almost every small two-stroke engine in the world in the immediate post-war years and until the mid-1960s.

The resemblance between the DKW and the early BSA Bantams is obvious, but the fundamental design of the port layout developed by Adolf Schnürle was also adopted for engines that had no outward similarity to the DKW.

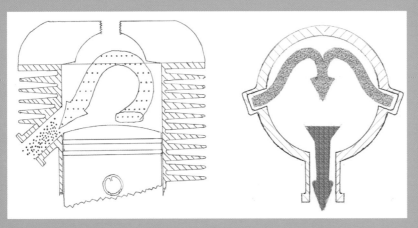

Fig. 2.1 Schnürle porting.

Fig. 2.3   DKW RT125.

POST-WAR VILLIERS ENGINES

The post-war E-series Villiers engines are examples of Shnürle port engines. While neither the 8E nor 9E motors matched the tidy, unit-construction design of the RT125, Villiers did go so far as to bolt the gearbox directly to the back of the crankcase, using gaskets in the joint to adjust the primary chain tension. At the same time, they retained the bob-weight, non-disc style of crankshaft used in the 14A, described in Chapter 1.

Fig. 2.4   Villiers 8E engine.

The 8E and 9E had a shorter stroke and a pressed-in crankpin by the time the twin-cylinder engines were produced. The large brass flywheel had been replaced by a smaller one, later contained within a teardrop-shaped aluminium casing, which gave a more modern, streamlined shape to the engine. Publicists at the time described the shape as 'air-smoothed'.

The cast-iron cylinder was a typical piston-ported item, a Schnürle-scavenged design. In fact, these engines were produced in vast numbers, as was the basically identical 11E used in the old blue three-wheeler invalid carriages, which had a Dynastart combined

starter and generator that allowed the engine to be started backwards for reversing. Many of these engines were sold on by the Health Ministry and recycled into motorcycles or into karts – often in very heavily modified form. For the sake of completeness, I should mention that there was also a 10E. This was a version of the 9E in which the cylinder was vertical instead of angled forwards.

The practicalities of working on the E-series engines are so very similar to those of the earlier models that it would not be particularly useful to go through them again. If you need a step-by-step guide to dismantling and reassembling the 9E engine, a full description can be obtained from The British Two Stroke Club. Contact details are listed in the Acknowlegements.

THE VILLIERS 2T ENGINE

In this chapter, we shall be looking at the Villiers twin-cylinder 250cc engine, the 2T. This engine and its variants, the 3T 350 and the later 4T, were used in a lot of motorcycles between 1950 and the mid- to late 1960s. They were built by such manufacturers as Ambassador, Cotton, DMW, Francis-Barnett, Greeves, James, Norman, Panther, Royal Enfield and Sun. The example I shall be using is a Greeves.

The bike was originally a 1963 Greeves Sportsman Roadster. Unlike the Francis-Barnett Seagull described in Chapter 1, which I knew for certain to be absolutely factory standard, this machine had clearly been modified, probably for actual road racing, but possibly as a café racer.

A picture of the 1962 Sportsman model on the Internet shows a bike with Ariel Leader-style 'spats' at the bottom of the traditional Greeves leading-link forks, together with a rather unattractive cigar-shaped handlebar fairing.

The bike described here is dressed as a Silverstone racer, with a combined tank and racing seat unit in fibreglass, which is a beautifully moulded Brear-

Fig. 2.6   Greeves Sportsman racer.

Fig. 2.5   Sectioned Villiers 8E engine.

Fig. 2.7   Light blue and yellow paintwork was not a marketing success.

ley-Smith aftermarket item that was available at the time. It is not one that I have seen on either an actual 250cc Silverstone or a 350cc Oulton, however.

Since the bike had been standing in a showroom for many years, it was felt that a complete check over was necessary, so the engine was removed and stripped. The procedures will help anyone working on any of the other twin-cylinder engines of the post-war era.

REMOVING THE ENGINE FROM THE FRAME

The major frame component in all of the traditional Greeves bikes is the cast-alloy 'front bone', which incorporates the steering head and a massive lug to support the top tube. The structure that looks like a battery box behind the carburettor does contain the battery, but primarily it is part of the structure of the frame, stiffening the area where the swinging-arm rear suspension pivot is mounted. Between the bottom of this structure and the bottom of the front bone, there are two long curved metal plates. These wrap around the engine mounting lugs and are a very tight fit on the lugs. For this reason, engine removal is made much easier if the studs holding the engine plates to the frame are loosened.

Disconnecting

Disconnect the clutch cable by slackening the adjuster at the handlebar end, slipping the inner cable through the gap in the lever and removing the barrel nipple from the lever. The other end of the clutch cable attaches beneath the engine and now will be slack enough to slip out of the clutch actuating lever. The adjuster underneath the engine can be unscrewed from the gearbox casing and the clutch cable pulled clear.

The electrical connections are inside the battery box. On this model, the rear mudguard completely covered the access to the battery box, so it was removed. The electrical connections had been made using screw terminal blocks, which is not ideal when they have to be connected by feel, inside a box. They were replaced by a modern multi-way plug on reassembly.

The carburettor is easily removed after slackening the pinch-bolt, and you should not forget to disconnect the spark plug leads and plugs. This does not give quite enough space above the engine to lift it clear of the engine plates, so it is a good idea to remove the rear ignition coil as well.

The Big Lift

Lift the front of the engine and slide it forward out of the rear engine plates. Then it can be lifted clear and placed on the ground. I recommend lifting it to the right-hand side, which is a little easier because the engine plates are not quite symmetrical.

There are a couple of tips that make things easier during this stage. Always wear grippy gloves for this job; it is very likely that by this stage your hands will be oily, and you don't want to drop the engine. I always prefer to lift the engine while standing astride the frame, especially if I am working on my own. This position prevents the possibility of the bike falling over while you have no hands free to catch it.

> ### *A SAFETY PRECAUTION*
>
> I am not a fan of kneeling on concrete, so I have a number of cushions and foam pads around the workshop. I like to place one next to the frame and put the engine on it as it comes free. This prevents any damage if the engine does slip. It is worth noting that the Villiers 2T is heavier than you might think, so this precaution is worthwhile.

DISMANTLING THE ENGINE UNIT

Fig. 2.8   Villiers 2T engine unit.

Partly because of the weight of the engine, and since the crankshaft was to be removed anyway, my first task was to remove the heavy flywheel. Only four slot-headed screws retain the flywheel cover, and there is no oil inside it, so the cover can simply be taken off. The dowels that locate it on the crankcase are a tight fit, and in complete contradiction to every piece of advice ever given on removing covers, it is removed by levering it free

Fig. 2.9   You can use a screwdriver here.

with a screwdriver – because a special slot is provided to allow this to be done without damaging the joint surface.

On removing the outer flywheel cover, you will find that the points simply pull off with the cover, leaving the ignition cam on the end of the flywheel. This cam must be removed before the flywheel nut can be undone. It is secured by a very small circlip and located by a tiny Woodruff key. You may need a cheap pair of circlip pliers with interchangeable jaws for this. Most circlip pliers are too big.

Villiers kept to their old practice by making the flywheel self-extracting, so the only tools needed to remove it are the strap wrench and a long 13/16in Whitworth ring spanner. Each of the separate cylinder heads is held down by four sleeve nuts, which screw on to studs. This design will be very familiar to people with experience of Yamaha two-strokes.

The cylinder head design shows signs of the progress made since the 1930s, since it demonstrates a knowl-

Fig. 2.10   A 'bathtub' head, with squish.

edge of 'squish', a concept developed by Sir Harry Ricardo from around 1918. The combustion chamber is smaller in size than the piston crown, and as the piston crown approaches close to the head, the fuel/air mixture is squished between the two and forced into the combustion chamber itself, creating massive turbulence there.

This particular version of a squish head is usually called a 'bathtub head'.

The Inlet Manifold

The Villiers twins, just like the Ariel and Excelsior engines, have a single carburettor in their standard form, and this example was fitted with the standard carburettor and manifold. The manifold links the cylinders together, so it must be taken off before removing the cylinders.

Inspecting the Cylinders and Pistons

After removing the cylinder heads, you will see that there are two separate aluminium head gaskets. The first thing that was obvious about these cylinders was the dark ring around the top of each cylinder bore. This marks the limit of piston ring travel, and it is often a sign of a worn cylinder.

The cylinders may simply be lifted off the studs, one at a time. With a long-stroke engine such as this, it is a good idea to remove the pistons straight away, especially on an old engine where the piston skirts are long. Careless handling, or even turning the crank too enthusiastically, may cause a conrod to hit the inside of a piston

Fig. 2.11   Cylinder spacer plate.

skirt, causing damage, perhaps even knocking a piece out of it. Pressed-steel circlips are used on this engine, so proper circlip pliers are needed to remove them. The type with the bent tips works best and slips off less often.

Beneath the cylinders on this engine is a thick steel plate. Such plates are often used when tuning an engine, but in fact they are standard on all 2T motors, although the reason is not known by anyone I have met, even the experts at Villiers Services. As a tuning trick, the plate is added to raise all the cylinder ports and increase the port-open duration for increased performance. This can be effective, as long as the shapes of the bottoms of the ports and cylinder top face are altered to suit and return the compression to standard.

Fig. 2.12   Rounded edges on piston rings.

Even the most superficial look at the pistons indicated that the engine had seized many times. The important part of diagnosing the causes of seizure is to look for the places where it has happened. In this case, the marks occurred in two places: below the piston-ring pins and in the areas of the piston that pass over the ports.

The cause of the problem became clear when the rings themselves were examined. They are of steel and chrome plated on the wear surface, but they displayed damage to both the top and bottom edges. Their corners were rounded off, and this rounding was very noticeable where the rings passed over the ports. A closer look at the cylinder ports showed that the edges of the ports joined the cylinder bore with a sharp edge. To ease the piston ring more gently back into its groove, these joints must have a smooth radius.

On measuring the bore, wear was evident. Not only was there a noticeable wear ridge at the limit of piston

Fig. 2.13   The cylinder bore – note sharp-edged ports.

Fig. 2.14   Measuring the bore for wear.

ring travel, but also there was a 0.005in ovality of the cylinder, as measured from front to back above the exhaust port, compared with the side-to-side measurement at the same point.

This was good news, however, since the cylinders were already 0.040in oversize, and the next oversize is +0.060in. That meant that a rebore to the next oversize would bring everything up to good condition. The port radiuses would be applied after the rebore.

The cylinders were sent to Villiers Services in Merry Hill for new pistons and a rebore. The flywheel was included, too, since the general advice is that loss of magnetism is very common in Villiers twin flywheels.

Clutch and Gearbox

In the meantime, dismantling and checking the rest of the bottom end could proceed. The drive side of the engine casing is full of gear oil, so this should be drained before removing the cover.

Once inside the casing, you will see the engine sprocket, the clutch and

the primary chain. You will not see any means of adjusting the primary chain, so if there is more than about 20mm (3/4in) of play, the chain will need replacing. Unless there is far too much play in the chain, the sprocket and clutch must be removed together.

There is a special tool for holding the clutch basket and engine sprocket (*see* 'Special Tools' later in this chapter). The genuine Villiers version takes the form of a block of aluminium with teeth cut into each end, which fits exactly between the teeth on the outside of the sprockets on the clutch and the engine sprocket, thus locking the two together and preventing them from turning.

In the absence of the Villiers tool, use a strap wrench to hold the clutch and then loosen the engine sprocket nut, but leave the sprocket in place for the time being. The fixing on the clutch is unusual, but rather elegant: there is a domed cap that contains the adjusting screw for the clutch pushrod, and it requires a pin spanner to turn it. On the sample engine, it was rather tight and needed a tap with a punch to start it turning.

To ensure that there is no pressure on the cap, loosen the locknut and unscrew the clutch adjusting screw in the centre of the cap.

Fig. 2.15   Use a pin spanner to unscrew the clutch dome.

Underneath the cap, you will find the nut that holds the clutch to the gearbox shaft. The clutch plates can be lifted off the central splined boss, leaving the clutch basket sufficiently open for you to be able to use a C-spanner to hold the central boss while you undo the nut. If you are likely to do this job often, the old trick of making a clutch centre holder by welding a handle to an old metal clutch plate will be a good idea. By this time, you will probably be wondering how you came to lose the clutch springs – they are inside the central boss.

Fig. 2.16   The clutch bearing has loose rollers.

Be careful when removing the clutch backplate, since the clutch bearing has loose rollers. If you lift off the basket and backplate as one unit, however, the rollers will remain together in one place for long enough for you to store them safely in a box. Remove the nut from the front sprocket, then remove the sprocket and the clutch at the same time, with the primary chain.

Fig. 2.17   The clutch springs.

The primary case will now be empty, and the three studs and two screws that retain the inner casing can be taken out, allowing the casing to be removed.

Fig. 2.18   Fixings for the inner primary case.

At this point, you will see that the engine and gearbox are not all in one piece, as perhaps you thought. In fact, they are separate, just as Villiers engines always used to be.

Fig. 2.19   Undo the nuts holding the gearbox.

There are two studs on each side of the engine. Having removed their nuts, a light tap with a mallet will encourage the gearbox to come free.

Unless you have already drained the oil from the gearbox, it will spill out – again! This shows the importance of the gasket to this joint. When the engine is reassembled, a new gasket set is highly recommended. They are readily available for these engines.

Splitting the Crankcase

A vital part of every multi-cylinder two-stroke is the seal between the cylinders. In most designs, this seal has to be assembled along with the centre bearing when the crankshaft is pressed together. In a more modern engine, where the crankcase is split horizontally, this is not a problem. The crankshaft can simply be dropped into the lower half of the case, then the top put on. In a vertically split crankcase, such as that of the 2T, the crank must either be made in two pieces, or the centre part of the crankcase must be part of the crank assembly. That is the Villiers approach in this case. There is a central divider that bolts between the halves of the case, and there is a pinch-bolt to squeeze the case tightly around the central divider as well.

Fig. 2.21   Undo the pinch-bolt.

Remove the cylinder base gasket and the Woodruff key from the drive side of the crankshaft, then undo the six nuts that hold the crankcase halves together. Before you pull the crankcase apart, turn the crank until the drive-side connecting rod is just past Bottom Dead Centre. There is a gap in the inner side of the case half, and in this position of the crank, the connecting rod will pass through the gap and allow the case to come free.

Fig. 2.22   Line up the connecting rod with the slot.

The state of the sample engine's crankcase was not very encouraging. In an engine in good condition, you would expect the crankcase to be relatively clean. There was some dark brown staining inside, however, and a pool of treacle-like oil in the bottom. The oil in the gearbox and primary case had been clean, but it was likely that this had been changed before the bike was put into storage. The dirty oil in the crankcase was almost certainly a result of oil being sucked in through leaking main-bearing oil seals. The centre main bearing and seal were now very suspect.

Fig. 2.20   Use a hammer gently to remove the gearbox.

Fig. 2.23   Remove the crank from the other crankcase half.

To remove the crank from the cases, release the three Allen screws from the centre plate and gently tap the end of the crank with a soft-faced mallet. Make sure that you guide the connecting rod through the gap in the cases.

CHECKING THE MAIN BEARINGS

After removing the crank, there are two simple checks to be made on the state of the centre main bearing and seal. First, hold the crank and spin the centre plate. There should be a definite resistance if the seal is in good condition. Second, the centre plate should be free to slide from side to side slightly, but it should not rock at all relative to the centre line of the crank.

Fig. 2.24 *The centre plate must not rock.*

In this case, both tests failed. There was brown staining on the rollers of the flywheel-side main bearing (and everything else, too), but on close inspection it was clear that this bearing had been replaced relatively recently. A picture of the history of the bike began to appear. What seemed likely to have happened is that the main bearing seals had started to fail, and the engine had lost power and started to smoke a lot. It had been stripped and the more easily replaced outer bearings and seals had been renewed. The centre bearing and seal, which are not so easily changed, had been left – but they had been the real source of the problem.

Typically, a bike in that state will start and run for ten or fifteen minutes, then lose power and eventually stop. The bike had been put away and added to the 'get around to it one day' list. It had never reached the top of the list – until I took it on.

There are two possible solutions at this point – ruling out the notion of just sticking it all back together and mak-

ing into a purely decorative object! The crank could be sent off for rebuilding or it could be exchanged for a rebuilt example from Villiers Services. In the interests of speed, the latter course of action was taken.

BEFORE REASSEMBLY

Prior to putting everything back together, it would be a shame not to take the opportunity of making a few modifications to the porting of the cylinders to make the life of the piston a little easier. I would recommend resisting any temptation to do anything that could be considered performance tuning on this engine. It is not a particularly robust design as compared with, say, a TZ Yamaha, and except on a wide open race circuit, a violent and narrow power band is not an easy thing to cope with – no matter how enjoyable it is, once you have learned to cope!

That said, there are some things that can be done to improve the engine that have been learned since the 1950s. The first thing to do, however, is to obtain an accurate idea of the existing state of tune. The key aspects are port timing and the width and shapes of the ports.

Begin by finding the port timing, that is the number of degrees through which the engine turns while each of the ports is open

Although a degree wheel on the crank works for determining port timing, when I was designing and making exhaust systems for race two-strokes, I became used to the more accurate approach of measuring the height of the ports. To do this, set the crank at TDC. On many engines, the crown of the piston will be exactly lined up with the top flange of the cylinder at this point. If it is not, make a note of the distance between the piston crown and the top flange. This distance is known as the deck clearance.

Now turn the crank until the point at which the exhaust port just starts to open. My usual way of determining this is to shine a torch up the exhaust port and watch from the top of the cylinder until I can see a line of light above the piston crown. I have also seen people open the port fully, put a thin feeler gauge into the port and then close it until the piston just grips the feeler gauge.

Fig. 2.25 *Using a vernier gauge to measure port opening.*

Having found the port opening point, measure the distance from the top flange of the cylinder to the piston crown. If there was a deck clearance, you must subtract that amount from the measurement you have just taken. You will now know how far the piston has travelled from TDC to port opening. Repeat the process with the transfer ports, checking carefully that both ports open at the same time. If they don't, then some unwise 'tuning' has been carried out. Balancing the transfers is really important for both power and fuel consumption. To convert these measurements into degrees is quite complex, requiring the use of sines, cosines and Pythagoras' theorem. You may not enjoy geometry and trigonometry, so I have provided a table to help you make the conversion (*see* Fig. 2.26).

The 'blowdown' is the difference between the exhaust opening and the transfer port opening. It is during this time that the pressure in the cylinder drops to allow the fresh mixture in the crankcase to come up the transfer ports to refill the cylinder for the next power stroke. It is absolutely vital to match the blowdown to the size and number of the transfer ports. The Villiers 2T has only two small transfer ports, and the exhaust port is small, too. It needs a lot of blowdown, and 24 degrees is plenty.

Port timing Calculator

		Villiers 2T	
Deck Clearance (mm)	0.75		
Stroke (mm)	63.5		
Exhaust opens (mm)	39.3	Ex port raised 2mm	
Transfers open (mm)	51.6	Trans port raised 1mm	
Inlet closes (mm)	21.3		
Rod length (mm)	140		

	Degrees ATDC		Degrees
Exhaust Port opens	95.77	Ex Total Duration	168.46
Transfer opens	121.18	Trans Duration	117.64
Inlet closes	63.6	Inlet Duration	232.80
		Blowdown	25.41

Fig. 2.26   Excel spread sheet of port timings.

The main thing that we learn from these port timings is that the engine is in a very moderate state of tune. A race engine might have total exhaust duration closer to 180 degrees. However, the existing ports are very square. It would do no harm to reshape the port tops into curves, lifting the centre of the exhaust port by 2mm and that of the transfers by 1mm. That would make a minor difference to the rev range, but it would make the life of the piston rings much easier and also soften slightly the tone of the exhaust note.

Fig. 2.27   Cleaned and modified exhaust port. The slight curve to the top of the port can be seen, also the beautiful crosshatch pattern on the cylinder wall created by the honing process after the rebore. These tiny scratches retain oil and improve the running-in process substantially.

ASSEMBLING THE BOTTOM END, DRIVE SIDE

Getting the steps in the right order is vital here. Begin with the drive-side crankcase. The outermost component is the drive-side oil seal. This fits up against a lip, and it can only be installed from the inside.

Fig. 2.28   Removing the oil seal and bearing.

To remove the old seal, whether you are replacing the drive-side main bearing or not, you must remove the large circlip inside the case (you will need a sturdy pair of circlip pliers for this – it is a strong fixing), then carefully and gradually drive the bearing and seal out of the housing. If you have a piece of tube of the right size, fine, but if not, tap the outer edge of the bearing ring with a punch or drift at four equally-spaced points around the ring, making sure that the bearing remains

Fig. 2.29   A smear of sealant on the joint; try to apply it more neatly than this!

straight in the case. Fit the oil seal from the inside, with the open face to the inside, making sure that only the metal outer rim of the seal is used to push it into place. Oiling the outer edge of the seal makes this easier, but you will still need to tap it lightly. Replace the bearing ring in the same way and then fit the circlip. Make absolutely certain that the circlip fits completely into its groove; it is worth tapping it in with a punch.

Next you can fit the crank. This needs to be close to BDC to pass through the gap in the case. Gently tap the centre plate into place and fit the Allen screws and spring washers to hold it. At this stage, it is a good idea to fit the cross-dowel and pinch-bolt. The cross-dowel is a short piece of steel rod with a threaded hole through it – it can be seen in the top right-hand corner of the case joint. It is easy to line up the threaded hole with the end of the bolt at this stage, but impossible once the case halves are together. Do not tighten the bolt yet. There is one more thing to do, and it is vital. There is a steel sleeve on the drive end of the crankshaft, which forms the surface against which the drive-side oil seal runs. Make sure you fit it at this stage.

ASSEMBLING THE BOTTOM END, FLYWHEEL SIDE

The inner race of the flywheel-side main bearing can now be fitted to the flywheel side of the crankshaft. Tapping it into place using a piece of tube of suitable size is the only way to do this. It should rest against the inner race, not the bearing cage. Make sure that the joint faces are clean, all traces of the previous sealant having been removed, then apply a smear of fresh sealant as neatly as possible. There is no gasket for this joint. The flywheel-side crankcase can be fitted next and the two case halves bolted together, using the long studs that have a nut and washer on each end. Tighten the pinch-bolt now.

FITTING THE CYLINDERS AND PISTONS

Fit one cylinder base gasket to the crankcase, then the steel plate and then another base gasket.

Fig. 2.30   The base gaskets and spacer plate.

The pistons have two rings, the lower one requiring an expander spring to be fitted in the ring groove first. These pistons have locating pins, so not only do the ring gaps and the pins need aligning, but also the rings need to be the right way up, since the pins are not on the centre lines of the ring grooves.

Fig. 2.31   Piston-ring locating pin.

Fit the rings to the pistons, not forgetting the expander springs in the lower grooves. You will find that the piston crowns have the word 'Front' stamped on them. The reboring process is done with the cutter set to the exact bore size that gives the correct clearance on the actual piston to be used in that bore, and manufacturing processes lead to slight variations in the diameter of the pistons. What this means is that the pistons should also be marked to indicate the cylinders in which they fit. In this case, the left-hand piston (when seen as if you were sitting on the bike, that is the nearside) was stamped with a letter 'L'. Fit the piston circlip to the inner end of the gudgeon-pin hole in each piston. With the piston cold, the pin is a little too tight to be pushed in easily. Warming the piston in hot water from a kettle, or with a heat gun, makes the pin a push-

fit. It will be hot enough to be uncomfortable, but not impossible, to hold!

FITTING THE CYLINDERS

Coat the insides of the cylinder bores with oil first. Fitting the first cylinder is relatively easy, since you have clear access and can see all round. The wall of the lower spigot of each cylinder is quite thin and there is not much of a chamfer on the bottom edge to help the rings squeeze into their grooves and slide into the cylinder. You need to be very careful to ensure that the rings are not trapped outside their grooves. Never use force to push the cylinders down. It is always useful to leave the rag in the top of the case to restrict the movement of the connecting rod. Sometimes it helps to lay two thin pieces of wood across the top of the case and let the pistons sit on them. This will keep the pistons straight and prevent them from rocking. If it is still difficult to get the rings in, try using a plastic tie wrap as a disposable piston ring compressor.

You are very likely to need this method for the second cylinder, since the gap between the cylinders is small and it is difficult to see exactly where the rings are.

Cut off the tie wrap and push the cylinders gently down into place, holding them down with your hand while

Fig. 2.32   A tie-wrap makes a useful ring compressor.

you turn the engine over. This not only confirms that you have remembered to remove the rag from the case, but also gives the pleasure of seeing and feeling how beautifully it all works now that everything is bright, shiny and new.

FITTING THE CYLINDER HEADS

When the cylinder heads were removed, they were covered with a dark brown deposit of burned gearbox oil. A quick rub over with fine wire wool restored the finish.

Fig. 2.33   The cylinder heads were cleaned.

Each cylinder head is held down by four sleeve nuts, which also locate and align the head on the top of the cylinder. There is a metallic gasket at the head joint. Tighten the eight cylinder-head nuts on the two heads together. Do it gradually and evenly in a diagonal pattern, as if you were dealing with a one-piece head. Since the crankcase is made of several pieces, it is important to avoid distorting it by uneven tightening. Tighten the head nuts to 20Nm (15lb ft).

Fig. 2.34 The standard (front) and Amal carburettors compared.

THE INLET MANIFOLD

When it was delivered to the workshop, this engine had been fitted with the familiar Villiers 20mm carburettor and the standard manifold. It came with a small box of spares, however, which included a special race manifold and a 26mm Amal Monobloc carburettor. Again, this confirmed that the crank seals had been a problem in the past. As the seals had begun to fail, there would have been a time when the inlet vacuum would have been insufficient to make a big carburettor work, while a smaller one might have continued to do so. With everything up to specification, the Amal race carburettor was the best option, so it was refitted.

Fit the inlet manifold, with its gasket and four nuts and washers, on to the four studs on the cylinders.

ATTACHING THE GEARBOX

Before attaching the gearbox, it is worth taking advantage of the rare opportunity to check its condition and operation, since the design allows a very good view of the dogs and gear teeth. A gasket is fitted to the face of the gearbox, and you should notice a small dowel in the upper left-hand corner of the joint face. There are corresponding holes in the gasket and the back of the crankcase, so there is no risk of fitting the gearbox upside down! In the bottom left of the joint face, you will also see a channel connecting the gearbox with the primary chain case. This allows them to share the same oil, so do not block it with sealant.

Fit the gearbox to the crankcase; if you have thin fingers, you will be able to fit the washers and nuts to the four studs. If not, a good method is to use a spot of grease to stick the nut to the flat of a screwdriver. Then hold the nut against the end of the thread on the stud and turn it with a spanner.

The same trick can be done with a magnet attached to the shaft of the screwdriver, or with a magnetic screwdriver.

THE PRIMARY CHAIN CASE

The inner primary case is fitted next. It is fastened to the crankcase with three studs, and to the gearbox with three screws. A paper gasket goes on the inner face.

When assembling the clutch and primary drive, everything has to be done in the correct order. The engine sprocket and the clutch basket must be fitted at the same time. It is not possible to fit one and then wrangle the primary chain on to the other. Before you do this, remember that the engine sprocket fits with the long boss to the outside and is located by a Woodruff key.

So, with the sprocket the right way round, put the primary chain around the sprocket and the clutch basket, line up the keyway in the sprocket with the Woodruff key and put the whole assembly on to the shafts. Collect all the clutch bearing rollers, which almost certainly will be loose in the box you stored the clutch in, and place them around the clutch shaft. The trick is to put the first rollers into the wider front part of the bearing and then push them around to the back. The slight tension on the primary chain will hold them in place while you fit the rest.

Fig. 2.36 One more roller to go (note that the backplate and chain are not in place).

The next item to add is the thicker clutch backplate. This fits on to the smaller, inner splined shaft. The splined outer sleeve goes on next. The centre boss with the springs fits on to the splined sleeve and is fastened down with the long sleeve nut. The centre boss can be held with a C-spanner if you do not have a clutch centre holder. Tighten the nut fully, then put in the clutch plates, steel plates and lined plates alternately.

Finally, fit the domed pressure cap and tighten it with a pin spanner, holding the clutch basket with the strap wrench, or the special locking tool. Tighten the sprocket nut at the same time.

Fig. 2.35 View of the gearbox internals.

SPECIAL TOOLS

Fig. 2.37   Special tools for the 2T.

Throughout this book, I have tried to avoid recommending that tasks should be done using highly specialized factory tools, particularly those that are likely to be unobtainable or rare. On the other hand, if you expect to keep a bike for some time, and will work on it often, it is a good idea to make your own special tools. A previous owner had done this for the sample 2T motor.

The photograph shows, on the left, a homemade clutch centre holder. The slot fits over a lug on the clutch basket, while the cutaway at the end engages with the clutch centre.

In the centre is the tool that fits between the sprockets to lock both the crankshaft and the clutch shaft. It is also homemade, from Paxolin, an old form of reinforced plastic, which is still obtainable online. The genuine works version is made from cast aluminium.

The item on the right is a very simple pin spanner. It was in the box that came with my angle grinder.

Since the clutch pushrod adjustment must be carried out with the cable attached, the outer case should be fitted when the engine is in the frame.

THE FLYWHEEL SIDE

The flywheel-side crankshaft oil seal is mounted in the centre of the magneto stator plate, and it is fitted with the open face to the outside. This means that the stator plate must be a pressure-tight seal on to the side of the crankcase. The gasket must be in perfect condition, and a little sealant is a good idea, too. Tighten the four screws evenly, making sure they are tight.

Fig. 2.38   The points and ignition cam.

To fit the flywheel, it is best to set the crank so that the keyway is at the top, with the Woodruff key in place, of course. The corresponding orientation was marked on the rim of the flywheel with a letter 'N', though there would have been no problem if there had been no marking, since the key and keyway are clearly visible through the windows in the flywheel. The flywheel will engage lightly with the keyway before the retaining nut engages with the thread. Secure the flywheel with an appropriate holder and tighten the centre nut. A torque of about 80Nm (60lb ft) is the target.

The outer case carries the contact points and capacitors, and also the basic wiring. The wiring on the sample engine bore no resemblance to the standard arrangement, so there is little point in going into it here. There will be wires to connect, including those to the ignition switch, which is mounted on this case as standard. The clutch operating lever fits through a slot in

the lower left-hand side of the case. Put the lever into the slot first, then fit the case over the kickstart and gearchange shafts, pushing it into place. There is a locating dowel around the upper case screw, and it may need a light tap to set it in place. There will be no difficulty with the points catching on the ignition cam, because the cam is fitted afterwards. It locates with a tiny Woodruff key, being held in place with a circlip.

FITTING THE ENGINE IN THE FRAME

The engine plates of the Greeves are a very tight fit on the engine lugs and there is very little space around the engine for wriggling it into place. The easiest approach was to slacken the bolts that fasten the plates to the rest of the engine, removing the front bolts altogether to allow the plates to flex outward. The only disadvantage was that without the plates, the frame became very flexible – to the extent that the front bolt holes no longer lined up. A car jack under the bottom of the front cast front frame member fixed that problem.

It only remains to connect the clutch cable underneath the engine unit, and fit the carburettor, kickstart, gear pedal and exhausts.

SETTING THE IGNITION TIMING

Both the points gaps and timing are adjustable individually. It is worth

Fig. 2.39   Use a car jack to support the frame.

checking that the two cylinders are timed identically, since it is possible that the crankshaft may not have been assembled with the crankpins set exactly 180 degrees apart. If you are not sure, you will need a timing gauge to find TDC on one cylinder, then mark the flywheel, turn it 180 degrees and check whether you have the same reading on the timing gauge on the other cylinder. Assuming this is correct, the standard Villiers procedure is to set the flywheel to the maximum opening of the points, then adjust the gap to 1/64in. That is just over 0.015in or almost exactly 0.4mm.

WHAT ABOUT THE OTHER TWINS?

The other British twin-cylinder two-stroke engines of the period were the Villiers 3T and 4T, the Excelsior Talisman (there was also a Talisman Three) and the Ariel Leader/Arrow.

The 3T is a bored-out 325cc version of the 2T, whereas the 4T is an upgrade, featuring additional fins on the higher-compression head and ported pistons to take advantage of the four transfer ports. These engines were originally intended for the Bond three-wheeler. They gained a couple of brake horse-power, but lost reliability because of the modifications. Incidentally, the sight of a Bond three-wheeler driver opening the bonnet to kickstart the engine when the battery was flat, or when the Dynastart was not working, is something never to be forgotten!

The Excelsior always seemed to be a better design. Certainly the seals between the crankcases were better, because the cranks were keyed and bolted together. The crankcase was in three sections, split along the centre line of each of the cylinders. The gearbox was attached to the back of the cases, Villiers style.

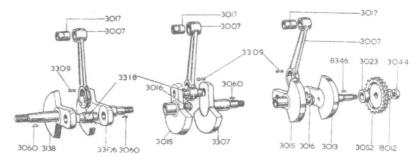

Fig. 2.41   A sketch of the crank from the Excelsior Talisman 3-cylinder version intended for the Bond Minicar. The twin uses only the outer sections.

Fig. 2.42   Talisman twin engine.

Fig. 2.43   The Excelsior Talisman Twin.

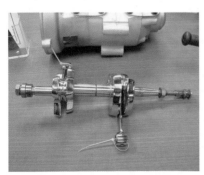

Fig. 2.40   Excelsior Talisman Twin crankshaft.

Fig. 2.44   Ariel Golden Arrow.

the exhaust were full of carbon deposits. Since the engine had been running with a leaking crank seal, this was quite likely.

The tailpipes had a split pin through the tip of each pipe, indicating that there was probably an internal baffle for silencing. Pulling out the pin and the internal pipe on the offside exhaust confirmed this. There was a tube inside, longer than the outer tailpipe, with a closed inner end and a ring of holes around the circumference. The holes were partially closed by carbon deposits, so the pipe was cleaned and the holes drilled a little larger.

Fig. 2.45   The over-efficient silencer baffle.

The Ariel twin-cylinder engine almost seems to revert to the Scott design, with the cranks assembled from the outside into a one-piece cast crankcase. The centre ball bearing and seals are fitted into the central wall, and then the cranks are inserted from either side. They are joined by a taper-and-key arrangement with a through-bolt down the centre of the two joining shafts. There is an extra flywheel outside the sealed case on the primary-drive end.

Like the Villiers engine, the Ariel had a single carburettor, but since there was a frame extension supporting the engine immediately behind the cylinders, the carburettor breathed through a passage in that extension. The clutch was unusual to look at, but operated conventionally. The gearbox was mounted in the same casting as the crankshaft, though it was actually a completely separate Burman unit.

THE FINAL STAGES OF WORK ON THE GREEVES

As mentioned at the beginning of this chapter, the aim with the Greeves was to get it going. Having assembled and fitted the engine, and gone through all the routine basic jobs of connecting the controls, adjusting the clutch pushrod, connecting and adjusting the chain and so on, it was time to see if it would run. It would not.

A complete rewire of the igni-

tion was needed to get it to spark on both cylinders, and this included the removal of the car-type ignition switch mounted on the flywheel cover. This is a standard item, but it made no difference to the ignition whether it was on or off. It was replaced by a race-style double-pole kill switch mounted on the instrument bracket The old wiring connected the outputs of both primary coils together. Clearly this is not a good idea when the plugs are supposed to fire 180 degrees apart. With both plugs sparking strongly, and after a quick push down the drive, it was immediately obvious that the engine was firing, but would not run.

Recalling that there had been a fuel blockage, I removed both fuel taps, which were very stiff to turn. In fact, both taps were blocked, one of them completely, with a dark brown solid deposit that had to be cleared out with a 4mm drill bit. Having done that and cleaned the cones that form the actual tap, one tap now leaked, despite lapping it in. Both were replaced with new items. Dripping petrol is not something I want in my workshop!

Now the fuel flow was good, but the engine would still only run for a few seconds. The bike was fitted with expansion chambers, but the sound of the engine was very different from the sharp crack that I would have expected from such an unsilenced unit. In fact, the sound was very subdued indeed – exactly as it would be if

The left-hand exhaust was more difficult; it was impossible to pull out the inner pipe. So I removed the pipe with the intention of driving the baffle tube out from the front end of the expansion chamber. The bar with which I was intending to drive out the tube would not go into the expansion chamber, and I discovered that the front of the chamber was blocked by a roll of expanded metal. I pulled this out, and another very rusty and oily tube was revealed. This was after a very thorough cleaning. It was a very effective silencer – the exhaust was forced to flow through four rolls of expanded metal as it passed in and out of the homemade silencer tube. The result was that the engine was completely silent – because it would not run at all.

After the tubes were discarded, the engine fired up easily. The bike is basically a race and parade machine, and the slight silencing effect of the tailpipe baffles is sufficient; if it were to be used on the road, a commercial aftermarket exhaust would be a far better option.

The moral of the story is that when you are looking for a solution to a problem, you must use all your senses – and expect the unexpected. The split pins were clearly visible, the sound of the engine was clearly wrong and the behaviour of the engine was exactly what would be expected of a bike with a blocked exhaust.

WHAT HAPPENED NEXT?

Not counting the unique design of the pre-war Scott, the Excelsior Talisman was the first of the post-war two-stroke twins, followed by the Villiers and then the Ariel. Of these, only the Ariel Arrow had any pretensions to being a sporting machine, but this situation would not last. As early as 1957, Yamaha was putting a 250cc two-stroke twin into production. The YD1 was very much a copy of the German Adler twin, and it was just as much a basic form of transport as any of the two-strokes of the 1950s, but it was the start of something that changed the motorcycling world.

By the early 1960s, Yamaha was making a YD2 that came with the letter 'S' – for Sport – added to the model number. Sporting YDS-series Yamahas became a worldwide sales success. At the same time, Suzuki was offering their own 250 twin, called the Colleda. Suzuki had the massive advantage of having signed up Ernst Degner, who had defected from what was then East Germany in 1961, taking some radically different ideas and technology with him. Mat Oxley's book *Stealing Speed* (Haynes, 2010) tells the tale in a highly readable way and is highly recommended.

After some great successes on the race circuits, in 1966, Suzuki released the Super Six, or T20. It was 'the fastest 250 in the world' and 'the first genuinely 100mph 250', as the papers put it at the time. The rule of thumb for a lightweight motorcycle in those days was that you needed 30bhp to reach 160km/h (100mph). The standard Super Six produced 29bhp, so it was a reasonable claim.

Both the Suzuki and the Yamaha could form the basis for a very successful clubman racer, though this was the era when the really complex Grand Prix bikes ruled the roost at the top level of racing. These included machines such as the 3-cylinder, 18-speed, 50cc Suzuki and the 250cc RD05 Yamaha V4.

As far as the club racer was concerned, Yamaha did the race prep themselves when they produced the TD series, race bikes very closely based on the current road models – with more power and fewer bits bolted on.

All of these twins, however, were still basic, piston-ported two-strokes, but the ports were bigger and more numerous, compression ratios were higher and, after Ernst Degner's input, the crucial role of the pressure pulses in the exhaust pipes were beginning to be understood.

Fig. 2.46   Works prototype, tube-framed Ariel Arrow.

Fig. 2.47   Ariel Leader.

Fig. 2.48   Moto Rumi Formichino 125 twin.

Fig. 2.49   Jawa/CZ 250 race version.

a radical rethink from Italy/1
Lambretta Li 125

It is almost heresy to say so in some circles, but one of the most important things that a powered two-wheeler can do is provide transport at relatively low cost. Throughout history, bikes have been either rich men's playthings or working people's transport for work and leisure. It is true that the former are often the classic bikes that capture the imagination – the Brough Superiors, Manx Nortons, Vincents and such, but the machines that have been the most important to the greatest number of people have been the cheap, step-through runabouts, such as the Honda 50 and the products of some radical design thinking in the post-Second World War era – yes, scooters!

Lo stile Italiano – Italian style – is world famous, and so is the Italian genius for engineering innovation. Put those two together, in a post-war world of growing employment, growing population and growing prosperity, where there was a need for a cheap and cheerful way of getting about, and the result was a clean and stylish machine in its own right that allowed the rider to travel while wearing stylish and fashionable clothing. A waxed cotton jacket or dirty old dispatch rider's coat did not cut it on the fashion-conscious streets of Milan.

Scooters were not a new idea, however. The concept of an easy-to-ride, step-through lightweight bike had been tried from the early years of the twentieth century, and in most parts of the world designers had experimented with a frame based on the push-scooter shape of the child's toy, as opposed to the bicycle's diamond frame. Some even retained the stand-up riding position!

In the years immediately after the Second World War, with many former aircraft designers (and aircraft components) having been released from war work, the Piaggio Company, based near Pisa, patented the design of a scooter that remains the basis of most of their machines to this day. The body was a single-piece structure, welded from pressed steel – a monocoque. The front suspension was similar to the nose wheel of a small aircraft and the engine was compact, fitting below the seat and driving the back wheel directly from the output shaft of the gearbox. The streamlined, hard-shell look of the finished machine was said to look a little like a wasp, and since small two-strokes often produce an insect-like buzzing sound, the name Vespa suggested itself to the manufacturers – the Italian for 'wasp'.

Fig. 3.3   Lambretta LD.

Meanwhile, in Lambrate, Milan, another scooter design was beginning to evolve. This was based on a frame made from a single large-diameter tube. Initially, it had only a small leg-shield and was open at the back. The Innocenti company, who developed this design, was originally a producer of steel tubing, hence the design. Various engine layouts were tried for the first four versions, designated the A, B, C and D models.

The real breakthrough came when a fully-enclosed version of the D model was produced in 1951, this was the Lambretta LD. With torsion-bar rear suspension and shaft drive to the back wheel, it was quite expensive to produce, so a simpler design that incorporated the function of the primary chain case with the rear swinging-arm was adopted for the Li and TV models. These were the classic Lambrettas.

Fig. 3.1   Vespa 152 L2.

Fig. 3.2   Lambretta Model A (three-wheeler).

Fig. 3.4   Lambretta Li parts on the bench.

The design of the engine units from these two iconic manufacturers is so different that we need to look at both separately. Bikes from the same era often have a lot of similarities, so that, for example, if you are familiar with a Yamaha FS1-E, you will not find many problems when working on a YB100 from the same factory, or indeed on an AP50 from Suzuki. In this case, however, Lambretta experience is not much help when working on a Vespa.

In this chapter, we shall look at a Lambretta, specifically an early Li model. In fact, it is a very early example – a 1958 Series One Li 125, from the first year of production of this model. In Chapter 4, we'll turn to a 'Super Sports' machine, the Vespa 90SS with advanced rotary-valve inlet and reverse cylinder.

First, though, the Lambretta. The brief was to renew and replace anything that would be needed to restore the machine to 'as new' specification. With this in mind, the engine had already been stripped and the cases bead blasted.

There are some important points to consider in dismantling a Lambretta engine unit, so it was fortunate that another similar engine was available, allowing the dismantling process to be shown.

DISMANTLING A CLASSIC LAMBRETTA

Space is very limited around the engine unit, so for most engine/gearbox jobs, it is almost always best to take the engine out of the frame, or to be more exact, to drop the engine down and wheel the frame away from it.

With the scooter on the centre stand (assuming that the stand brackets are in good condition – if not, you will be able to get them welded up while the engine is out), disconnect the clutch and gear cables by slackening the Allen screws in the solderless cable nipples in the control levers on top of the chain case.

Loosen the carburettor clamp and pull off the carburettor. Suspend it out of the way with its cables still attached.

It is easier to detach the rear brake cable at the pedal end. Do this by loosening the cable clamp nut and pulling the inner cable free. Leave the back brake cable attached to the engine unit for now. If the front end of the inner cable is in good condition, that is not frayed and not twisted, it will go back into the hole in the clamp bolt easily. (I recall soldering the ends of new inner back brake cables to keep the strands from fraying so that they would be easy to refit in the future.)

Unplug the bullet connectors where the generator wires plug into the regulator rectifier and disconnect the HT wire from the plug.

Remove the rear shock absorber and the nuts on the suspension pivot spindle, using a thin bar to drive out the spindle. Pull out the bar.

The frame can now be lifted away, leaving the engine unit, complete with exhaust and rear wheel. Take off the rear wheel by unfastening its four nuts.

Remove the 8mm screws that hold the fan casing to the engine case, and the bolt that holds down the cylinder cowling to the cylinder-head nut. Remove both cowlings.

Remove the two nuts that hold the exhaust to the cylinder flange, and the three nuts that hold the exhaust box to the chain case – there are two on the bracket at the front and another further back on the tailpipe.

Removing the Rear Hub

This is the first point where anyone working on a Lambretta hits difficulty. The rear hub, incorporating the brake drum, fits on to splines on the gearbox output shaft. On its own, this arrangement would not be enough to stop the hub from wearing loose on the shaft and allowing the rear wheel to wobble. To prevent this, there is also a cone collet. The cone is split, and as the hub is tightened on the shaft, it is squeezed by the tapered hole in the hub, clamping tightly around the shaft. This gives good support to the hub and wheel, but it makes the hub very difficult to remove from the shaft.

When I was a student in Liverpool, I worked for a couple of years in a scooter shop. I lost track of the number of times I had to fit a new rear hub to a Lambretta after someone had smashed the original by trying to remove it with a hammer while attempting to change the rear brake shoes. You *must* use an appropriate puller. The usual version has a flange with screws that fasten into threaded holes around the centre of the hub. They are still available.

Sometimes the hub is so tight on the cone that you can strip the threaded holes around the hub centre. In the Liverpool workshop, we had a large spider-style puller that attached to all four of the wheel studs. Regardless of the type, you really cannot do without it.

Both of the engines arrived with the hubs removed, which saved a job.

Dismantling the Top End

The cylinder head and cylinder are held down by four long studs with nuts that bear on the cylinder head. The bottom nut on the opposite side to the flywheel is longer, because it fits

---

LAMBRETTA LI ENGINE SPECIFICATIONS

Bore and stroke: 52 × 58mm (Li 125); 57 × 58mm (Li 150)

Actual cubic capacity: 123cc (Li 125); 148cc (Li 150)

Compression ratio: 7:1

Claimed power: 5.2bhp (Li 125); 6.5bhp (Li 150)

Carburettor size: 18mm (Li 125); 19mm (Li 150)

Cooling: fan

Gearbox: 4-speed, operated by twistgrip

Transmission: chain primary drive to multi-plate clutch

Ignition: flywheel magneto with external HT coil

Fig. 3.5   Cylinder-head nuts.

Fig. 3.6   The condition of the piston.

the bolt that secures the engine cowling.

Loosen the nuts gradually and pull the head off the studs. The cylinder can be removed easily in the same way.

The standard Lambretta piston (made by Borgo) has flat circlips to retain the gudgeon pin, so you will need circlip pliers to remove them. On the sample engine, there had been a very great deal of blow-by past the rings, which had caused carbon staining on the piston skirt. This was a sign that at the very least the engine needed new rings, but more likely a rebore.

Although you can remove just one gudgeon-pin circlip, sometimes it is better to remove both, because this makes it easier to push out the pin.

GUDGEON-PIN CIRCLIPS

Although it is always good policy to renew wire circlips each time they are removed, reusing flat circlips is perfectly acceptable. One thing you must never do is fit a flat circlip in a piston meant for a wire one, or a wire circlip in a piston meant for a flat one. The groove for a flat circlip is square, while that for a wire circlip is semi-circular. Fitting the wrong type will wreck any two-stroke motor.

The Flywheel Side

The centre of the flywheel is covered by a spun-aluminium cover, which is held in place by a large wire ring. One end of the ring has a tail that can be grasped with pliers, allowing you to wind it out. The cover can then be removed.

Fig. 3.7   Removing the flywheel with a puller.

The flywheel is held by a nut that has a left-hand thread, so turn it clockwise to undo it. The conventional holder for the flywheel is a device that engages with the two access slots in the flywheel, but if you are careful, you can use a tommy bar passed through one slot and bearing against the end of one of the generator coils' pole pieces.

After that, you will need a flywheel puller to remove the flywheel from its tapered shaft. The puller has a conventional right-hand thread and has flats on the top that allow you to prevent the flywheel from turning with a spanner, while you tighten the extractor screw with another.

With the flywheel out of the way, you can undo the three screws that hold the stator plate. Before you can take the stator out, however, you need to free the seal for the wiring loom. The wire comes out of the flywheel case through a watertight seal, fastened to the top of the casing with two screws. Undo the screws, remove the top plate and slide the rubber grommet off the wire. You will then be able to pull the wires gently through the hole and remove the stator. Put it back inside the flywheel to preserve the magnetic field.

The Chain Case

On the other side of the engine unit, fourteen 10mm nuts and studs attach the chain case cover. There are two

Fig. 3.8   The fourteen nuts on the chaincase. Note the brass oil drain plug at lower left.

other M8 studs at the upper right; these hold the bracket that supports the silencer. Before releasing the nuts, make a quick check that the oil has been drained. This can be done by removing the brass drain plug from the case. The plug has a magnetic insert, and an examination of the magnet will give an idea of the condition of the gears and kickstart mechanism, since it will have captured any steel debris inside the casing.

With the nuts and washers removed, an easy way to break the seal and lift the cover away from the inner case is to pull on the clutch operating lever on the top. This will press on the clutch and lift the outer cover. The kickstart shaft will come out with the cover. You do not need to remove it at this stage.

Fig. 3.9   Examine the teeth on the kickstart. In this case, there are definite signs of wear, making replacement of the plunger necessary.

Lift the cover away and turn it over to examine the condition of the teeth on the kickstart mechanism. In the sample engine, the teeth were showing definite signs of rounding over and wear, and the plunger was due for replacement as a result. Put the outer case on a tray to allow the remaining oil to drain off where it will not cause problems.

Fig. 3.10   *The components inside the chaincase.*

Fig. 3.11   *The cush-drive components.*

It is best to remove it at this stage to prevent it from falling off and becoming lost later.

The five clutch springs are held under pressure by a large flat circlip that fits into a groove around the inside of the clutch 'spider'. This means that if you remove the circlip, the whole assembly will fly apart and might hit you in the face. You need to compress the clutch centre to take the load off the circlip and then release the pressure on the springs in a controlled manner.

HAND PRESSURE

I have seen a clutch centre compressed by hand when, during an emergency clutch repair miles from anywhere, a friend took a stranglehold on the chaincase and pressed the clutch centre down with his thumbs sufficiently to allow me to replace the circlip! This is not recommended, and may not even be possible, unless you are exceptionally strong (this man was!).

The Clutch and Primary Drive

The chain case contains the crankshaft cush drive, the primary chain and chain guides, the clutch and the gearbox.

To remove the cush drive, whose job is to smooth out the torque fluctuations as the engine goes through its cycle, and also to protect the engine and transmission from road shocks, simply undo the bolt in the centre of the outer cap. The spring is strong, but the bolt is a long one. This allows the pressure on the spring to be reduced gradually, so the whole assembly is not going to fly off and hit you in the face.

The components of this assembly are the outer cap, the spring, the outer face-cam, the inner face-cam (which incorporates the sprocket) and the splined sleeve. Once the bolt is removed, the cap, spring and outer face-cam can be pulled away easily, though you may need to slacken the chain tension by moving the chain guide downward before you finally remove the sprocket. Locking strips

with bent-up tabs secure the screws that hold the chain guide, so you will need to flatten the tabs to slacken the screws. The upper chain guide is adjustable, so slide it downwards to slacken the chain. The splined sleeve that drives the outer face-cam fits on to a smaller spline on the end of the crankshaft, and it can be pulled off easily. Because there is very little clearance between the casing and the chain, it is far better to leave the sprocket and chain in place until the clutch is removed, when both assemblies come out easily together.

Dismantling the Clutch

The first thing to notice is that in the centre of the clutch pressure plate there is a small – about 8mm (0.3in) diameter – thimble-shaped cap that fits over a pin protruding from the pressure plate. This is important, since it forms a thrust bearing for the clutch release mechanism. Without it, the pin would wear a hole in the release lever.

The official tool for the job is a device that attaches to the four studs that sit on opposite sides of the casing surrounding the clutch. A strong bar bridges the clutch and a central screw can be tightened to compress the springs. These tools are relatively inexpensive; if you are a Lambretta owner, you should have one in your toolbox.

However, if you are lucky enough to have a well-equipped workshop, there is another way. Level the engine unit on wooden blocks on the bed of

Fig. 3.12   *You can use a bench drill to compress the clutch.*

a bench drill, then fit a socket over the chuck jaws, using this and the feed lever to compress the springs so that you can remove the circlip with narrow-nose pliers or, failing that, a small screwdriver. Left-handed people will find this easier, since every drill press that I have ever used has the operating lever on the right.

Once the circlip has been removed, release the pressure gradually and remove the clutch plates. With the clutch plates out of the way, the central nut and locking tab should be tackled next.

Fig. 3.13   A cold chisel flattens the tab washer.

A small cold chisel can be used to bend the locking tab away from the nut. This is a more effective tool than a screwdriver.

An old tyre lever can be used to hold the clutch centre while the nut is loosened, resting between the gaps in the clutch centre (the spider) and the clutch basket. The curve of the tyre lever will prevent it from blocking access to the nut.

Once both parts of the clutch are free, the clutch and front sprocket can be removed, along with the primary chain. It is worth examining the chain guides for wear and general condition.

There have been accidents in the past with some poor-quality aftermarket chain guides, where welds have failed and the guide has ended up wrapped around the sprocket, causing a disastrous transmission lock-up. I have never encountered this problem with original Innocenti parts, despite some serious abuse in competition engines. On the other hand, much more substantial cast-aluminium chain guides are available and are recommended for the very high-powered modern scooter racing engines.

The Gearbox

Fig. 3.15   The iron gear plate.

The Lambretta gearbox is possibly the easiest gearbox to understand in the history of motorcycle transmissions. To gain access to it, you must remove the iron gearbox end-plate that lies behind the clutch. The plate is held in place by six 10mm nuts and studs. There are also two other threaded holes at the top and bottom of the plate. These allow you to screw two M6 screws into the holes to force the plate away from the main casing. With the end-plate removed, the large gear that carries the kickstart ratchet teeth can be lifted off the final-drive shaft. There is not very much room around the gears, so it is helpful to use a small hook. (The hook was designed to make it easy to fit the exhaust-pipe springs that hold the pipes to the cylinders of race bikes.) Use the hook to lift the rear side of the gear as you lift the front side by hand.

An important point when removing the gear shafts is to make a careful note of the shim washers on the ends of the shafts. These are used to set the correct end-float for the shafts. There may be one on each shaft or, most often, one on each end of the two shafts, or sometimes none at all.

Fig. 3.17   The sliding-spline gear selector.

Remove all four gears, then the other gearbox shaft with the fixed gears. You will now be able to see that there is a 'sliding spline' that can engage with square notches on the inner side of each gear pinion. This slider simply selects which pair of gears actually drives the rear wheel. You will also see that there is a lever that fits into a grooved ring on the slider. That lever links to the bell crank that connects to the cables that run to the gearchange twistgrip. You will probably realize that the condition of the hardened ends of the slider has a very important bearing on whether the bike has a tendency to jump out of gear. It is important that there is only minimal rounding

Fig. 3.18   Remove the split cone from the drive shaft. The rectangular plate that holds the drive-shaft bearing can also be seen.

Fig. 3.14   Preventing the clutch from turning.

Fig. 3.16   Removing the gear pinions.

Fig. 3.19   Examine the slider carefully. This one shows signs of wear.

off of the slider ends. You will be able to inspect the slider more thoroughly with the final-drive shaft out of the casing.

After removing the split cone that centres and secures the rear hub, the shaft can be driven out of its bearing from the outside, using a soft-faced mallet of course.

The slider in the sample engine was in acceptable condition, but it displayed signs of wear. It would be replaced as a matter of course during a full engine reconditioning.

Replacing the Slider

It is not immediately obvious, but the final-drive shaft consists of several concentric components. The slider itself has five notches on the inside of the legs – one for each of the four gears and a smaller one for neutral. The central part of the shaft has a hole drilled across its diameter, which contains two ball bearings and a spring. The ball bearings press against the notches in the legs of the slider and hold it in the correct positions to select the gears (see Fig. 3.19). This detent mechanism also provides the 'click' feel at the gearchange twistgrip that informs the rider that they have changed gear successfully. However, this means that if you simply pull the slider out of the

final-drive shaft, the ball bearings and spring will fly out and lose themselves in a far corner of the workshop. If you know about this, you can keep your hand around the shaft and catch them. Otherwise, put the shaft in a plastic bag before removing the slider.

To fit a new slider, you need to put the spring and the two ball bearings into the cross-hole, compressing the spring so that the ball bearings are level with the bottom of the spline grooves. This can be done by using the flats of two smallish screwdrivers (the blades need to fit into the slots in the shaft) to hold the bearings and spring while the slider legs are slid on to the shaft.

The Drive Shaft

The drive-shaft bearing is secured in the casing by a rectangular plate bolted to the outside of the case, in the centre of the rear brake backplate. Once the cone and shaft are out of the way, remove the four nuts and retaining plate. After warming the case gently, the drive-shaft bearing can be tapped outwards from the gearbox side.

The Crankshaft, Main Bearings and Seals

Turning to the other end of the engine/ gearbox casing, the design of the Lambretta makes the job of replacing the main bearings and seals relatively easy. Indeed, if this is the only task that you need to do, all of the procedures for dismantling the gearbox described so far can be ignored. It is only necessary to remove the outer cover and the front sprocket/cush-drive assembly. Any readers who own engines of conventional motorcycle design will feel a touch of envy at this point!

Instead of splitting along the centre line of the crankcase, Lambrettas mount the flywheel-side main bearing and seal in a large 'plug' incorporating the backplate of the fan housing. The three nuts that hold this housing to the main casing lie between the screws that secure the stator plate.

Remove the three nuts and insert M6 screws into the two threaded holes at top and bottom of the plate. This will jack the backplate away from the joint between the two parts of the crankcase, but you will need to tap very gently around the backplate to remove it completely from the main casing.

The crankshaft can then be tapped out of the drive-side main bearing from the other side.

Fig. 3.22   The condition of the crank.

The condition of the sample engine's crank was not pretty! It was completely coated with carbon deposits, which meant that combustion products must have been leaking past the piston. It was also very likely that the drive-side oil seal had been allowing gear oil into the crankcase, meaning that the combustion had been very oily as well. Examine the seal. The two key aspects are the garter ring, the little spring ring that squeezes the seal on to the shaft, and the lip of the seal itself. The lip, which is the part that actually touches the shaft, must be sharp. If it is even

Fig. 3.20   You can hold the ball bearings with two screwdrivers.

Fig. 3.21   Three nuts between the stator-plate screws.

Fig. 3.23   The seal plate inside the crankcase.

slightly rounded or flattened, it will leak. Any damage or distortion to the garter ring is also the seal's passport to the dustbin.

To replace the seal is a simple job, since it is carried in a round plate held to the inside of the crankcase by three countersunk screws. You will need an impact driver to undo them, though. Remove the plate and push the old seal out, replacing it with the new one. Of course, the open face of the seal faces to the inside. The plate also holds the bearing in place, so having warmed the case a little, tap out the bearing and replace it.

Fig. 3.24   The inner race remains on the shaft.

The flywheel-side bearing can be more difficult to change. The inner race of the bearing remains on the left-hand end of the shaft. Most of the time, the inner race can be removed from the shaft by using a cold chisel to wedge the inner race away from the shoulder on the shaft. Do this very carefully, because you do not want the chisel to touch the shaft itself. In a difficult case, you might need to grind a notch in the race to split it. Use a grinding point in a Dremel or electric drill for this, being

---

BEARING VARIATIONS

It is worth noting that although the bearing used in the sample engine had a plain sleeve as the inner race, with the rollers and cage retained in the outer race, this is not always the type of bearing used. Sometimes, as will be seen with the Vespa in the following chapter, the outer race is the one that is free while the inner race holds the rollers. I know of no reason why one type should be preferred over the other.

---

even more careful not to damage the shaft. If you are lucky enough to have a full set of bearing removal pullers, it may include a suitable tool; an ordinary three-legged sprocket puller will not be able to grip the bearing race.

To replace the inner race easily, place the crank (discreetly, in a clean bag, for the sake of domestic harmony) in the freezer. When it is thoroughly chilled, heat the inner bearing race in boiling water; you will find that it drops freely on to the frozen shaft.

EXAMINING THE CRANK

As always, you need to check the condition of the crank, especially the taper and keyway that drive the flywheel, the sealing surfaces where the crank seals rub against the shaft itself, and most of all the big end.

Fig. 3.25   Examine the taper and keyway.

Sometimes, the flywheel does not bed down closely enough on to the taper on the crank. Sometimes the fixing nut is not tightened properly. In this situation, the flywheel can chatter from side to side on the taper as the engine speeds up and slows down, because of the acceleration of the piston as it goes through the power stroke and deceleration on the up stroke. This repeatedly batters on the sides of the Woodruff key, the only purpose of which is to locate the flywheel in the correct place while it is tightened up on the taper, so it will not tolerate such treatment. The key is not meant to drive the flywheel; the friction of the taper does that. This repeated battering eventually will shear the key, and most likely the remains of it will damage the taper as the flywheel spins on the shaft. The chances are that an uninformed owner will blame the key and buy another one. Even worse, he or she may decide to get a stronger one, made of harder steel. With a scarred

taper from the previous event, there is even less chance of the flywheel fitting snugly to the taper, so the next time the key fails, it will probably ruin the keyway, and that means a new crank. In the sample engine, the keyway was in good condition.

The big-end bearing can be checked for play. There should be no noticeable up-and-down movement, and anything more that the slightest side-to-side rock is a bad sign.

Fig. 3.26   Checking for play in the big-end bearing.

A dial gauge is used to measure up-and-down play in the big-end bearing while the crank is held between centres in a lathe. There was no measurable play in the sample engine's big end. Side-float at the big end is a little more complicated. Early Lambrettas use 'bottom guided' connecting rods. That means there is only a small clearance between the sides of the big-end bearing and the cheeks of the flywheel. There are soft thrust washers in the clearance to guide the connecting rod and keep it straight in the cylinder. On some of the later, bigger engines, there is a lot more clearance, intended to allow more lubrication to reach the big-end bearing. So in this case, the connecting rod is 'top guided' by thrust washers on the gudgeon pin on either side of the small-end bearing, between the small-end eye and the inside of the piston boss. Opinions are divided about which is the better design, top guided or bottom guided.

REASSEMBLING THE BOTTOM END

The first step is to install the main bearing into the main casing. Warm the casing, preferably with a heat gun rather than a blowtorch.

When the casing is hot, the bearing will *almost* drop into its housing, though first you must wipe around the housing with a clean cloth to ensure that there is no dirt or grit that would prevent the bearing from fitting all the way. If you need to tap it into place, use a small pin punch against the outer race, switching around the circumference to ensure that it remains straight as it goes in. Next fit the plate that carries the new seal. (The open side of the seal faces inwards, towards the crank, of course.) Wipe the three countersunk screws clean and apply some locking fluid to the threads. Fit the screws and tighten them well.

The crank is a stiff sliding fit on the inner race of the bearing, so once you have applied a spot of oil or grease to the lip of the seal, it should slide into the bearing. Clearly you have to position the connecting rod at BDC and tilt the crank to fit the rod through the cylinder base, but after that it should slide straight in.

Clean up the flywheel side of the crankcase and fit a new gasket to the joint. The procedures for replacing the bearing and seal were described previously. Line them up with the studs and fit them to the main casting. Once again, the seal should be lubricated, while a hot main case and a cold flywheel side will ensure easy assembly. Fit the nuts to the three studs and tighten them to about 10Nm (7.5lb ft).

ASSEMBLING THE CLUTCH AND GEARBOX SIDE

The Gearbox

The first component to go into the casing is the drive-shaft bearing. However, if you have removed the rectangular plate from the centre of the back brake backplate, you should replace this first, since it locates the bearing in the housing and stops it from being pushed out of the casing when the drive shaft is fitted. Drop the bearing into the heated casing and tap it down to rest against the plate. It is a good idea to replace the O-ring that forms the oil seal on this shaft. Lubricate it well before you fit the shaft.

1. Put the shim washer on to the shaft.
2. Slide the drive shaft into the bearing, carefully lining up the little pivoting blocks on the gear change-lever forks with the ring groove on the selector slider.
3. Fit the fixed-gear shaft, with its shim washer, into the blind bearing housing with the needle-roller bearing in it.

Fig. 3.27   The gearbox assembled outside the cases.

4. Unfortunately, without making a sectioned crankcase, it is not at all easy to photograph the gearbox internals to show how they are assembled inside the casing. However, Fig. 3.27 shows an assembled gearbox outside the casing. When assembled in the casing, however, this is the other way up. The shaft fits into the bearing, the selector-groove ring engages with the gearchange lever and the small gear shaft goes in before any of the bigger gears. The smallest free gear, which is the fourth-gear pinion, goes in first. The slightly thicker boss in the centre of the gear goes downwards, towards the rear hub.
5. Fit the third-gear pinion, also with the thicker boss downward, then second-gear pinion, fitting them over the dogs of the slider. The second pinion has the drive dogs cut away on the upper side to give clearance for the selector dogs to provide a neutral gear. There is a similar cutaway on the lower side of the first-gear pinion, which has ratchet teeth on the upper side to engage with the kickstart mechanism.
6. Finally, the iron bearing plate fits over the upper ends of the shafts and is fixed by the five nuts and studs.
7. Check that all the shafts turn smoothly in all four gears. You can operate the gear change by turning the gearchange lever on top of the case.
8. To check the end-float, you will need to fit the clutch spider to the clutch shaft, making sure it is quite tight.
9. With a feeler gauge, measure the gap between the iron gearbox bearing plate and the boss of the first-gear pinion. It should be 0.5mm, plus or minus 0.2mm. If it is significantly more than this, you need to add shim washers; if it is less, to fit thinner shims. Genuine shims come in 2.0, 2.3 and 2.4mm thicknesses.
10. Remove the clutch spider again and tighten the bearing plate nuts to 5Nm (3.5lb ft).

The Clutch

During the dismantling process, you will have noted that the drive chain runs very close to the casing and is difficult to wrangle through the gap, so it is well worth fitting the chain on to the teeth of the clutch basket before you fit it to the shaft. Also, the clutch basket

Fig. 3.28   The clutch centre bearing(s).

runs on a pair of needle-roller bearings that in turn run on a boss on the clutch spider, so these four components can be assembled together and then fitted on to the clutch shaft of the gearbox. The spider engages with splines on the shaft and is secured with a lock washer and nut. A mirror image of Fig. 3.14 would illustrate the process of holding the spider while the nut is tightened. A torque of 65Nm (48lb ft) is the recommended setting for this nut before it is locked by bending up the tab washer.

At this stage, you need to set up the arrangement that you used to compress the clutch springs to dismantle the assembly. The first thing to note is that you need to assemble the springs, the pressure plate, all the lined plates, the thicker top plate and the circlip, in the correct order before you fit the springs under the pressure plate and compress them, either with a spring compressor or a bench drill. In a standard clutch, a lined plate goes at the bottom of the pile, followed by a steel plate, then alternate plates until the thicker steel plate goes on top.

BEEFING UP

Adding an extra steel plate at the bottom of the pile is a cheap fix for a clutch that needs to withstand the extra load of a slightly uprated engine. Clutch upgrades go much further than this for the modern high-performance hybrid 250cc-plus motors!

Persuading the springs to sit nicely in their recesses in the spider and pressure plate is easy if the clutch is horizontal, but it can be a problem if the engine is still in the frame with the clutch vertical. In this case, you can buy, or make, a holder with a circle of pegs that fit through the holes in the pressure plate and locate the springs while the clutch is compressed.

Compress the pressure plate and fit the clutch plates into their notches in the spider (the steel plates) and the clutch basket (the lined plates). When everything is in place, fit the circlip. Just work around with a screwdriver to make sure it is well settled into its groove before releasing the pressure.

Finally, fit the little thimble release-bearing cap to the peg in the middle of the spider.

The Cush Drive

Fit the front sprocket on to the splined sleeve, engage the chain with the sprocket and fit the sleeve on to the spline on the drive end of the crankshaft.

The other part of the cush-drive face cam, the spring and the top plate (shown in Fig. 3.11) go on next, then the bolt can be fitted and tightened. The spring has to be compressed slightly, but this takes very little pressure. Tightening torque for this bolt is 30Nm (22lb ft).

The Kickstart

Before refitting the outer cover, the kickstart assembly must be renovated with a new ratchet plunger. This is a simple task, but really it needs two pairs of hands. The plunger is held in a retracted position when the kickstart pedal is in the up position.

A pin sticks out of the side of the plunger and runs into a slot in the bracket shown in Fig. 3.29. The angle of this slot pushes the plunger back, away from the ratchet teeth on the first-gear pinion.

To remove the plunger, you need to move the kickstart mechanism so that the pin on the plunger is out of the slot. The simplest way to do this is to fit the kickstart pedal to the shaft, then persuade someone to hold the cover and operate the pedal, holding it against the tension of the kickstart return

Fig. 3.29 The kickstart plate.

spring. When the pin is free of the slot, it can be unscrewed from the plunger with an 8mm spanner. The plunger will then spring out of its housing, under the pressure of its own internal spring. Assembly is the reverse of this process.

The job can also be done single-handed by mounting the boss of the kickstart pedal in a vice and using your body to hold the cover against the kickstart return spring, leaving your hands free to remove and replace the plunger.

To replace a broken kickstart return spring, you have to remove the kickstart shaft from the cover. First, you must remove the circlip and washer that holds the kickstart shaft in place.

After that, the process is similar to that described previously, by turning the shaft so that the pin clears the slot, then pulling the kickstart shaft out of the cover. To turn the shaft, the only method that I have found effective is to clamp locking pliers to the plunger housing and use them to turn the shaft.

Installing a new spring is a matter of fitting the ends of the spring into holes

Fig. 3.30 Winding up the kickstart spring can be done by one person.

Fig. 3.31 Fit the washer and circlip to the kickstart shaft.

in the cover and shaft respectively, and then winding the spring up until the plunger shaft can be pushed past the end of the bracket with the guide slot in it. The shaft can then be pushed all the way into place and the washer and circlip replaced.

The drive-side outer cover can be fitted next, with a new gasket, the M6 nuts being tightened gradually and evenly to 5Nm (3.5lb ft).

The Flywheel Magneto Assembly

The first task is to thread the generator wires through the hole in the top of the casing. The seal that prevents water from running into the generator consists of two metal plates with cup-shaped dimples in them and a rubber gland grommet. Fit the lower plate over the cable, then the grommet and finally the top plate. The seal assembly is held to the casing by two slotted screws – but do not fit them yet!

The stator plate must be lined up, and the three M6 nuts and washers fitted finger-tight to the fixing studs. Next the cable should be adjusted so that it is neither stretched nor kinked too loosely. Only then can the seal screws be fitted and tightened. These squeeze the plates together and squash the grommet tightly around the cable, making a watertight seal. Leave the stator nuts finger-tight for now, since you will need to be able to move the stator to set the ignition timing later.

Wipe both the crankshaft taper and the inner surface of the flywheel hub to make sure that there is nothing to prevent the taper from fitting snugly. If the front end of the key is a millimetre or so lower than the back, that might help the key to engage with the key-way in the flywheel.

Taking great care to line up the key on the crankshaft with the keyway in the hub of the flywheel, fit the flywheel on to the crankshaft. A little gentle jig-gling could be needed, but when the flywheel is fully on the crank, just turn it to ensure that the crank moves with it. Fit the washer and nut, tightening it slightly and temporarily while holding the flywheel by hand.

SETTING IGNITION TIMING

This is the point at which the timing should be set. The first step is to set the maximum points gap. Turn the fly-wheel until the points are at their maxi-mum gap. This should be very close to 0.35mm (0.013in). A screw secures the plate that carries the fixed contact. Loosen it just sufficiently to allow the adjustment. Then, using a screwdriver in the notches provided, adjust the gap to the correct value, as measured by a feeler gauge. A safe timing for an early Lambretta on modern petrol will have the points opening when the piston is 2mm Before Top Dead Centre. If you prefer to use a timing degree wheel, 2mm BTDC represents 18–19 degrees of advance. To adjust the timing, move the stator plate in the curved slots into which the three studs fit. If you have left the nuts loose, you will be able to move the stator with a screwdriver through the windows in the flywheel. Of course, you will need to remove the flywheel again to tighten the nuts on the stator plate once the timing has been set correctly, but it will pull off easily because you did not tighten the flywheel nut.

With everything correctly set and tight, refit the flywheel again and replace the nut and washer. Prevent the flywheel from turning with either a Y-shaped Lambretta flywheel holder or a strap wrench, then tighten the flywheel nut to 68Nm (50lb ft). This is important.

Fig. 3.32 The generator cable and sealing gland.

Normally, the next step would be to fit the aluminium flywheel centre cover, but the sample engine was to be fitted with electronic ignition before installation in the frame, and neither the ignition nor the chassis had yet been delivered. On very early Li models, this cover is secured by two slot-headed screws instead of the big wire circlip used later.

ASSEMBLING THE TOP END

This is a very straightforward task on a Lambretta.

1. Fit the rings to the piston, noting that they do have a right way up – the ring locating pins are in the lower edge of the ring groove.
2. Fit the far-side circlip to the piston. Turn it a little in its groove to make sure that it is seated fully.
3. Fit the small-end roller bearing to the connecting-rod small end.
4. Warm the piston.
5. Making sure that the arrow on the piston crown points towards the exhaust port, put the piston on the end of the connecting rod and push the gudgeon pin through.
6. Fit the other circlip to the piston. Again, check that it is fully seated.
7. Fit a new cylinder base gasket.
8. Make sure that the piston rings are resting nicely with the gaps astride the piston-ring pins.
9. Smear a little oil around the inside of the cylinder.
10. Fit the cylinder on to the long studs.
11. Squeeze the rings with your fingers and ease them into the chamfer around the base of the cylinder.
12. Slide the cylinder all the way down, then turn the engine to check that everything moves smoothly.
13. Fit a new head gasket.
14. Fit the cylinder head so that the plug is at the top.
15. Fit the washers and cylinder-stud nuts. Tighten them in a diagonal pattern, gradually working up evenly to a torque setting of 20Nm (15lb ft).

At this stage, the sample engine was put back on the shelf to await installation in the restored chassis and bodywork.

Fig. 3.33   *Make sure the rings are located on their pins.*

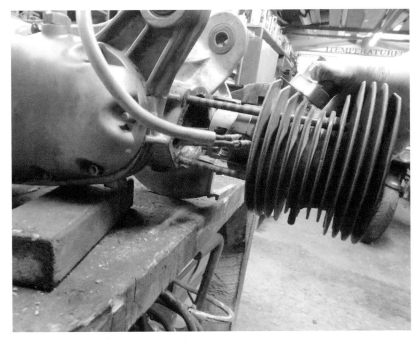

Fig. 3.34   *The cylinder should slide on easily.*

Fig. 3.35   *The cylinder head – this side up.*

Fig. 4.1 The Vespa 90SS.

a radical rethink from Italy/2
Vespa 90SS

Since the introduction of the first GS models in 1955, there have been only two basic body styles for Vespas: the larger ones, with detachable side covers over the engine and spare wheel, and the small-body models introduced in the early 1960s to satisfy the market in those countries that allowed young people to ride 50cc bikes at sixteen. To be honest, these small-body Vespas have always been my favourite scooters. I like them for their lively performance, together with their lightness and nimbleness in traffic, and in competition. In their day, they were all conquering in off-road scooter competitions.

The iconic small-body Vespa is the 90SS, which has a spare wheel on the footboard and a little dummy tank above it. Thanks to Andrew Butler of The Vespa Club of Britain, whose 90SS is shown here, you can see the process of renovating the engine unit. Like many of the projects in this book, it had not been run for some time, but it was complete and turned freely.

DISMANTLING

Whenever working on a complete engine on the bench, the first step is to remove anything that makes the unit bulkier or heavier, or that is liable to be damaged. In this case, undo the clamp bolt underneath and remove the kickstart pedal.

The nut that holds the rear brake hub is underneath a little metal dome in the centre of the hub, and it is locked with a split pin, which must be pulled out first.

The hub must be held to prevent it from turning as you loosen the nut, which can be done quite easily by holding the brake on. This can be achieved with a screwdriver in the shock absorber bush and a tyre lever against the brake lever. This method leaves a hand free to undo the nut.

Fig. 4.2 The rear hub.

VESPA 90SS ENGINE SPECIFICATIONS

No. of cylinders: 1
Bore and stroke: 47 × 51mm
Cubic capacity: 88.5cc
Compression ratio: 8.7:1
Power: 6bhp at 6,000rpm
Cooling: forced air
Induction: rotary
Carburettor: 16mm
Fuel/oil mixture: 2 per cent
Ignition: flywheel magneto
Starting: kickstart
Clutch: multiple-disc in oil bath
Gears: 4-speed, operated by twistgrip
Claimed performance: maximum speed, 93km/h (58mph); acceleration,
    0–80km/h (0–50mph) in 13sec; fuel consumption, 3.14ltr/100km (90mpg)

Fig. 4.6   *Carbon inside the cylinder head.*

Unlike the Lambretta, the Vespa rear brake is mounted simply on a splined shaft, not a spline and taper, so a sharp tap on the shaft end with a soft mallet will be enough to allow the brake hub to be pulled clear.

Fig. 4.3   *Omega clips on the brake shoe pins.*

The brake shoes are retained at the pivots by wire omega clips, which should be removed carefully without bending them.

The single brake spring is very strong, so to remove the brake shoes, turn the brake lever so that the brake cam holds the shoes fully apart. Then gently lever the shoes up. Be careful! They will come clear of the pivot pin with a snap. Make sure your fingers are not in the way.

The screws that hold the ignition coil are inside the flywheel casing, so turn the unit over and remove the flywheel cover next. Remove the slotted screws from around the edge of the cover and lift it away, exposing the flywheel. The lower part of the cover is visible when the bike is assembled, so it needs to be examined carefully. Put it aside safely.

Removing the Cylinder Assembly

A quick inspection of the piston through the exhaust port suggested that this engine would need a rebore, so the next step was to remove the cylinder head, cylinder and piston.

The cylinder head is fastened by four studs with hex screws measuring 11mm across flats. It was thoroughly coated with carbon.

Note that the cylinder fits with the exhaust port on the upper side of the engine – it is a reverse-cylinder motor! The inlet does not fit to the cylinder; it is bolted to the crankcase, where it is controlled by a specially machined and cutaway crankshaft web that acts as a rotary inlet valve.

The head should be set aside for a good clean-up later.

The inlet tract does not need to be removed at this stage, although taking it off does give you slightly better access to the cylinder base nuts, which should be loosened evenly and gradually to prevent possible distortion.

The cylinder can now be pulled off the studs and the condition of the bore and piston examined.

Fig. 4.7   *Removing the gudgeon-pin circlips.*

The gudgeon pin is held in place by flat circlips, so circlip pliers are needed to remove them. Once the circlips are out, the piston can be warmed gently to allow the gudgeon pin to be pushed out with a pin punch.

Fig. 4.4   *Lever off the brake shoes.*

Fig. 4.5   *Undo the cylinder-head nuts.*

Fig. 4.8   *Blow-by on the piston skirt.*

There was carbon staining below the rings, which is evidence of blow-by – burning gases leaking past the rings. There were also signs of piston seizures on the upper side.

The small-end bearing can be removed from the small end of the connecting rod, and in this case, since a new gudgeon pin was to be fitted with the new piston, it was discarded. It displayed some wear marks to the rollers, and there was measurable (with a micrometer) wear to the pin.

The cylinder was measured in the manner shown in previous chapters, and this indicated that it had close to 0.2mm variation in bore between the best and worst parts of the cylinder. That meant that it was worn beyond the point of being restorable by a rebore to the first oversize of 47.2mm. After obtaining a second-oversize piston, the cylinder was sent to a rebore specialist to be bored to give the

PATTERN PARTS

Many owners have had issues with pistons and other pattern-part components of dubious quality sourced from countries with 'developing' economies. At the present time, buying such parts is rarely a good option if original manufacturer's parts are obtainable instead. However, it is important to realize that Vespa, for example, did not make all the components in their machines. Manufacturers always buy in many of their components, and it may be possible, as in the case of the sample Vespa engine, to buy a piston that was made by the same firm that sold them to the manufacturer. You can find the same thing with Japanese machinery, and it is well worth seeking OEM parts in this way.

On the other hand, I remember when Japanese components were regarded with the same suspicion as those from India or the Far East today. I hope that in the foreseeable future, metallurgy and quality control will be brought up to the highest standards in these developing countries, too, and that warnings like this will be no longer needed.

proper clearance fit at the second over-size of 47.4mm.

Removing the Flywheel and Stator

Two types of flywheel are used in the small Vespas. The early models, such as the subject of this chapter, have a self-extracting flywheel just like the Villiers engine covered in Chapter 1. Later examples require the use of a screw-in type of flywheel puller like the Lambretta. The only problem in this case was that the wire circlip that fits above the flywheel nut was missing, so the nut could not extract the flywheel. However, it was a simple matter to take a length of piano wire, wind it around a brush handle to produce a smooth circle, cut it to length and fit it into the extraction groove on the inside of the flywheel centre. It would have been possible to order a replacement circlip, of course, but the materials to make one were at hand.

Fig. 4.9   Remove the flywheel nut.

With the circlip in place, you need to hold the flywheel to prevent it from turning, and a strap wrench is ideal. The factory flywheel holding tool bolts to the casing and incorporates an arm welded at right angles that engages with the fan blades on the flywheel.

Fig. 4.10   Three screws secure the stator plate.

With the flywheel removed, the three screws that hold the stator plate can be unscrewed and the stator plate lifted out of the casing.

The ignition and lighting wires are connected to the main wiring harness in a black plastic connector block fastened to the swinging-arm part of the engine casting. These will have been disconnected from the main harness when the engine was taken out of the frame, but the wires now need to be disconnected from the block so that they can pass through the hole in the case. The wires are fed through a rubber sleeve that fits through the rearmost of two holes in the casing. Normally the wires and the sleeve could be eased out of the hole, but in this case the rubber was disintegrating and it just came apart. A replacement was added to the spares order.

WIRING WOES

The problem of disintegrating insulation and sleeving occurred frequently with the projects in this book. The solutions varied from simply fitting a heat-shrink sleeve over the top of a brittle and cracking outer sleeve to creating a complete new wiring harness with modern wires, and even to replacing an entire stator assembly to obtain a new shiny cable. The Internet is full of advice on how to replace stator wiring, and many rebuild specialists offer this service relatively cheaply. It is a task that requires some soldering equipment and the skill to use it, and the ability to follow a logical sequence of operations. Of course, many restorers choose this opportunity to fit a modern electronic ignition system in place of the points ignition at the same time.

Removing the Clutch

The one downside to the very compact design of these engines is that access to some components is restricted. That is why the first step in removing the clutch is to take off the rear brake backplate. After releasing the three nuts that hold it in place, the backplate can simply be pulled away, exposing the gasket and the drive-shaft oil seal.

Fig. 4.11   The clutch cover is behind the brake backplate.

You will now be able to access the six screws that secure the clutch cover. Vespas are a little unusual in that their M6 screws and nuts require an 11mm spanner instead of the more usual 10mm size. Operating the clutch release lever by hand will separate the cover from the main casting.

Under the cover, you will see the clutch, and another big difference from the conventional design is that this clutch is removed as a complete assembly, not one plate at a time.

Fig. 4.12   Remove the clutch centre plate.

Fig. 4.13   Undo the clutch centre nut.

To access the clutch nut, remove the round release plate in the centre of the top clutch plate. It is held in place by a wire clip with ears that fit under the inner edge of the plate. A small screwdriver will free the clip, allowing the plate to be lifted off.

To unfasten the clutch nut, you will need to prevent the clutch from turning. Various methods can be employed, some more primitive than others, but I prefer simply fitting a ring spanner to the nut on the end of the crank while using a socket on the clutch nut.

Next, flatten the tab of the tab washer and remove the nut and washer. You will need a special puller to remove the clutch from the taper on the shaft. This has an internal thread that screws on to a threaded boss in the centre of the clutch.

Fig. 4.14   You must use the proper puller.

Now you can lift out the clutch, though you will need to wrangle it out from under the overhanging part of the main casting. To dismantle the clutch itself, you will need to compress the clutch, though this does not require any special tools. You will need a long bolt, or a length of 'all-thread', around M8 size, with nuts and a couple of sturdy washers.

Fig. 4.15   Threaded boss on clutch centre.

The washer that goes on top should be small enough to fit inside the aluminium oil shield, but large enough to bridge the hole in the outer plate.

The long bolt or threaded rod should be passed through the centre of the clutch and the nut tightened down to compress the clutch spring. The circlip can then be taken out and the nut slackened off to allow the 'compressor' to be removed and the clutch to be taken apart. These clutches have to work hard, so replacing the lined plates and the single central spring is a good idea at this time.

Splitting the Cases

The main parts of the engine case are held together by bolts with flats on their heads that fit against the edge of the casing to prevent them from turning. They have 11mm nuts on the other end. Some of the bolts are fitted from the flywheel side and some from the clutch side, so search very carefully for any that you might have missed if the cases seem difficult to split. Frankly, even with all the bolts and nuts removed, the cases are still stubborn to separate.

Fig. 4.16   Separate the cases gradually. Tap here.

There are two places where it is safe to tap the case gently – and 'gently' is the important word in that phrase. One point is below the engine, the other is at the front. Other useful techniques involve the use of small wooden wedges to widen the gap, and holding the cases while using a plastic mallet on the ends of the shafts. Mostly, it is a question of being patient and content with splitting the cases a millimetre at a time until eventually everything comes free. You will end up with the crank and gearbox output shaft in the clutch-side case, and the input shaft of the gearbox in the flywheel side. However, the kickstart gear, with ratchet, and the outer clutch shaft will remain in the clutch-side case. Removing the circlip over the kickstart gear will allow it to be extracted, after which the clutch shaft can be removed from the other side.

Removing the Crank, Bearings and Seals

The crank cannot be taken out of the clutch side of the cases until the primary gear has been removed. It is secured with a nut and tab washer. Flatten the tab and hold the crank while you unscrew the nut – a firm hand on the crank web should be enough or, of course, a strap wrench on the crank web will do the job perfectly. There is a Woodruff key between the crankshaft and the gear, so take care not to lose it. You will need a copper mallet to drive the crank out of the bearing; alternatively, use a piece of wood between the hammer and the end of the crank. Never hit a threaded shaft with a steel hammer. That would damage the thread, possibly beyond repair. Heating the case does not help much, unfortunately.

When the crank is free, examine it carefully, concentrating especially on the flywheel taper and the machined

Fig. 4.18 *Remove the gears one by one, and keep them in order.*

BEARING LUBRICATION

If you look carefully at the main bearings of this engine, you will notice that they are lubricated in two different ways. The flywheel side carries the oil seal outside the bearing, so it is lubricated by oil in the premix that pools in the bottom of the transfer passage and dribbles into the bearing through a drilled hole. The drive-side bearing has the seal on the inside and receives its lubrication from the oil in the gearbox.

surface on the drive-side crank web that acts as a rotary inlet valve.

If the crankcase casting is warmed thoroughly, it will be quite easy to drive the bearings and seals out of their housing. However, you need to hook the seal out of the drive-side case first, because there is a large circlip beneath it, which holds the bearing in place. The flywheel-side seal can be hooked out from the outside and the bearing driven inwards.

Dismantling the Gearbox

Once the cases have been split, you will find that the two gearbox shafts are in opposite sides. Start with the output shaft with the separate gears. Remove the circlip and the special washer, then lift off the gears one by one. Put them

down carefully, making sure that they remain the right way up. If you are storing the gears in a box, use a piece of wire to keep them together and the right way round.

Take out the kickstart shaft and remove the kickstart gear from the clutch shaft. Behind the gear, there is an arrangement of a spring between two interlocking washers to hold the ratchet gear against its counterpart on the first-gear pinion.

Fig. 4.19 *The kickstart gear and its washers.*

The entire kickstart gear assembly can be seen in Fig. 4.19. Underneath the gear, there is a circlip. Removing this allows the clutch basket to be taken out of the other side of the case. There is only just room to get it out, but it is possible.

The drive shaft can then be tapped out of the bearing, which will allow you to check the condition of the slider (Vespa call it a 'cruciform'). Changing the cruciform is carried out in a very similar manner to that described for the Lambretta, though with the Vespa,

Fig. 4.17 *Examine the crankshaft.*

Fig. 4.20   Fit the circlip to the clutch shaft.

Fig. 4.22   Replace the gears one by one and the right way up.

Fig. 4.23   Use pliers to wind up the kickstart spring.

the old one can be left in place and the new one slid on to the shaft to replace it without ever allowing the detent balls and spring to escape – if you are lucky!

During the rebuild of the subject engine, with everything removed from the cases, this was the stage at which the engine was blast cleaned. It should look cleaner from this point on.

REASSEMBLING THE GEARBOX AND TRANSMISSION

The first item to reinstall is the clutch basket, which is not easy. There is not really enough space between the outer part of the casing and the edge of the bearing. The procedure is to tilt the clutch basket so that the tangs of the basket go under the edge of the casing. The clutch shaft will not quite slip into the bearing, so you will need to put a thin pin punch under the basket and give the side of the bearing a gentle nudge into its bearing.

Once the basket is in place, fit the circlip to the inner side of the shaft, then the kickstart gear. The gearbox input shaft goes into the other case half. If you fit it to the drive side at this stage, you will not be able to install the gears on the output shaft, nor put the cases together.

Fit the gears in order, and the right way up, then the circlip that retains them.

Fit the kickstart shaft, then use a good pair of pliers to wind up the kickstart spring and drop the end of it into the notch in the shaft.

Temporarily fit the gearbox input shaft and check the operation of the kickstart. Then put the input shaft back in the other half of the casing.

Replacing the Bearings and Seals

The bearings are a shrink-fit in the casing, so the case must be heated to install them. Oil seals also fit more easily into a warm case, and a smear of oil or grease around the outside of the

Fig. 4.21   Then fit the kickstart gear.

Fig. 4.24   A suitable size of socket can be used to safely drive the seal into place.

seal is always desirable. Warm the case evenly up to about the temperature you would get if you poured a kettle of boiling water on it. You could actually use a kettle, but employing a heat gun keeps the cases dry as well as hot.

Push the seals into the case with the open face to the inner side. The ideal device to install them is a socket that is just a little smaller than the outer diameter of the seal. An extension bar in the socket allows some gentle tapping to seat the seal fully in the case.

The same process is used to insert the bearings. Fit the retaining circlips where necessary. The bearing used on the flywheel side is one of the type referred to in the previous chapter, where the inner race is a close fit on the shaft and the bearing rollers are a sliding fit on the inner race. Heating the inner race and chilling the shaft makes the job easier, though often you do need to use a piece of tube that fits over the shaft to drive the inner race all the way on to it. An old steering stem from a Lambretta makes a perfect tool for this job.

Fig. 4.25   Fitting the bearing sleeve.

Carefully fit the crankshaft. An excellent recommendation is to put the crank into a bag and put it in the freezer for a couple of hours before you do this. This makes the shaft fractionally smaller, and thus easier to fit into the bearings.

You can now put the cases together. Use a little sealant on the joint.

Different lengths of bolts are used to hold the cases together, but given that the bolts are a slip-fit in their holes, it is very easy to see which bolt goes where.

Fig. 4.26   The clutch compressor is set up in the vice.

Assembling the Clutch

Assembling the clutch with its spring and plates can be done on the bench, using the homemade clutch compressor.

The clutch assembly can then be fitted into the basket, and the centre nut fitted and tightened. Bend up the tab washer to lock the nut and replace the clutch pressure disc in the centre. Fit a new gasket to the clutch cover and replace the cover.

The back brake backplate can be fitted next.

While you are on this side of the engine, fit the Woodruff key to the keyway in the crank end, followed by the primary gear with its washer and nut. Lock the engine and tighten the nut to a torque setting of 18Nm (13lb ft).

Assembling the Flywheel Magneto

Fit the generator wire through the rearmost hole in the casing and work the grommet into place. Line up the stator plate and fit the three screws.

Fig. 4.27   The stator plate fits this way round.

In the correct position, the moveable contact of the ignition points is in line with the axis of the cylinder. Fit the Woodruff key to the keyway in the shaft and gently align the keyway in the flywheel with the key, then fit the flywheel on to the shaft. Check that the flywheel does turn the shaft and, therefore, that the key is correctly in place. Tighten the nut to seat the flywheel firmly on the taper. Hold the flywheel and tighten the nut to a torque setting of 13Nm (10lb ft).

Assembling the Cylinder and Piston

Fig. 4.28   Align the rings with their pins.

First, fit the new piston rings. The ring pins are in the upper edge of the ring groove, so make sure that the rings are fitted the right way up. Next insert the far-side circlip, warm the piston, fit the small-end bearing to the eye of the connecting rod and push the gudgeon pin through the piston and small end. Then fit the other circlip, using circlip pliers.

The port edges of the cylinder had been radiussed properly by the reboring company, an advantage of using a specialist. Accordingly, no preparatory work was necessary on the cylinder. Fit a new base gasket. Coat the inner surface of the cylinder with two-stroke oil. A rebored cylinder will need all the lubrication it can get in the first few minutes of running. Remember that the exhaust port goes to the top of the engine, not the lower side as you might expect.

Fig. 4.29   A magnetic screwdriver will help you fit the cylinder base nuts.

Fit the cylinder, making sure that the ring gaps are seated astride the ring pins; squeeze the rings into the bore. Slide the cylinder all the way down on to the studs. Then put on the washers. Access for refitting the cylinder-stud nuts is poor. It helps to put each nut on the blade of a magnetic screwdriver, then use the screwdriver to place the nut on the stud and hold it there while you turn the nut with an open-ended spanner. Alternatively, you can attach magnets to a non-magnetic screwdriver shaft – a tip to remember.

No torque settings are given for these nuts, because it is so unlikely that anyone would have a tool that could measure the torque applied to nuts with so little access. They should be tightened gradually, evenly and very

Fig. 4.30   The cylinder head fits this way round.

tightly. The spark plug hole goes to the upper side on the clutch side.

Fit a new head gasket and the head, tightening the four hex-headed screws gradually in a diagonal pattern to a final torque setting of 13Nm (10lb ft).

The inlet port can then be fitted to the crankcase.

It only remains to refit the fan cowlings, the rear hub and, in this case, the back wheel, and the engine unit is ready for installation in the frame. Note that on small-bodied Vespas, the carburettor is not installed until the engine is in the frame, since it fits inside the frame cavity, under the fuel tank.

Fig. 4.31   Vespa and Lambretta engines compared.

TORQUE SETTINGS FOR THE 90SS AND SIMILAR VESPA MOTORS

Crankcase bolts: 6Nm (4lb ft)
Cylinder-head screws: 13Nm (10lb ft)
Exhaust flange: 18Nm (13lb ft)
Kickstart lever nut: 18Nm (13lb ft)
Clutch centre nut: 21Nm (16lb ft)
Primary-gear nut: 18Nm (13lb ft)
Clutch-cover bolts: 6Nm (4lb ft)
Flywheel nut: 13Nm (10lb ft)
Stator-plate screws: 2Nm (1.5lb ft)

Fig. 4.32   A Series 3 'Slimline' Lambretta.

Fig. 4.33   A Maicoletta 250cc scooter.

Fig. 4.34   A Series 2 'Wideline' TV175 Lambretta at the Manx 400.

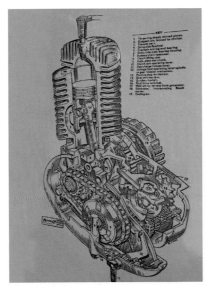

Fig. 4.35   A sectioned diagram of the Maicoletta engine.

Fig. 4.36   Modern automatic scooters.

Fig. 4.37   The author in his student days, on a 100cc Lambretta Cento.

Fig. 4.38   Vespa 90SS bikes at the finish of the Cambrian Rally.

Fig. 4.39   A 75cc Lambretta Vega sand racing in the Isle of Man.

the sixteener years
Yamaha FS1-E

Until 1960, a young person of sixteen could go out and ride any motorcycle that he or she could get their hands on. The late 1950s were the era of rock and roll, coffee bars, black leather jackets and the 'ton-up' kids – boy racers who rode their 650 Triumphs and BSAs, 700cc Royal Enfields or, if they were really lucky, 1000cc Vincents, thundering around the city ring roads trying to achieve 100mph (160km/h).

Actually, most youngsters puttered around on 150cc Bantams, 200cc Tiger Cubs or ex-military dispatch-rider bikes, dreaming of occasionally touching 129km/h (80mph). Many of them became casualties in accidents, but even when this was not the case, the sight and sound of them was enough to cause the sort of press panic that all youth cults seem to arouse. So it was that in 1960, learner riders of any age were restricted to 250cc machines. No doubt, the legislators expected this law to force learners on to the aforementioned Bantams, and the like. In 1961, however, Honda began to produce the CB72, a 250 that was a match for the vast majority of the British bikes

Fig. 5.2   This is a genuine racing Van Veen Kreidler. The 'Sixteener' version was nearly identical, except for the pedals.

that the ton-up kids rode. By the end of the 1970s, all the major Japanese manufacturers had genuine 100mph (160km/h) 250s.

More restrictions were called for. In many countries, however, especially in mainland Europe, it was legal for young people to start their riding life at a much earlier age than seventeen – provided they were limited to the little motorized bicycles or simple mopeds, which are still common in France and Spain. The ages of fourteen or fifteen

were common. The gallery at the end of this chapter shows some typical examples.

In the UK, it was decided to raise the age limit for riding motorcycles to seventeen, the same as for driving a car, but combining a government wish for a touch of Euro-cool with British caution, in 1971, it remained legal for a sixteen-year-old to ride a moped. The definition of a moped at that time was: 'A machine not exceeding 50cc and equipped with pedals by means of which it is capable of being propelled.'

Please note that this is no longer the legal definition, and has not been since 2013. The current definition restricts both engine size and speed. Today, a moped is defined as having a maximum design speed over 24km/h (15mph), but not exceeding 45km/h (28mph). The engine capacity can be no greater than 50cc.

None of the bikes in Figure 5.1 is a moped under the current definition, and none can be ridden legally at the age of sixteen.

SIXTEENERS!

The Sixteener specials were born – they were fifties, they had pedals, but they were closer to a Grand Prix 50cc

Fig. 5.1   A line-up of FS1 and FS1-E machines.

Fig. 5.3 An FS1-E in showroom condition.

FS1-E ENGINE SPECIFICATIONS

No. of cylinders: 1
Bore and stroke: 40 × 39.7mm
Induction: rotary disc valve
Compression ratio: 7:1
Carburettor: 16mm Mikuni
Cooling: air-cooled
Gearbox: 4-speed with foot change
    (N, 1, 2, 3, 4)
Ignition: flywheel magneto
Transmission: gear primary drive to
    multi-plate clutch

Dismantling the Flywheel Magneto

Fig. 5.5 Use the correct puller to remove the flywheel.

racer than a Mobylette or a Velo Solex. There were a lot to choose from, too, with Minarelli engines from Italy powering many of the European bikes, with the notable exception of the Kreidler, which was directly related to the multiple world championship-winning Van Veen Kreidlers.

However, the iconic bike of the era was the Yamaha FS1-E, always affectionately known as the 'Fizzy'.

The first picture in this chapter shows an almost complete history of the Fizzy. In fact, the two blue and white bikes and the first two gold coloured ones are not actually FS1-E models; they are European-specification FS1 SS models, with 5-speed gearboxes, standard footrests (no pedals) and a 6bhp engine. I have been told that the pedal conversion, which made the FS1 into an FS1-E to suit the UK definition of a moped, was originally performed in the Netherlands, Yamaha's centre of European operations. The SS, Super Sports designation of the FS1 was

changed to 'Sixteener Special' on posters for the FS1-E.

I am very grateful to Per Brandt of the FS1-E Owners Club for his help in collecting information for this chapter – and for the loan of the engine, which now we shall examine in detail.

BEFORE WE START

The subject engine was a typical 'back from the dead' restoration. It had been left partly dismantled for years and would be put back into good running order by a complete renovation with new parts.

Fig. 5.4 The FS1-E engine as collected.

A CLEAN START

I should mention that the engine was one of the dirtiest I have ever seen. This was not actually a bad thing, since most of the dirt seemed to have come from the attempt to preserve the engine during storage. The crankcase had been filled with grease, and a thick layer of greasy dust covered the engine cases. The engine was soaked in a parts washer, the worst of the dirt was scraped off, then it was scrubbed with an old nailbrush and finally pressure washed. Final cleaning was done later, after stripping down, when the bare cases were gently bead blasted.

The outer covers over the carburettor and the flywheel magneto were missing from the subject motor, but normally they would have been the first items removed. Thus, in this case, the first task was to remove the flywheel. It is possible to do this with a general-purpose three-legged puller, since there is room for the puller to grip under the edge of the flywheel, but if you do use one of these, you will need to lock the engine to prevent it from turning. A simple way to do this is to put a bar (such as the extension bar of a socket set) through the small-end eye and turn the engine until the bar rests on the top of the crankcase. I prefer to put two strips of wood between the crankcase and the bar to prevent damage to the cylinder base joint.

Since changing the points is quite a routine task, however, and you may need to remove the flywheel quite often, it really is worth using the genuine works flywheel puller (*see* Fig. 5.5). The part that screws into the flywheel has a left-hand thread, that is, you turn it anti-clockwise to screw it in. This means that you can hold a spanner on the flats of the extractor and turn the bolt in the normal, clockwise, direction to extract the flywheel, and you do not need to lock the engine.

The Stator

Disconnect the wire that connects to the neutral light switch. You do not have to take the screw right out because the wire terminates in a forked connector. Next undo the two screws that hold the stator plate in place. This proved not as simple as it sounds. The fixings used on machines of this era are made of what is politely called 'free-cutting steel'. There are far less polite names too, but the fact is that the metal is very soft, and it is very easy to damage the slots in the screws in particular.

The crosshead screws holding the stator plate were badly damaged and could not be removed by any non-destructive means. They are counter-sunk screws, so there was no way to grip the outer edge of the screw head, and they would not turn even when tapped around with a centre punch, so they had to be drilled out.

> ### DRILLING OUT A DAMAGED SCREW
>
> The idea is to drill through the screw head, in the dead centre of the cross, using a drill that will not damage the threads. The maximum diameter of the threads of M5 screws (the size used in this case) is 5mm. The size at the root of the threads is 4.2mm. Thus a 4.5mm drill was used to remove the screw heads, drilling carefully and testing to find the depth at which the screw head would easily snap off from the threaded part of the screw. You can always hope that there will be enough of the screw left to grip to remove it. This time, there wasn't! Removing the remains of the screws was a job for later.

The Clutch Side

The FS1-E is a rotary-valve engine, so there are more components inside the clutch side of the casing than you would normally find. At this stage, you

Fig. 5.6   The carburettor would be here.

cannot see any of them. When the engine is fully assembled, you would see the carburettor in the location that is shown in Fig. 5.6. Just to the right of the inlet stub, there is a hole in the front edge of the casing, fitted with a rubber plug. This provides access to the screw that secures the carburettor clip.

Now is the time to ensure that the gearbox oil has been drained. It is always useful to have a good look at the old oil. It can tell you a lot about the problems you may find later. The oil from the subject engine was completely black, but it smelled clean and 'oily'. That indicated that the clutch plates were probably worn, but that the crankshaft oil seals had not failed, so the main bearings were probably fine, too. Failed seals allow burned fuel to mix with the oil, which is left with a sour, smoky smell.

The clutch cover is retained by typical pan-head screws. The posi-drive-type heads are very easily damaged, and another snag with them is that trying to remove them by chiselling them from the outside is not very effective. This is because the shanks of the screws are narrower than the threads, so they

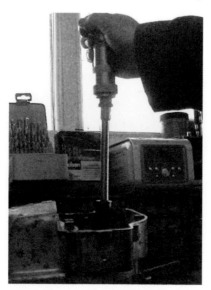

Fig. 5.7   An extension bar on the impact driver.

can bend sideways in their holes if you hit them from the side. Then they become tighter than they were before. The answer is an impact driver.

Some of the screws holding the clutch cover are very close to the casing, so it is a good idea to use an extension bar from your socket set to give you a little more room. Only one would not come out, and luckily it was accessible. The head of the screw was cut with a hacksaw to create a full-width slot, then the impact driver was fitted with a flat-blade screwdriver bit to remove it.

The clutch cover is dowelled, so it may need to be gently eased off by tapping it with a soft mallet.

The Kickstart Mechanism

To remove the kickstart mechanism, unhook the return spring from the post cast into the casing, after which the kickstart shaft and Bendix gear can be pulled out as one unit. Unless there are problems with the kickstart, this can be left in one piece. An idler gear connects the gear on the kick-start shaft with one on the back of the clutch, but this cannot be removed until the clutch is out of the way.

Fig. 5.8   Components inside the clutch side of the case.

Removing the Clutch

The clutch-side components can be seen in Fig. 5.8. It also shows the block of wood that is useful when you are working on one of these engines. Long shafts protrude from either side, and the engine will not rest properly on its side unless it is supported on something.

The first step is to release the four screws holding the clutch springs in place. They are likely to be really tight, so you may need an impact driver to move them initially. If they are very tight, or stuck, you will need to lock the engine (as described previously) to keep the clutch from turning. Once they have been loosened, save a little time by using an electric screwdriver to take the screws out. The top pressure plate, and the steel and fibre clutch plates can then be removed, revealing the clutch boss. Set the clutch plates aside for a thorough check later. If you have not locked the engine before, do it now.

At this point, you will need to hold the clutch boss to keep it from turning.

BAD PRACTICE

I would never recommend trying to hold the clutch boss with a screwdriver through the slots in the clutch basket and jammed against the splines of the boss. This can often break the clutch basket.

Fig. 5.9   Clutch holder made from an old clutch plate.

It is possible to make a holder out of a strip of steel bent into a Z-shape to hook over the lug of the basket and fit into the splines on the boss. The better and safer way is to scrap one of the steel plates and fasten a handle to it to make a holder that engages with all the splines on the boss. Since the steel plates in this engine were rusty and needed to be replaced, making one into a clutch holder was no loss. Old clutch plates are plentiful at the breakers' shops, too.

Take out the clutch pushrod 'mushroom', then undo the nut. The clutch hub nut is locked by a tab washer, so the tab must be flattened before you can remove the nut. A hammer and a small cold chisel are the ideal tools, but use a screwdriver if you must! The nut

needs an 18mm socket to undo it, and you can expect it to be tight. With the nut undone, you can pull the hub off the splined shaft, and you will find a bronze thrust washer. The clutch basket can then be removed, followed by the drive gear for the kickstart along with the bearing sleeve in the centre of it. Behind the bearing sleeve, there is another thrust washer. Keep all the clutch bits together. Now you can remove the idler gear for the kickstart and the wave washer that sits behind it. This gear is held to its shaft by a circlip.

The Primary Gear

The primary-drive helical gear on the end of the crankshaft must be removed next.

This was the first serious difficulty encountered during this job. With the engine locked, the nut could not be turned using the usual 18mm socket and ratchet wrench. It would not turn with the socket set fitted to the impact driver. It would not turn with a 1/2in-drive socket and a long tommy bar.

Fig. 5.10   Use a drill to split the nut.

At this point, the amount of force being applied to the crank, possibly twisting it out of alignment, was becoming a concern, so it was decided to split the nut. It is possible to buy a specialized nut splitter, but in the absence of one of these, the task was completed using a drill and cold chisel.

The first stage is to drill into the top face of the nut. Use a centre punch, then, with a sharp bit, drill into the narrow part of the nut, between the angles

of the hexagon shape. Use a drill that is smaller than the thickness of the metal, and drill as close to the flat on the outside of the nut as you can. You do not want to damage the threads on the crankshaft. Hold the drill at an angle (*see* Fig. 5.10) so that the bit will break out of the flat of the nut. You do not need to drill all the way through the nut, and it is best not to. Then use the cold chisel to split between the drilled hole and the flat of the nut.

Fig. 5.11   The stubborn nut after splitting. Note the undamaged thread. The large notch in the nut both stretches and loosens it; it also provides a good purchase so that the chisel can be used to knock the nut around.

The stretched nut is shown in Fig. 5.11. After this treatment, it could be turned easily with a socket spanner. It had to be replaced by a new one, though.

Removing the Rotary Valve Assembly

The rotary valve is covered by an iron plate that incorporates the inlet stub, and it is held in place by four pan-head screws. Use an impact driver to remove the screws and lift off the cover. Note that the offside crank oil seal is fitted in this plate. The plastic composition rotary valve is underneath the cover. It is driven by a splined sleeve, which locates on the crankshaft with a tiny drive pin that fits into a hole in the crankshaft. Remove the valve and the splined sleeve. It is difficult to pull the pin out of the crank, so you will need a pin punch (or a nail) to push it out from the other side of the crank. The hole is drilled right through, so this is easy to do.

Splitting the Crankcases

Twelve pan-head screws hold the two halves of the crankcase together; all are on the flywheel side of the engine, and

Fig. 5.12   The screws holding the cases together.

Fig. 5.13   Remove the gearchange mechanism.

they come in three different lengths. Two, which cannot be seen in Fig. 5.12, are adjacent to the cylinder studs.

Before you start to split the cases, there is one more task to perform. Behind the clutch, on the other side of the engine, is a detent mechanism that holds the gear-selector drum in the correct position for each gear. You must unhook the spring and move the detent claw out of the cage on the end of the selector drum. You can then pull out the gear-change shaft.

The cases will need some effort to split. Hold the engine and use a copper-faced mallet to tap gently on the end of the crankshaft and the output shaft alternately to persuade them to slide out of their bearings. As the gap between the cases widens, you will be able to part them by holding the cases in your hands and pushing the shafts with your thumbs.

The Crankshaft

The unusual state of the crankshaft and case can be seen in Fig. 5.15. The flywheel end of the shaft displayed signs of surface rust, and the colour of the grease on the face of the crank disc suggested that it also could be rusty. The condition of the crank and its usability was suspect, and it needed checking very carefully – especially in the light of the struggle to remove the nut holding the helical gear. It seemed likely that the grease had been packed into the crankcase after the components had already started to rust.

Fig. 5.14   A light tap with a copper hammer will help when splitting the cases.

Fig. 5.15   The condition of the crank – greasy!

Any sign of rust or marking on the big-end or small-end bearings means that the crank has to be rebuilt with a new connecting rod and bearing kit. This is a specialized job that has to be farmed out.

Using a DTI (dial gauge) on a magnetic stand, the crank can be checked. Make sure that the flywheel end is running true, within 0.025mm (0.001in), then move the DTI to the bearing surface on the drive end and check that.

With this crank, it was surprising to find that there was a small error, and it was identical in both size and position on both ends. It proved to be the result of a small distortion in the centre hole, which was easily remedied using a centre drill in the lathe. Damage to the centre hole can be caused by using a steel hammer on the crank end, or even by a poorly designed puller when removing the flywheel. At the same time, the DTI was set up to check the play in the big-end bearing. It was too small either to feel or to measure. The crank was slightly rusty on the faces, and the flywheel rims were cleaned up in the lathe, using a hand scraper. After that, it was fit for reuse.

ASSEMBLY

Replacing the Crankshaft in the Cases

The condition of the main bearings was beyond restoration, so new bearings and seals were fitted. As always, the method is to drive out the old ones and fit the new ones, using a drift that is the same size as the outer bearing ring. In practice, this will often be a large socket.

For both removal and replacement, it does help to warm the cases. A heat gun is the preferred method.

The gearbox bearing was also renewed at this time.

The Flywheel-Side Crankcase

Starting on the flywheel side, and having installed the bearings and seals,

---

TWO-STROKE CRANKSHAFTS

Four-stroke engines, especially the multi-cylinder types used in big bikes and cars, tend to have one-piece forged crankshafts and split plain big-end bearings lubricated by a forced oil feed. Since there are very few two-strokes that feed pressurized oil to the big end, the usual practice is to employ a roller bearing in the big end. Roller bearings can survive a much less generous oil supply. Some two-stroke engines in outboard motors use a split big end design with roller bearings. Bike engines have to be much sturdier, and they have a one-piece connecting rod with a multi-piece 'built up' crankshaft. Although crankshafts were bolted together in the past (*see* Chapter 1 for an example), the most common design since then has been pressed together. This involves forcing a crank pin into a hole in the crank disc. The hole is very slightly smaller than the pin – an interference fit. In the case of the FS1-E, there would be about one hundredth of a millimetre difference. It takes a force equivalent to more than a ton to press the crank pin home. It is very unlikely that this could be done except in an unusually well-equipped home workshop.

The other issue that arises with this type of construction is the problem of alignment. If the crank discs are twisted relative to each other, the crank ends will not be in line, and if the engine were run like this, it would vibrate badly and the main bearings would fail rapidly. The stresses could even cause the crankcases to crack.

Crankshaft alignment is something that can be checked, and even adjusted, relatively easily. The best way is to set the shaft in V-blocks, arranging them to support the shaft's main bearings. Unfortunately, the way in which engines are normally assembled, with the bearings a close fit in the cases, means that they are difficult to remove without damaging either the bearing or the bearing housing. Using V-blocks, which support the main bearing surface of the crankshaft, is nearly as good.

In fact, I did not use either method for the subject engine. The dial gauge is set to measure movement at the rims and edges of the flywheel discs in this method. Because the flywheel rims were rough and rusty, it would be difficult to obtain an accurate reading from them, so I supported the crankshaft between centres, using a lathe as an accurate pair of pointed 'centres' that fitted, with only the lightest pressure, into the centre holes in the ends of the crankshaft.

Fig. 5.16   Checking the crank with a DTI.

Fig. 5.17   Fitting the new main bearings.

carefully insert the crank into the fly-wheel-side bearing – the end with the taper on it, obviously!

A smear of oil on the shaft will make extra sure that it can be fitted through the seal without causing any damage. It should be a close fit in the bearing, but no more than a gentle tap with a soft-faced mallet should be needed to get it all the way in.

Assembling and Fitting the Gearbox

This is a tricky operation, because almost the whole assembly has to be fitted at the same time. Begin by holding the two gearbox shafts in your hand, with the gears meshing together, then position the selector drum on top. Next place the selector forks so that their pins engage in the slots in the selector drum and their forks fit on to the channels of the gears. All of these components must be fitted into their respective bearings at the same time – and kept in their proper places while this is done. The spindles for the selector forks can be added afterwards and wriggled into their holes in the inner side of the casing. Once everything is in place, you can actually check that it all operates properly by turning the selector drum by hand and selecting all four gears, and neutral. Finally, give everything a spot of oil.

Reassembling the Cases

It is quite usual for there to be no gasket between the crankcase halves, but this does mean that the joint face must be cleaned very carefully and a thin smear of sealant applied to ensure that there are no leaks. You do need to realize, though, that sealant that shows on the outside of the cases will spoil the look of the engine – and the reputation of the assembler, too! So always wipe away any dribbles! Position the clutch-side casing on top of the other side and, keeping everything square, squeeze the cases between your hands to join the two halves. For the last few millimetres, you will need to tap them gently into place with a soft mallet.

Next turn the assembly over, because the twelve pan-head screws are fitted from the flywheel side. Tighten them evenly. The short ones are fitted adjacent to the cylinder, the middle-sized ones at the back and the longer ones along the top and bottom – if you marked the holes as suggested in Chapter 2, you would not need to know that!

Turn the engine over again and put together the rotary valve assembly.

The Rotary Valve Assembly

First, replace the little drive pin in its the hole in the crankshaft, then fit the drive collar on to the shaft.

The rotary valve, made of a brown composition material, is set up by aligning the two dots on the disc with the pin that drives the drive collar. Oil both sides of the disc well before fixing the cover in place. Make sure that

Fig. 5.18 The gearbox components in the case.

Fig. 5.19 Fit the case halves together carefully.

Fig. 5.20 The drive for the rotary inlet valve.

Fig. 5.21 The rotary disc valve in place.

the carburettor stub on the cover is in line with the inlet port. The valve cover has a large O-ring, so as long as this is in good condition, you do not need to use sealant on this joint. As previously noted, this case also carries the drive-side crankshaft oil seal, with its open face inwards.

The Clutch-Side Components

One item needs to be fitted from the other side, before starting on the many components inside the clutch-side casing. This is the long clutch push-rod, which is simply pushed through the small oil seal from the flywheel side.

The first step is to fit the bearing retainer plate over the gearbox bearing. It is secured with two screws.

The selector shaft can now be fitted. It passes right through the cases to come out on the flywheel side.

Fig. 5.22   Comparison of new and old splines on the gearchange pedal shaft.

The splines on the gear-selector shaft are easily damaged where they engage with the gear pedal, If the pedal pinch-bolt is loose and the rider a little heavy-footed. This was replaced by a new one on the subject engine.

The pedal return spring fits over the slotted peg seen on the left of Fig. 5.23, and the detent claws engage with the pins on the end of the selector drum.

Fig. 5.23   Replace the gearchange mechanism.

From here on, every component fitted covers or obscures the previous one, so instead of an account in which every sentence starts with 'Before' or 'Don't forget', the tasks will be presented as a numbered list.

1. Fit the kickstart shaft. Below the kickstart gear, there is a spring-wire clip with a small loop that has to fit into the notch at the top of the casing (*see* Fig. 5.24). Having pushed the kickstart shaft in, wind up the kickstart spring and loop it over the peg at top left.
2. Fit the idler gear. A wavy washer goes on the shaft first, followed by the gear, a plain washer and the circlip.

Fig. 5.24   The kickstart gears.

3. Fit the thrust washer to the clutch shaft, followed by the spiral bearing sleeve, then the clutch gear for the kickstart, positioned with the drive dogs upwards. Then fit the clutch basket on to the sleeve, making sure that the dogs on the back of the basket engage with the dogs on the kickstart gear.
4. Fit the bronze thrust washer to the shaft, then the clutch hub. Put the tab washer and the nut on the shaft and use the clutch holder to prevent it from turning. Tighten the nut to around 40Nm (30lb ft) of torque. Lock the nut in place by bending up the edge of the tab washer.

Fig. 5.25   Tighten the clutch nut to the correct torque.

Fig. 5.26   The 'mushroom' goes in after the ball.

5. Drop the single (5mm or 3/16in) ball bearing into the hole in the centre of the clutch shaft. Then fit the short mushroom clutch push-rod. The long pushrod, which is already in the hole, prevents the ball bearing from dropping straight through.

6. Fit the first lined clutch plate, the steel plate, the second lined plate and then the pressure plate. A Fizzy pressure plate can be fitted any way round, but note that this does not apply to other Yamaha clutches that have five springs.

7. Fit the four clutch springs and screws, tightening them evenly and all the way in.

8. Finally, fit the helical primary gear to the end of the crank, followed by the plain washer, the spring washer and the nut. With the engine locked, tighten the nut to around 40Nm (30lb ft) of torque.

9. With the locking bar removed, use the crank nut to turn the engine over and check that everything rotates smoothly and easily.

10. Fit the gasket and the clutch cover casing, tightening the seven pan-head screws that hold it in place. The carburettor and its cover will not usually be fitted until the engine is installed in the bike.

Fitting the Magneto

A new stator and flywheel were supplied with the engine, so these were fitted. One of the stator fixing screws had been drilled out and retapped to 6mm, but a new 6mm countersunk screw was found to fit into the stator with no need for further modification.

The important factor in fitting the flywheel is the crankshaft taper. This was cleaned up with wire wool while the crankshaft was being inspected and cleaned. If it had been decided to refit the original flywheel, it would have been a good idea to lap it on to the taper with some fine grinding paste, such as you would use to grind in valves on a four-stroke.

Replace the Woodruff key in the crankshaft keyway, line up the key-ways and fit the flywheel. Fit the spring washer and nut. With the engine locked, tighten the nut to around 40Nm (30lb ft) of torque.

Assembling the Top End

As the subject engine was delivered without the cylinder assembly, all new components were fitted at this stage. Anyone restoring a Fizzy will be pleased to learn that new and remanufactured parts are readily available.

The original cylinder studs were bent and one was missing, so a new set was fitted.

Fig. 5.27   Two nuts locked together to install the new studs.

The technique for fitting studs is to use two nuts, locked together, to allow the studs to be screwed into the cases. Fit the cylinder base gasket and then put the small-end bearing into the connecting-rod eye. It is often advisable to stuff a clean rag into the crankcase mouth in case the circlip is dropped when fitting the piston. This is less likely to happen with a horizontal engine, but sometimes it is useful to use the rag to hold the connecting rod still during assembly.

Fitting the Piston

Fit the circlip into the piston so that it will be on the far side when the piston is installed.

This engine uses wire circlips in a sort of G-shape. To fit them, grip the cross-tail of the circlip with a pair of narrow-nose pliers, hold the piston in the other hand and tilt the pliers so that the opposite end of the spiral enters the gudgeon-pin hole. Put your thumb on the end of the circlip and wind it into the hole, turning and squeezing it in with the pliers. Once the clip is in the hole, use the pliers to turn it and settle it completely in its groove.

After fitting the first circlip, install the piston rings. They are identical, so it does not matter which groove they go in. They do have a way up, though, because the piston-ring pins are off-centre in the groove. The rings are made of iron, so they are brittle and need to be fitted carefully, though it can be done with bare hands.

Fig. 5.28   Fitting G-shaped gudgeon-pin circlips.

Fig. 5.29   The complex fitting of the sprocket – the splined sleeve.

Fig. 5.30   The sprocket in place.

The piston itself does have an orientation. The arrow on the piston crown should point downwards, towards the exhaust port.

Warm the piston, but not so much that it cannot be held in the hand without burning yourself. Fit it over the small end of the connecting rod and push the gudgeon pin into the piston. Line up the piston and small-end eye, then push the pin straight through until it reaches the circlip on the far side.

Fitting the Cylinder and Head

Before fitting the cylinder, oil the bore to provide some lubrication for the initial few seconds of running when the engine is first started.

With the exhaust port to the bottom, fit the cylinder over the studs. It has a good chamfer at the base of the bore, so as long as the piston rings are correctly set up, with the ring gaps positioned over the piston-ring locating grooves, the rings can be slid into the bore by simply squeezing them between your fingers.

Push the cylinder right to the base joint, then turn the engine over to make sure it rotates smoothly.

The cylinder-head gasket is metallic. Place it over the studs, followed by the cylinder head. Fit the washers and the four head nuts, tightening them evenly.

Fitting the Drive Sprocket

The drive sprocket fits on the long output shaft, and the installation is a little unusual. The sprocket fits over the splines of the shaft, followed by a tab washer. A threaded sleeve goes on next and then a pair of semi-circular collets, which locate in a groove on the shaft and a recess on the end of the sleeve. A nut goes on the threaded sleeve and is tightened down against the washer and sprocket. This pushes the sprocket down the shaft and the sleeve up against the collets. Everything is now firmly attached to the shaft, the tab washer preventing the nut from coming loose.

It is worth pointing out that Fig. 5.29 shows the old sprocket, which you can see is badly worn. It was replaced.

Summary

That completes the work on this engine. The air cleaner was sandblasted and given a quick coat of aerosol paint to prevent any further rusting. It was refitted for a full 'before and after' comparison.

WHAT HAPPENED NEXT?

After 1977, when pedals were no longer needed, there was a tendency for 50cc bikes to revert to more conventional looks and layouts. Machines like the Yamaha RD50, the Suzuki X1 and the

Fig. 5.31   *The finished engine ready to return.*

All of the bikes had restricted engine power in standard form, though it was not unknown for that restriction to be removed (illegally). The fact that all of these bikes had 80cc versions made this easier still. The larger-capacity models were not always sold on the UK market, since the extra capacity put them out of the reach of sixteen-year-olds and into competition with 125cc bikes for seventeen-year-old learner riders.

Across the motorcycle market, the 1980s and early 1990s were the era of the superbike and sports-bike styling. This fashion spread to the 50cc class. Both the Yamaha RD and DT, and the Suzuki RG and TS appeared in water-cooled guise, though not in the UK, and a new breed of European ultra-lightweights took over the market. First Aprilia, and then Derbi and Gilera produced tiny race-style bikes based on the latest water-cooled development of the Minarelli engine. Rieju joined the list, and Yamaha produced a TZ 50 road bike using the Minarelli engine.

Kawasaki AR50 had slightly inclined upright cylinders, various forms of reed-valve induction and typical road-bike looks. There were also trail bike versions, often using the exact same engines as the road versions – Yamaha had the DT50, Suzuki the TS 50 and Kawasaki the AE50.

ABOVE: Fig. 5.32   *A typical traditional moped.*

LEFT: Fig. 5.33   *Motorized bicycles – Velo Solex, etc.*

Fig. 5.34   *A rare Giulietta, with the Minarelli P6 engine.*

Fig. 5.35   Puch were the first to produce a 'Sixteener'.

Fig. 5.36   Garelli used their own established engines, which were fast.

Fig. 5.37   A late entry from Suzuki, an RG50 Gamma.

Fig. 5.38   The Aprilia RS50. The engine is a water-cooled version of the P6, the AM6 Minarelli.

race developed!
Yamaha RD350LC & 250 YPVS (RZ250)

While Kawasaki and Suzuki were adding cylinders and building bigger engines, Yamaha were working on improving the designs that they already had. Porting and, in particular, the control of the induction system were the areas in which they already had experience and expertise, from their GP race bikes. It is no coincidence that their next step in design was called the 'race developed' series, the RD models.

I have always considered the RDs to be the equivalent in bike evolution to the cat in the animal world. From the Bengal tiger to the moggy curled up by the fire, a cat is a cat; evolution has produced the perfect ambush predator, and there is no need for anything more than tweaks in the details. With the basic RD design, Yamaha developed a machine that works on the racetrack, on the road, in motocross, in trials. There are minor variations, but it is always recognizably the same design.

Actually, it is not entirely accurate to describe all of these designs as ancestors of the RD series. Early Yamaha twins were copies of the German Adler twin-cylinder motors; it was not until the YDS5 that the current clutch layout was adopted. Previous models carried the clutch on the end of the crank – a hangover from the German design, which the MZ and CZ/Jawa two-strokes clung to until the last. By the time the

YDS7 came out in 1970, the style was set as far as the bottom end and transmission were concerned. Only details have needed to be changed since that time. Cylinder porting development continued, however, and power improved, helped by the fact that the TD (250) and TR (350) race bikes were completely based on the road bikes at that time.

Rotary valves were known to be a big improvement on an inlet controlled by the piston skirt, and they had been featured in many bike engines already, often very successfully, both in racing and on the road. The FS1-E and its close relatives were prime examples, but there were excellent disc-valve motors from Kawasaki for their Samurai twin 250, and we must not forget the wonderful Bridgestones with their 90, 175 single and 350 twin engines. There were also many exotic road-race bikes, such as the 50cc Kreidler, and the jewel-like MBA and Morbidelli 125cc twins.

However, Yamaha were exploring a different, cheaper approach. 'Torque Induction' was the name that they gave to the idea of fitting a reed-valve block into a much widened inlet port. It was not actually a new idea: a reed valve had been patented in 1906, but this had been for use in a pulse jet – a forerunner of the engine that powered the German V1 during the later years of the Second World War.

As far as can be discovered, the first person to use a reed valve in a two-stroke engine was Rudolph Evinrude (son of the pioneer of outboard motor development, Ole Evinrude). This was produced in 1935 and, as you might expect, it was fitted to an outboard motor. From then onwards, reed valves became the standard arrangement for outboards, the reed block being mounted in the base of the crankcase. The normal arrangement for an outboard power head is to have the crankshaft running vertically; thus the cylinders generally point backwards and the carburettors forwards. By the end of the 1940s, reed valves had also been widely adopted for small industrial engines used in chainsaws, generators, etc.

The big advantage of the Torque Induction system is that the inlet opening time varies according to engine demand, which provides much better gas flow at high revs. At low rpm, because the inlet port is open while the piston is going down, a piston-controlled port allows blowback. At the very least, this either makes a mess behind the carburettor or clogs up the air cleaner. There is a worse problem, though. As the piston descends, it can push the mixture in the crankcase back out through the carburettor. As the mixture passes the jets, it picks up an extra dose of petrol. The next upstroke of the piston pulls in the already too

Fig. 6.1   An early RD350.

Fig. 6.2   The 'coffin tank' DX version of the RD250.

Fig. 6.3   The RD350LC.

**ENGINE SPECIFICATIONS:
RD350LC**

Type: liquid-cooled, parallel twin
    cylinder
Capacity: 347cc
Bore and stroke: 64 × 54mm
Compression ratio: 6.2:1
Carburettors: 2 × 26mm Mikuni
    slide/needle
Ignition: flywheel magneto CDI
Starting: kickstart
Max. power: 47bhp at 8,500rpm
Max. torque: 3.8kg m (27.5lb ft) at
    8,000rpm
Transmission: gear primary drive to
    multi-plate clutch and 6-speed
    gearbox; chain final drive

**ENGINE SPECIFICATIONS:
RD250 YPVS**

Type: liquid-cooled, parallel twin
    cylinder
Capacity: 247cc
Bore and stroke: 54 × 54mm
Compression ratio: 6.7:1
Carburettors: 2 × 26mm Mikuni
    slide/needle
Ignition: flywheel magneto CDI
Starting: kickstart
Max. power: 35bhp at 8,000rpm
Max. torque: 3.0kg m (21.7lb ft) at
    8,000rpm
Transmission: gear primary drive to
    multi-plate clutch and 6-speed
    gearbox; chain final drive

rich mixture through the carburettor yet again, and it becomes even richer. The result of this is that when the throttle is opened after a period of low revs, the engine will be running far too rich and will bog down for a while, four-stroking until it can finally clear out the over-rich mixture. A reed valve in the inlet prevents this and gives the engine a much crisper pick up. Yamaha took the idea further, though, making the reed cavity do the job of an extra transfer port by including a passage from the inlet port up to the height of the existing transfers.

There was a whole range of RD Yamahas: RD50 and RD125 singles, 250cc and 350cc twins, and eventually the longer-stroke RD400 twin. Initially, these had air-cooled engines, and they were very successful, but the series really took off with the liquid-cooled versions, the LC (or 'Elsie').

THE PRACTICAL PROJECT

We shall be exploring two engines in this chapter: a 350cc LC, the model numbered 4L1; and a 250cc YPVS

Fig. 6.4   A 4L1 RD350LC engine.

model, known in the USA as the RZ250.

Both subject engines belonged to Norbo Lea, organizer of the RDLC Crazy club and website. They had been on the shelf for some time, but were complete and were thought to be in running condition prior to removal from their frames. The strip-down was done primarily for the benefit of this book, though the opportunity was taken to renew any damaged or suspect components that were found during the process.

THE RD350LC

Initial examination of the 350 indicated that the wiring harness from the generator had been chafed. One of the wires was completely worn through and the insulation was missing from two of the others. To repair them required at least 30mm (1¼in) to be removed from all of the wires, and even the undamaged ones would have had to be cut and resoldered. Instead, short sections were cut from the damaged wires and wire of the correct colour soldered in, using heat-shrink tubing to cover the joints. A fresh piece of sleeving was split and fitted over the gap in the old sleeving, being held in place with insulating tape. This ensured that the harness retained its original length.

Dismantling the Engine

The first step is to remove the cylinder head. It is held by eight long sleeve nuts, which hold down and locate the

cylinder head. It is not unusual for LC cylinder heads to warp and blow gaskets, so it is important to slacken the bolts gradually and evenly. Taking the head nuts to be numbered one to four, from left to right across the top, and five to eight across the bottom, slacken them in the order 2, 7, 3, 6, 1, 8, 5, 4. No thermostats were fitted to these models, but it is worth removing the water

Fig. 6.5   Remove the head nuts in order.

Fig. 6.6   Damage to the cylinder head.

Fig. 6.7   Remove the head gasket carefully.

Fig. 6.8   The pistons are undamaged.

outlet to ensure that the water passages are clean and clear. Before removing the head, once the head nuts have been taken out, you must slacken the hose clip that holds the water hose to the spigot on the underside of the head.

It was clear that this engine had suffered a blow-up. The left-hand cylinder head had been battered by debris, most likely from a broken piston or piston ring. In an ideal world, this could be restored completely by cutting back both squish bands to clean metal, then skimming the whole head to restore the correct compression ratio. The important aspect of this sort of damage, however, is the fact that roughness on the inner surface of the cylinder head can cause a problem with detonation, which would do even more damage. The main problem lies in the places where the aluminium of the head is pushed up into little spikes, which become hotter than the rest and can trigger premature ignition of the mixture. Unless the engine is to be highly tuned, it is sufficient to remove the spikes. The depressions in the head are less important.

The spikes were removed with a bearing scraper and the head was polished with a Dremel power tool. Having scraped off the remains of the old gasket, the head face was cleaned up using 400-grade wet-or-dry abrasive paper taped to the top of a piece of kitchen worktop, the head being rubbed in a circular motion while pressing it down on to the paper.

The Cylinders

Once the bridging tube between the carburettor rubbers has been pulled out of the rubbers, and the rest of the head gasket has been removed, the cylinders can simply be pulled off their studs and the pistons. It does not particularly matter whether the carburettor rubbers and reed blocks are removed before or after taking off the cylinders.

Whatever had happened to the cylinder head, it was clear that the pistons had not been there at the time. They displayed very little wear, but the studs were rusty, as were the sleeve nuts, suggesting that there may have been a water leak in the past. Both studs and nuts were cleaned up with a rotary wire brush on a bench grinder.

Removing the Pistons

The pistons have tailless circlips with extraction grooves, so the circlips can be removed very easily with a small screwdriver – remembering to hold your thumb over the circlip to prevent it from vanishing into a far corner of the workshop as it comes free. The gudgeon pins can be pushed out of the pistons with a pin punch (or possibly the tommy bar from your socket set). If the pin is tight, warm the piston with a heat gun.

Once the pistons are free from the connecting rods, set them aside, marking them 'L' and 'R' to ensure that they go back into their original cylinders. In this case, the crank was to be changed, so the old small-end bearings were not to be refitted. If they are to be reused, the small-end bearing and gudgeon pin should be left together in the correct piston.

Removing the Generator

Remove the flywheel cover from the left side of the engine. Three different lengths of screw secure this cover, so marking the cases to identify which screws fit in which holes will be a major time saver (*see* Chapter 2).

The flywheel fits on a taper and cannot be removed without the correct puller, that is one with a 27mm, fine-pitch, left-hand thread. These can be bought online relatively cheaply at the time of writing. Having undone the flywheel nut, and used your favourite method of preventing the flywheel from turning in the process, retract the centre bolt of the puller and screw

Fig. 6.9   Use the correct flywheel puller.

the tool anticlockwise into the thread in the centre of the flywheel. Holding the puller body with a suitable spanner, screw in the centre bolt of the puller until it presses on the end of the crank. For the sake of the photograph, the two spanners are shown in Fig. 6.9 about 180 degrees apart. In fact, it is far more effective to place them only about 20 degrees apart and squeeze them together. This still requires a lot of force, and often you have to give the puller a smart tap on the centre screw to jolt the flywheel free from its taper.

With the flywheel out of the way, the stator can be accessed. It is held in

Fig. 6.10   Remind yourself of the orientation of the stator.

> ### THINGS DO NOT ALWAYS GO TO PLAN
>
> At one college where I worked, we had a very useful hydraulic puller, which greatly amplified the force applied to the centre bolt. A student who had been struggling to remove the flywheel of a 350LC with a conventional puller asked to borrow the device. There was a policy of not lending out tools, but in this case it was no problem because he had the engine in the back of his car in the college car park. We all adjourned to the car park and set up the puller on the engine, which was still in the back of the car. The flywheel showed no sign of moving. More force was applied, again without success. One more turn of the screw and there was a loud bang as the taper finally released. The whole assembly now contained a lot of energy, however, and both flywheel and puller jumped up violently – straight through the tailgate window of the car!

place by three screws in slotted holes, which allow it to be rotated to adjust the ignition timing. The position of the stator should be marked so that it can be refitted in exactly the same place. Before the stator can be removed, you need to push the large round rubber grommet in through the casing so that the wiring harness can be eased through the hole.

Keep the flywheel and stator together so that there is no loss of magnetism while the items are stored. The magnetic flywheel makes a very good place to keep the Woodruff key, too.

Fig. 6.11   Disconnect the neutral switch.

Finally, before removing the stator, disconnect the wire from the small screw on the neutral warning lamp switch.

The stator is a close fit in the housing and will need to be gently prised out with a screwdriver.

The Final Drive Sprocket

While you are working on the flywheel side, it is a good idea to remove the sprocket. This is retained by a large nut and a tab washer. Flatten the tab, hold the sprocket, and loosen and remove the nut. The method of holding the sprocket with a strap wrench is shown in Fig. 6.12.

Fig. 6.12   Removing the sprocket.

The Clutch Side

Having made sure that the gearbox oil has been drained, remove the clutch cover, noting or marking the screw positions.

After removing the cover from the subject engine, it was clear that there was a problem. The first step is to unscrew the six screws and remove the clutch springs. Unfortunately, there were only five. A previous owner had attempted to remove the clutch without a holder and had broken one of the bosses from the clutch centre.

Fig. 6.14   Keep the parts together.

the basket. A length of wire will keep these items together and in the right order until it is time to reassemble the clutch.

Preparing to Split the Crankcases

The gearchange shaft can simply be pulled out once the claws have been disengaged from the pins on the end of the selector drum. If the shaft is difficult to remove, it is probably because the other end, where the gearchange pedal fits, has become corroded or coated with greasy dirt.

If you intend to reuse the shaft oil

seal, it is a good idea to clean the shaft and lubricate the end before pushing it through the seal, since a gritty or rusty shaft will tear the lip of the seal.

Apart from the gearchange shaft, only one component bridges the joint in the horizontally-split cases, and that is a little sheet-metal cover that retains the clutch-shaft bearing. This retainer is fixed by two screws on either side of the clutch. It must be removed before the cases can be split.

The next step is to turn the engine upside down and unscrew the eight 12mm nuts on the bottom of the crankcases. The joint between the cases is vital to the engine, so you must take great care not to distort the cases when splitting them. Slacken the bolts gradually, working in a diagonal pattern from the centre outwards.

Turn the engine the right way up again and loosen the 10mm-head bolts on the top in the same way. Yamaha have made this easy by numbering the bolts in the correct order. The YPVS has the underside fixings (and the cylinder-head sleeve nuts) numbered as well.

SCREW AND GLUE

If a broken clutch-centre boss is still present, it may be possible to repair it. I have succeeded in doing so in the past, using a countersunk screw on the back of the clutch centre and a good epoxy adhesive. In the case of the subject engine, however, there was no boss, so a replacement centre was obtained.

Fig. 6.13   Lock the clutch with a homemade holder.

After removing the five remaining springs, the clutch plates were pulled out. Each friction plate is fitted with a rubber ring between the plate and the clutch centre. The clutch can be run without these, but they do cut down on clutch rattle at tickover. The clutch centre is held by a nut and tab washer.

Flatten the tab washer and use a clutch holder to prevent the clutch centre from turning. There is a thrust washer beneath the clutch centre, a bearing sleeve inside the clutch basket and another thrust washer underneath

Fig. 6.15   Pull out the gearchange shaft.

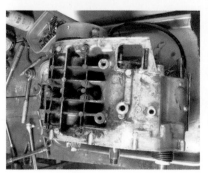

Fig. 6.16   The bottom of the cases.

Fig. 6.17   The number tells you the order of releasing the crankcase top bolts.

Fig. 6.18   All the internals in the top case half.

Fig. 6.19   A good view of the crank and gearbox.

Splitting the Cases

Start with the engine upside down. The easiest way to get the case joint to start opening is to hold the lower half of the casing up, clear of the bench, then use a copper mallet on the ends of the studs that hold the two halves of the case together. Once the joint has separated, it is just a question of keeping the case halves level while they are eased apart. All the shafts will then be exposed for inspection.

The only other component that joins the two halves of the case is the kick-start spring. Unhook the spring and pull out the kickstart assembly.

As mentioned, the subject engine had been standing for some time, and after discussion with the owner, it was decided to change all the bearings and seals. Like the Greeves (*see* Chapter 2), the key items are the seals and bearings of the crank. It is very difficult to check the seals between the two halves of the crankshaft; they are only renewable during a crank rebuild, so a replacement crank, bearings and seals were fitted to be on the safe side.

Removing the Water and Oil Pumps

The engine cases were to be blast cleaned, so every moving part had to be either removed or very thoroughly protected to ensure that none of the abrasive found its way into any bearings or especially oil or water passages. In fact, the seals and bearings of both pumps were suspect and due to be changed. Accordingly, removing the water pump and the oil pumps were the next tasks.

WHY DO OIL SEALS BECOME HARD?

I have made a couple of references to the fact that oil seals become hard over time. Without delving into organic chemistry, the hardening is a result of the way that certain molecules, called polymers, behave. A simple substance like water is made up of molecules, and although each molecule consists of two hydrogen atoms and one atom of oxygen, the molecule is complete like that, and the molecules are separate and free to move relative to each other. In polymers, like plastics, however, the molecules link together chemically. In a flexible substance, they often link up in long lines, or chains.

If you imagine a substance made up of a lot of short lengths of string, joined end to end and all tangled up, you can see how that substance would hold together in a lump, but would be flexible. There are two things that could go wrong with this. If something came along and chopped the strings into much smaller lengths, it would not hold together any more – it would effectively turn to dust. Alternatively, suppose that the string became sticky, so that all the pieces stuck together side by side as well as end to end. In polymerization terms, this is called cross-linking, and it is what happens when you add the hardener to fibreglass body filler.

The synthetic rubbers used to make oil seals suffer from both problems. They contain plasticizers, chemicals that prevent their molecules from cross-linking, but these evaporate over time, causing a seal to become hard, at which point it will no longer flex enough to grip and seal the shaft. As proof, try to bend an old plastic petrol pipe!

Heat, sunlight and certain petrol additives (alcohols mainly) can actually de-polymerize some materials completely, and they will turn to dust. When this happens to rubber, which is a natural polymer, we say it has perished. When I took the rubber insulated wiring off the Francis-Barnett, there was evidence that the rubber had perished and been taped over some time in the 1950s. That would indicate that it had lasted no more than twenty-five years in biking conditions.

By the way, both problems also occur in your tyres over time. That is why you do not go racing on thirty-year-old tyres.

Fig. 6.20   The oil pump gear and clip.

The two pumps are fitted to the clutch cover. In both cases, the plastic drive gear is retained on its shaft by a spring E-clip, and in the case of the oil pump, there is a form of tab washer to prevent it from coming off accidentally. The tab washer must be straightened and the E-clip removed. Each gear is driven by a pin that passes through the shaft and fits into a groove on the underside of the gear. Remove the E-clip with a small screwdriver, making sure that you keep your thumb on it so it does not disappear, then lift off the gear and remove the drive pin.

Fig. 6.21   Two screws hold the oil pump.

The oil pump is fastened to the casing by two screws on the outer side of the clutch cover, and with these removed, it can simply be pulled out of its bearing. The water pump has a removable cover, fastened with four 10mm screws. With the cover off, the pump's impellor can be removed.

Fig. 6.22   The water pump was rusty – not what it should look like.

The pump was in a sorry state. The impellor was very carefully cleaned with a wire brush, while the cover was sandblasted. Then it was faced up, using a sheet of fine sandpaper on a flat surface to ensure that the joint was true and level. The inside of the pump was also cleaned. The entire pump

Fig. 6.23   The housing was rusty, too.

compartment was stuffed with rag and then sealed thoroughly with gaffer tape on both sides before it went into the blast cabinet.

ASSEMBLY

Refitting the Gearbox to the Cases

Assemble the components into the lower half of the crankcase.

1. The first item to go in is the gear-selector drum, slid in from the fly-wheel side.
2. The front gear selector shaft and its selector fork go in next, from the same direction. Fit the E-clip before the shaft is pushed home fully. The pin on this selector engages with the middle selector groove.

Fig. 6.24   A clip holds the selector shaft.

Fig. 6.25   Fit all three selector forks first.

3. Fit the rear selector shaft, with its two selector forks, engaging their pins with the outer grooves in the drum.
4. The two gear shafts, complete with their bearings and seals, can be dropped on to the selector forks and bearing housings.
5. Make sure that the grooves in the bearings line up with the half-circle clips in the bearing housings, and that the selector forks line up with the grooves of the sliding gears. All of this is easier if both the selector drum and the gears are in the neutral position.
6. Once the gears are in place and rotating freely, try turning the selector drum to check that the gears select properly. (In fact, you may spend several minutes just amusing yourself, watching while you go through all the gears!)
7. There is a small oil seal on the blank end of the gear shaft that has the clutch on the other end. This is the seal for the clutch pushrod, and it can be fitted now.

Fig. 6.26   The little oil seal fits at the end of the shaft.

The working part of the gearbox is now assembled, as shown in Fig. 6.27. The components for the selector-drum detent cam and roller can be seen lying

Fig. 6.27   All the gears in place and working.

Fig. 6.28   *This plate holds the selector drum.*

ready to be installed just beyond the case. Those components are attached next.

A small plate locates the selector drum. It is attached to the case by two countersunk screws and stops the drum from moving endways by engaging with a groove.

Fig. 6.29   *Assemble the detent mechanism like this.*

The detent cam goes on to the end of the drum next, followed by the detent roller and spring. This assembly can be seen in Fig. 6.29.

Changing Seals and Bearings

One of the great advantages of a horizontally-split crankcase is the ease with which the bearings and oil seals can be changed. Crankshaft main bearings and their oil seals can simply be fitted on to the crankshaft ends. It is always a good idea to lubricate the shaft before putting on the seal. This will prevent any damage to its lip.

Fitting the Crankshaft

The crankshaft main bearings of Yamaha twins are fitted with pins to prevent the outer races from rotating in the cases, while half-circle clips locate the outer bearings endwise.

Fig. 6.30   *Align the pins on the main bearings to face forward.*

Just check that the pins are not facing downwards before you lower the crank into place. Once the crank is in position, the pins need to point forwards. They fit into a recess machined into the lower part of the case joint.

Putting the Lid On

The tachometer drive shaft needs to be fitted to the top half of the cases before it is replaced on the bottom half.

Fig. 6.31   *The tachometer drive must be fitted in the top case.*

It is a good idea to apply a light smear of sealant to the very large joint between the case halves, and it is much easier to apply this to the upper half, because there is nothing to get in your way.

Having carefully fed the connecting rods through the upper case, it can be lowered on to the bottom half. It should slide down easily. If it does not, make sure that everything is in place. Never force it or try to pull it down with

the studs. Check that the joint is fully closed all around before attempting to tighten the studs. One possible sticking point can be the tachometer drive gear failing to mesh properly with the idler gear behind the clutch.

Fig. 6.32   *Check that the cases fit snugly before bolting it together.*

Now the cases can be bolted together. Start with the large nuts on the bottom, tightening them gradually. Yamaha did not number them on this model, but you need to work in a diagonal pattern from the middle. Run all the nuts up to finger-tight first, then go around again in the same pattern, taking them to about 10Nm (7.5lb ft) torque, and then to about 20Nm (15lb ft).

Turn the engine the right way up and fit the thirteen top screws. These are numbered (*see* Fig. 6.17), so keep to the order cast into the case. Tighten the screws to about 10Nm (7.5lb ft), then go back to the lower nuts and take them to the final value of 24Nm (18lb ft).

Fig. 6.33   The kickstart gear and tachometer drive.

Assembling the Clutch

1. The first items to be fitted are the gears that drive the tachometer shaft and the idler gear of the kickstart assembly. They are held on their shafts by circlips.
2. Fit the kickstart shaft, ensuring that the friction clip underneath engages with the slot in the casing. Wind up the kickstart return spring and hook it over the pin.
3. Install the gear-selector shaft. The claws on the selector engage with the pins on the detent cam.
4. Fit the thrust washer and bearing sleeve to the clutch shaft. Then, making sure that the gear on the back of the clutch basket meshes properly with the kickstart idler gear, install the basket.
5. Fit the primary-drive gear to the end of the crank and tighten the nut slightly. The final torque set-

Fig. 6.35   Tighten the centre nut to the correct torque.

ting for this nut is 75Nm (54lb ft), but it is better to wait until both the nuts that need the engine to be locked can be torqued up at the same time.

6. Add the other thrust washer, the clutch centre, the tab washer and nut, and tighten the nut to 75Nm (55lb ft). It is vital to use a clutch holder.
7. Insert the clutch pushrod, the ball bearing and then the mushroom into the hole in the centre of the clutch shaft.
8. Fit the clutch plates, friction plates and steel plates alternately. A rubber ring fits between each friction plate and the centre. These prevent clutch rattle as the friction plates move back and forth in their slots in the basket. This would wear out the basket and eventually indent the slots, producing a very 'snatchy' clutch. With the dry clutches used on the racing TZ series, clutch rattle used to break the friction plates; any racer of this era will remember paddocks paved with old broken clutch plates!
9. Before fitting the pressure plate, confirm that you have installed the clutch pushrod mushroom. The top pressure plate fits over the splines of the clutch centre, and it must be fitted so that the arrow on the top plate lines up with the circle stamped on the top of the centre. When installed correctly, the top plate will rest tightly on the top of the clutch plates.

Fig. 6.36   The top pressure plate must fit snugly.

10. Install the clutch springs. Norbo Lea (owner of the subject engine) recommends an upgrade to the standard springs, to prevent clutch slip, especially with a tuned

Fig. 6.34   Install the clutch bearing sleeve on the shaft.

engine, so the springs fitted were three standard 350LC springs and three slightly longer springs from the Yamaha R6. To ensure that the clutch releases and engages evenly, the springs must be installed alternately.

11. With the springs in place, fit the six screws and tighten them down evenly and completely.

Fig. 6.37   Three standard springs and three from the Yamaha R6.

Refitting the Flywheel Assembly

Fig. 6.38   The Woodruff key and taper are in good condition.

Set the crank so that the slot for the Woodruff key faces upwards, then install the key. It is much easier to do this first.

Fit the stator on to the lugs in the casing; it is a tight fit. *See* Fig. 6.10 for the correct orientation of the stator.

In this case, the stator was replaced in its original position, using the marks made when it was dismantled. As you fit the stator, feed the wiring harness

through the hole in the casing and work the grommet into place to seal it.

Install the flywheel, making sure that the Woodruff key fits into the keyway in the centre. This is easier if the front of the key is very slightly lower in its keyway in the crankshaft – not too much, or it will tip up and be pushed out of the keyway, just a couple of millimetres only.

Use a holder to stop the flywheel from turning, or lock the engine with a bar through one of the connecting rods. Then add the washer and nut, and tighten the nut to 75Nm (55lb ft).

Do the same to the primary-drive nut, which will not have been tightened yet, remember?

Fitting the Pistons and Cylinders

1. First fit the cylinder base gaskets on to the cylinder studs, making sure that they are the right way round so that the transfer ports are not blocked.

2. Fit the circlips to the sides of the pistons that are going to be on the inner side of the engine. The pistons are marked on the crown with an arrow that must point forwards, towards the exhaust port.

3. Warm the pistons slightly so that the gudgeon pins are an easy push-fit, insert the small-end roller bearings in the connecting rod eyes, fit each piston to its rod and gently

Fig. 6.39   Warm the piston to about 80°C.

push the gudgeon pin through the small-end bearing. You will find it easier to align the pin with the small end if you rock the piston on the rod a little.

4. Unless you are very good with tailless circlips, stuff some clean rag into the crankcase before you try to fit the outer circlip.

FITTING TAILLESS CIRCLIPS

My method with this type of circlip is to hold it with the gap uppermost, grasping it with narrow-nose pliers at the 10-o'clock position. Push the other end of the circlip into the hole at the top of the bore in the piston (12-o'clock). Then, while my right thumb is firmly clamped over the loose end, I push and turn the clip clockwise with the pliers, winding it into the bore. Once it is in, I settle it into the groove with a small screwdriver.

It is worth mentioning that I am left-handed, so if you are unfortunate enough to be right-handed, you will need to work out a reverse version of this. Sorry about that!

With the pistons and circlips in place, install the piston rings. The top and bottom rings are different. The bottom ring is thicker and has an expander ring beneath it. As always with a two-stroke, it is vital to align the ring gaps with the ring pins once the rings have been fitted to the pistons. No special precautions are needed to fit the rings. It can be done quite easily by hand.

When the subject engine was dismantled, it was clear that the cylinders and pistons were in good condition, so no significant work beyond a quick clean up was needed before they were refitted.

Although, in theory, cylinders could be honed at home, using an expanding hone and an electric drill, to do the job properly requires a constant flow of oil into the cylinder, so in my opinion it is work that is best sent out to a specialist. Ideally, the treatment should be carried out with a bottlebrush-type known as Flex Hone, which produces a far better crosshatch pattern.

IGNITION TIMING

You will need to fit the cylinders and pistons before you can set the timing, but for reference, the ignition timing for a *standard* 350LC is set by moving the left-hand piston to a position 1.8mm before TDC and adjusting the stator plate by turning it, using a screwdriver in the slots in the plate (having loosened the screws that secure the stator). The ignition timing is correct when the timing marks on the lug next to the wiring harness (*see* Fig. 6.10) and those on the stator plate align perfectly.

Fig. 6.40   *Using an expanding hone with an electric drill.*

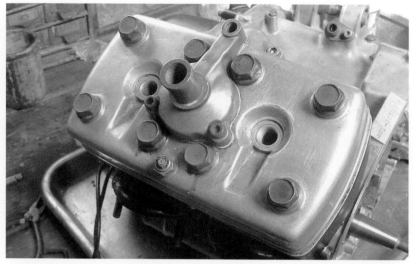

Fig. 6.43   *The cylinder head in place.*

Whichever type of hone is used, the cylinders must be thoroughly washed before being installed on the engine. The edges of the ports should be checked for sharp corners, too, and radiussed if necessary.

Fig. 6.41   *Fitting the cylinder.*

Fig. 6.44   *Tighten the nuts in this order.*

Always lubricate the cylinder walls with a film of oil before fitting the cylinders, which is another easy task on a Yamaha. There is room between the cylinder studs to grip the piston rings between thumb and finger, and squeeze them in enough to slide the piston into the cylinder.

Start with the piston at Top Dead Centre. Once the piston has entered the cylinder, you can squeeze the rings in fully. This allows you to feel if the rings catch on the ports as they pass. Of course, if everything has been aligned properly, they should not do so!

With both cylinders in place, add the cylinder-head gasket and fit the cylinder head. Insert the eight sleeve nuts and tighten them gradually in a diagonal pattern, as indicated in Fig. 6.44.

The reed valves and carburettor rubbers attach to the back of the cylinders.

Fig. 6.42   *You can squeeze the rings with your fingers.*

Fitting the Oil and Water Pumps

The oil and water pumps are fitted inside the front of the clutch cover.

Fig. 6.45   The water-pump cover has been cleaned up.

The water pump casing is part of the clutch cover. The impeller is driven by a gear on the inner side of the cover (*see* Figs. 6.20–6.23 for details of the installation). It is a good idea to replace the bearing and seal in the water pump, since they are subject to a lot of wear, and a water leak into the engine is always bad news.

Install the cover plate with a new gasket. The oil-pump spindle and its driving gear must also be fitted into the clutch cover (*see* 'Removing the Water and Oil Pumps' for how it all goes together). Then the clutch cover can be added, with a new gasket, of course.

The oil-pump body can then be fitted on to the worm-drive gear that drives it and screwed to the cover with two crosshead screws.

At this point, the engine was assembled and ready to return to its owner.

Fig. 6.46   The completed engine, out in the sunshine.

Fig. 6.47   The ten fastenings on the YPVS version.

Fig. 6.48   The underside of the head.

WHAT ABOUT THE YPVS MODELS?

As mentioned, Yamaha twins have a lot in common, so there are far fewer differences than you might imagine, and many parts are interchangeable.

However, there are some obvious differences in the case of the YPVS:

- Ten nuts secure the cylinder head, not eight.
- The water outlet on the head is taller and contains a thermostat.
- The water pipe from the pump to the head is bigger.
- There are studs, nuts and a flange to hold down the cylinders.
- The clutch actuating lever is different.
- Last, but most importantly, there are rotating drums in the exhaust port, which vary the exhaust-port timing.

Servicing the Powervalves

To gain access to the powervalves, the cylinders must be removed. The cylinder-head sleeve nuts (shorter than the LC) are numbered, so undo them in that order.

Remove the head and gasket. An artist's palette knife is a good tool for lifting the gasket without damaging it.

The cylinders are separate, but they are joined by a central coupling that connects the spindles of the power-valve drums. This must be removed

Fig. 6.49   A palette knife is good for removing the gasket.

Fig. 6.53   There should be a drive flat on the end of the drum.

Fig. 6.50   The coupling connects the two powervalve drums.

There is a housing for the pulley for the cables of the powervalve servo on the left side of the left-hand cylinder. Unscrew the two cap-head screws and remove the housing. There is a similar blanking cap on the right side of the right-hand cylinder. This must also be removed. On the inner sides of the cylinders, there is a long cap-head screw that runs down the centre of the powervalve drums. Removing the screw allows the two halves of the drum to be pulled from each side of the cylinders.

Fig. 6.52   A very dirty powervalve drum.

before the cylinders can be taken off. Undo the two Allen screws and separate the two halves of the coupling.

The cylinder base fastenings are separate from the head studs on this model. Tuners, who have worked with the earlier models, are very aware that the cylinder studs restrict the amount by which the ports can be widened. For the YPVS, the ports were made wider but without the need to alter the crankcase completely. You will need a combination spanner to undo the base nuts – there is no access for a socket spanner.

The cylinders can then be lifted off the crankcase.

It is vital that the drums can turn freely in the exhaust ports, so they must be kept clean. The bike is designed so that the servo cycles the powervalves open and closed to ensure that they are free to move every time the ignition switch is turned on. The powervalves of the subject engine were thoroughly cleaned with a rotating wire brush on a bench grinder. There was a noticeable build up of carbon in the ports, too, and this was cleaned out with a small wire brush on a Dremel.

The powervalves are sealed with O-rings and lip seals, and all the previous remarks about the problems encountered with aging oil seals are very relevant here. The powervalve

shaft seals were actually crumbling, while the O-rings were stretched and loose.

On reassembling the powervalves into the cylinders and connecting the shafts, a further problem became apparent. It is obvious that both powervalves must operate at exactly the same time. Their shafts are D-shaped and fit into matching holes in the coupling, but in this case the coupling was badly worn, preventing simultaneous operation. It was replaced.

Fig. 6.54   This coupling should have a D-shaped end.

Fig. 6.51   The powervalve pulley housing.

A BETTER COUPLING

In the days of TZ racing, I recall fitting to a TZ250 an Oldham coupling, which is a device that allows free movement between two shafts that are not quite accurately aligned. If these are still available, it would be a good choice in a situation such as this.

The task on the YPVS engine was only to examine the powervalves, so a written report on the parts needed was provided and, after a quick clean up, the engine was reassembled for return to the owner.

Fig. 6.55 *The clutch on the YPVS is very similar to the LC.*

However, purely to prove the point that the basic design of these two engines is the same, the clutch cover was removed. One difference that could be seen was the presence of two torque stays beneath the crankcase. These were fitted to counter the tendency of the engine to twist in the frame during the ferocious acceleration for which these bikes are famous, and to reduce vibration the rest of the time.

WHAT HAPPENED NEXT?

During this period, two-strokes entered an 'arms race': bigger cylinders, more cylinders and more technology led to some of the most exciting bikes in history.

Suzuki introduced its T500, an air-cooled 500cc twin to go with its GT250 models, which were followed by the very light and nimble X7. The water-cooled RG250 models marked

the next step. The series having started with a parallel-twin version, the final RGV was a jewel-like V-twin. They are very powerful, but a little fragile – the engine is also used in the RS250 Aprilia.

Honda were late to the two-stroke party, but the NSR250s, in their many variants, were glorious machines.

Yamaha moved on from the RDLC YPVS to the smaller and lighter TZR250. This bike graduated to a reverse-cylinder version and then a V-twin. Many of the more elaborate late versions of these bikes were never officially sold in the UK. Some were available in other parts of Europe, while others were for the Japanese market only. That has not stopped them from being imported, cherished and traded for high prices.

The ultimate twin must be the Bimota V Due. The name is even better in Italian, where 'V' is pronounced 'Vu', so the name sounds very like 'Voodoo'. It is beautifully engineered, as is everything made by Bimota, and it is powered by a 500cc V-twin.

On the other hand, work on the Scott continued, and it was still possible to buy a British two-stroke twin, in 600cc or even 750cc versions, in the form of the Silk Scott.

Fig. 6.56 *The author's Suzuki T500 around 1976.*

Fig. 6.57 *A Suzuki GT250, the version without the 'Ram Air' cowling.*

Fig. 6.58   A Bridgestone 350GTR in need of restoration.

Fig. 6.59   A fully restored Honda NSR250.

Fig. 6.60   A view under the fairings of a reverse-cylinder TZR250.

Fig. 6.61   The engine from a reverse-cylinder TZR250.

Fig. 6.62   The Bimota V Due. It was retrofitted with carburettors by the factory.

Fig. 6.63   An Aprilia RS250, using the Suzuki RGV engine.

Fig. 6.64   One of the last of the Silk Scotts.

Fig. 6.65   'Like a Swiss watch inside.' An MBA 125 twin.

bigger engines and more cylinders
Kawasaki S2 (350 Triple)

Between 1968 and 1984, every 250cc world road race champion won the title riding a twin-cylinder two-stroke. It is a very similar story with the 125cc class between 1970 and 1988, when the 125s were restricted to a single cylinder. Meanwhile, until 1974, Giacomo Agostini was still winning the 350 and 500cc classes on a four-stroke MV.

Two-stroke manufacturers wanting to expand into the larger-capacity market needed a bigger bike. Yamaha, following Honda's lead, had always produced a bigger-bore 350cc version of their 250cc machines. From their introduction into the UK, Honda had offered their CB72 250, along with a CB77 305cc version, but big bikes started at 500cc in those days.

In the two-stroke world, Suzuki made the first move with the bike that became successful as the T500, but it was still a twin-cylinder machine. In 1969, Kawasaki raised the stakes in a big way with the mighty H1. Designed to be the most powerful bike in its class, it was a 500cc 3-cylinder, air-cooled two-stroke, and it set the pattern for a whole series of Kawasaki triples. Five years later, the H2 was released. It was a 750cc version and it became famous for its violent power band, uncertain handling and tendency to wheelie with very little provocation. In this respect, it was more appealing to the American market, where drag racing seems to be the more popular inspiration for riding style. In the UK, we tend to model our ideas of riding on the Isle of Man TT style of racing, preferring a bike that can swoop around fast bends.

THE KAWASAKI S2

Road testers of the time felt that the best of the triples, as far as balance of power to weight and rideability were concerned, were the 350 and 400cc versions. The 350cc Kawasaki S2 was introduced in 1972, though the example described here is a disc-braked model from the following year.

A well-known New Zealand tuner, Wayne L. Wright, who trades under the name Wobbly, described the Kawasaki S2 in these words:

> The S2 in its day was one of the best bikes on the road. It would destroy an RD350 and the engine power vs. chassis capability was near on perfect.

As classic two-strokes are becoming difficult to find, it is increasingly likely that anyone looking for one to restore will need to turn to one of the businesses that import them from the USA and Japan. One of the biggest in this field is DK Motorcycles of Newcastle-under-Lyme in Staffordshire. The bike shown in this chapter was one of theirs. It was a 'barn find', imported from Kansas, and was both rusty and seized. The aim of this strip-down was not to perform a full restoration, but to free up the engine if possible and provide a full report on its condition for any prospective purchaser.

KAWASAKI S2 ENGINE SPECIFICATIONS

Type: air-cooled, transverse 3-cylinder
Capacity: 346cc
Bore and stroke: 53×52.3mm
Compression ratio: 7.3:1
Induction: $3 \times$ Mikuni 24mm carburettors
Ignition: battery and coil
Starting: kickstart
Max. power: 45hp at 8,000rpm
Max. torque: 4.2kg m (30.4lb ft) at 7,000rpm
Transmission: Gear primary drive, multi-plate wet clutch, 5-speed gearbox, chain final drive

TAKING THE ENGINE OUT OF THE FRAME

The very first task, which had to be faced before the bike had been in the workshop for more than fifteen minutes, was to remove the seat. The seat cover was missing, as were parts of the

Fig. 7.1   The Kawasaki S2 as it arrived.

Fig. 7.2   The seat base was rotted through.

Fig. 7.3   Removing the cylinder heads provides more room.

seat foam. But it was not the way it looked that was the problem.

It was the smell!

Lifting the seat did reveal the missing carburettor air hoses, which was good, but the seat itself was a shocking sight. The base was almost completely rusted out, and from the smell and appearance, it seemed that the seat had been home to rats.

The seat was removed by extracting the hinge pins and then stowed away under cover outside. The atmosphere in the workshop improved after that!

Disconnecting the Engine

Engines in Kawasaki triples are fixed to the frame in four places, using long through-bolts. To make removal and refitting easier, small engine plates are used, so that the engine does not need to be wriggled in and out of close-fitting brackets around the engine lugs.

Provide extra space and visibility by removing the fuel tank. Three separate fuel pipes connect to the petrol tap, and it is easier to disconnect them once the tank has been lifted away from the frame slightly.

Try to be systematic when disconnecting everything. Starting from the front of the engine and working around it clockwise, you will come across items to be disconnected in this order:

1. The exhaust pipes are separate from the silencers, so remove the exhaust flange nuts. There should be clamps that seal the down-pipes to the silencers, but these were missing, so the pipes could simply be pulled away from the stubs. The pipes are all the same, so you do not need to number them or mark them 'Left', 'Right' and 'Centre'. There are copper gasket rings inside the exhaust ports. In a proper restoration, these should be replaced on reassembly.

2. Disconnect the tachometer drive cable by unscrewing the fastening ring.

3. It will be easier to lift the engine out if you can reduce the height and weight a little, so I recommend removing the cylinder heads. I hope it is not too much

like stating the obvious, but if you remove the outer heads first, the 13mm nuts that fasten the centre head will be easy to reach.

4. Remove the carburettors. They are a stub-fitting type with clamp bolts that can be undone with a screwdriver. You can drape the carburettors, still attached to their cables, over the top of the frame.

5. The rear brake pedal obscures the lower rear engine mounting bolt, so loosen off the adjuster at the rear brake arm to allow the pedal to drop out of the way.

6. Continuing to the back of the bike, and switching to the other side, remove the chain. The subject bike did have a split link, but the clip had rusted to nothing, and after a good shot of penetrating oil, the link could be driven out with a hammer and pin punch. The quicker approach would have been to cut off the chain with an angle grinder, since it was only fit for scrap.

7. Moving forward, remove the chain guard. It is secured with a hex-head bolt at the back and a pan-head posi-drive at the front.

8. Take off the air cleaner. In this case, it was due for an encounter with a pressure washer! (*See* panel, 'Mobile Home.')

9. There is one main wiring cable to disconnect, with three multi-way plugs. They are all different in colour and shape, so there is no need to worry about making the wrong connections later. The only other electrical connection is the neutral-switch wire, which attaches to a screwless connector on top of the crankcase. Press down on the spring-loaded ring on the top

---

MOBILE HOME

This bike had another surprise for me. The entire space around the ignition coils was packed with hard, dried mud, full of little holes. The desiccated corpses of dozens of hornets filled some of the holes. As it turned out, there was another colony in the air-cleaner box, and more in the space in front of the engine sprocket. Perhaps this was why the bike had been abandoned to rust!

of the connector and pull out the wire. Now that the chain guard and air cleaner are out of the way, the engine end of the wiring harness can be pulled clear of the frame, having removed any cable ties first. The original Kawasaki cable ties have release tabs and can be used again.

10. Disconnect the gear lever. There are two ways of doing this. One is to take off the retaining clip on the brake pedal itself and then, having removed the clamp screw from the lever on the gearchange spindle, pull off the whole assembly. Alternatively, you can remove the adjuster rod and leave the pedal in place. The adjuster rod has left- and right-hand threads, so if you loosen the locknuts and turn it anti-clockwise, you can unscrew it simultaneously from both ends. Then the gear lever can be removed from the shaft.

Fig. 7.4 You can disconnect the gearchange by removing the adjuster.

11. Remove the sprocket cover and disconnect the clutch cable. It is not easy to do this under normal circumstances, since the space is constricted and it is difficult to see what you are doing, but in this instance it was impossible because of the mud! Consequently the clutch cable was disconnected at the lever end and the cable pulled clear of the steering head, etc.

12. Start to remove the engine bolts. The front one has nuts on both ends, and the nut on the nearside end must be removed, because it will not pass the screw boss on the casing. I was working on the bike while it was on its side stand, so it was leaning slightly to the left. I prefer to work this way because

Fig. 7.5 There is a removable engine plate at the front.

it gives easier access to the bolts underneath the engine. It also provides a tiny amount of gravity assistance when the engine is moved to the left. For this reason, remove the left-side engine plates from the front and upper rear fixing points. The bolt head and the loose engine plate are at the front left fixing point.

13. The last engine bolt to be removed will be carrying the whole weight of the engine and will be stubborn. Use a lever or a socket extension to lift the engine in the frame slightly to take the weight off the bolt and allow it to be pulled out.

14. Having removed all four bolts, stand astride the frame and lift up the engine at the front and forwards to clear the rear engine mounts. Then lift the engine up and out of the frame. As you carry the engine away from the bike, be careful of the handlebars, particularly if it is a US version, which commonly had unusually long bars.

Fig. 7.6 Lift the front of the engine first.

Fig. 7.7   One piston was seized at TDC.

FREEING A SEIZED CYLINDER

With the engine on the bench, it was time to explore the reasons why the engine would not turn. Mention a seized Kawasaki triple to any motorcyclist, and the response is likely to be 'Middle cylinder'.

In this case, however, the middle cylinder could be removed easily, as could the right-hand one. The left cylinder, the one at TDC, was solid.

The task of freeing a seized piston should be tackled in stages. The first stage is to proceed on the basis that the piston is to be freed up without damaging it, so it can be used again. Accordingly, the piston crown was liberally sprayed with penetrating oil, left for half a day to allow the oil to sink in, then heated with a heat gun and tapped with a soft-faced mallet.

This produced a movement of the piston of about 2mm, and it provided some good news. It was now possible to turn the crank fractionally, and it was clearly turning easily. More penetrating oil was sprayed on to the piston crown and also into the exhaust port, and left overnight. No further movement of the piston was achieved the following day, however, the conclusion being that it was unlikely that the piston would be removed in a useable condition.

Knowing that the crank could turn meant that the next stage in the process would not damage the crank or connecting rod, so more force was used. A technique with two hammers was employed. The soft-faced mallet was rested on the piston crown and then the other end of the mallet head was struck with a heavier hammer. The purpose of this was to allow the hammer

blows to be very firm while avoiding the danger of a missed blow damaging the top of the cylinder. Unlike the use of a straight bar as a drift, there is little danger of hitting your hand either!

In fact, the piston fought every inch of the way. Apart from a ring of corrosion at the very top of the bore, however, the cylinder was in good condition.

Fig. 7.9   The piston was partially cleaned to show the thick deposits.

The piston, on the other hand, was dented on the crown (hardly a surprise considering!) and the skirt was coated all over with a rusty white crust about half a millimetre thick. The rings were completely stuck in their grooves.

If the pistons are reuseable, it is a good idea to mark them to ensure that they go back into their own cylinders. These pistons have tailless circlips, and they are best removed by inserting a small screwdriver in the circlip extraction notch. To prevent a sudden 'ping', followed by the circlip doing a high-speed vanishing act and a frantic search among the debris under your bench, put your thumb over the gudgeon-pin hole while you do this.

Removing a Stuck Piston Ring

The first thing to say about removing a stuck ring is that if it is stuck because of debris from a piston seizure, detonation damage to the edge of the piston crown or from broken bits of metal from, for example, a lost gudgeon-pin circlip, don't bother. The engine will need a rebore, probably some work on the cylinder head and a new piston and rings. In this case, the piston had been damaged in removing it, so the task of unsticking the rings was done purely as an exercise, and eventually as

Fig. 7.8   Using a soft mallet on the seized piston.

an experiment with a technique mentioned on the Internet.

The first step is to try soaking the piston in penetrating oil, but before you do this clean out the gaps above and below the ring so that the oil can penetrate more easily. You can do this with a sharp knife, though I prefer an artist's palette knife. Repeatedly heating and cooling the piston will often free a ring, as will gently tapping it all around the circumference of the piston. If you can see any slight movement as you do this, more soaking and finally a very gentle prising at the ring ends with an electrical screwdriver may create the space to slide the palette knife under the ring and lift it out of the groove.

If the penetrating oil seems to be having no effect and the ring is stuck as a consequence of the engine standing idle, many people on the Internet advise soaking the piston in brake cleaner. This incorporates organic solvents such as acetone, and it will dissolve the 'varnish' caused by the oxidation of some two-stroke oils – the much-loved Castrol R is an example. You find a similar 'varnish' in old carburettors.

I tried soaking the piston in cellulose paint thinners, which contains similar solvents, but since the problem was corrosion, it had no effect.

Some websites suggest that soaking the piston in a glass of cola will work. There is some reason behind this, since the majority of colas contain a low concentration of phosphoric acid as flavouring. Phosphoric acid is also used as a rustproofer, since It converts iron oxide (rust), which is flaky and absorbs water, into iron phosphate, which does not. Another use is as a cleaner for bricks and concrete. (It dissolves concrete if you are not careful!)

Fig. 7.10   Using the acid reduced the piston diameter.

As a final experiment, the top of the piston was soaked in neat brick cleaner. An hour later, the top of the piston was black and two millimetres smaller (!), while the rings were free enough to be persuaded off.

The conclusion is that a dilute solution of phosphoric acid might be useful in freeing a corroded ring that is stuck in its groove, but a concentrated one is certainly effective. Unfortunately, it destroys the piston itself.

RESTORING THE CYLINDER BORES

The ideal way to restore a dirty but otherwise perfectly useable cylinder bore is by honing. Ideally, this should be done with a bottlebrush-style flexible hone. These are sold the under the name Flex Hone and are readily available. By moving the hone up and down the bore, a crosshatch pattern of fine scratches is created to make a perfect surface for retaining oil on the inner wall of the cylinder.

Unfortunately, a different hone is required for each bore size, requiring a substantial outlay, although expanding hones with three spring-loaded stones are also available, but they are less effective in creating a crosshatch finish. Moreover, a constant supply of oil is needed to the cylinder during the process, so realistically you would need to send the job to an engine reconditioning firm.

However, now a scrap piston of the correct size was available, and this offered the opportunity to try a cheap, home-based technique that was popular in my father's day.

The first stage is to make a wooden 'connecting rod' so that you can hold

Fig. 7.11   Make a wooden 'connecting rod' to use as a handle when honing the cylinder with an old piston.

Fig. 7.12   Push and twist to lap the bore clean and create a crosshatch pattern.

and twist the piston. Fit the handle and apply some coarse grinding paste to the scrap piston. You will probably need to use some light oil as well to make this lapping process easier.

Using a twisting motion, work the piston up and down the bore, making sure to take the piston beyond the top of the cylinder. Twist the piston clockwise going up and anticlockwise going down for a few strokes, and then reverse the motion to anticlockwise up and clockwise down for the same number of strokes. This will give you a very acceptable crosshatch pattern. Wash the cylinder clean *very* carefully, including the insides of the ports, using engine cleaner or paraffin.

Fig. 7.13   The finish on the bore is good as a result.

The previously seized cylinder, which had a thick ring of corrosion around the top 5mm of the cylinder bore, was cleaned up using this method and can be seen in Fig. 7.13.

Obviously, a piston would be totally unfit for use in an engine after such treatment. Abrasives can become impacted into the surface of aluminium, and they will turn a piston into a permanent honing tool. In this case, however, the piston was the perfect tool for cleaning up the other two cylinders.

Fig. 7.14   *The points mount on the alternator end plate.*

CRANKCASE, ALTERNATOR SIDE

The crankcase on this engine is split horizontally along the centre line of the main bearings. This makes dismantling a much easier task. When splitting the crankcase, however, it is important to remove the generator and points casing first, since it connects the two halves of the case.

Undo the casing screws and remove the casing along with the stator windings for the alternator. Next, undo the screw that holds the ignition cam to the shaft and pull the cam from the centre of the alternator rotor.

There is a small locating pin to set the basic timing of the ignition cam.

The alternator rotor is fitted on to a taper on the end of the crankshaft; a puller is needed to remove it. Sorting through my selection of pullers, I found that the centre screw from a hub puller was the correct size and thread to fit into the extraction thread tapped into the centre of the rotor. It was a little too short, however, so a small piece

Fig. 7.15   *Note the locating pin on the face of the ignition cam.*

of scrap steel was put into the hole first to increase the reach of the thread.

The rotor was held with a strap wrench while the extractor was used.

Three other components bridge the two halves of the crankcase, so these

must also be removed. The first is the clutch release mechanism. It could not be seen for mud at this stage, but it is located just ahead of the sprocket (*see* Fig. 7.35). It is secured with two cross-head screws, which almost certainly will need to be removed with an impact driver, being in a very dirty place.

The next item is the gearchange mechanism; unfortunately, this is close behind the clutch, so the clutch must be removed first.

Removing the Clutch

Probably you will not need to lock the engine to release the five screws that hold the pressure plate. If you do, it is easy to hold the crank with a spanner on the nut that holds the drive gear. Undo the screws and lift off the pressure plate.

You will notice that there are wavy rings between the plates to help them separate when the clutch lever is operated. Keep all the plates and rings together.

Fig. 7.16   *Extracting the rotor with the centre screw from a puller.*

Fig. 7.17   *Undo the clutch spring screws evenly.*

Fig. 7.18 Note the broken and missing lug.

You will definitely need a clutch holding tool to lock the clutch centre while you undo the nut in the middle. The clutch basket is made from cast aluminium, and the tabs are very brittle – as a previous owner had already discovered. As mentioned previously, it is easy to make a clutch holder from an old steel clutch plate; plates for most models are easy to find at the breakers.

A tab washer prevents the centre nut from loosening. Flatten the tab and remove the nut and the clutch centre. Make a note of the order of the sleeve and thrust bearings. Taking a photograph will help, though the items will be listed in the correct order in the description of the reassembly process.

With the clutch out of the way, you can gain access to the gear selector mechanism. Unhook the claws of the selector pawls from the drum and remove the gear-pedal shaft. The shaft was quite tight in the casings of this engine, so after removal, it was thoroughly cleaned with a wire brush and lubricated with a smear of oil ready for reassembly. It must turn freely for a smooth, slick gearchange.

SPLITTING THE CRANKCASE

Turn the engine over. The fastenings are all on the lower side of the crankcase.

Eight large studs with 14mm nuts and thirteen smaller ones with 10mm nuts hold the halves of the crankcase together. It is good practice to loosen the nuts gradually in a diagonal pattern to prevent the cases from distorting. Having removed all the nuts, however, you will find that the cases still fit tightly together. There is nowhere to safely tap the cases or use a lever to prise them apart, so my recommendation is to insert a rod, or one of the engine bolts, through the mounting lugs on the bottom crankcase half, lift the engine by the rod and tap the studs with a copper hammer. Once the joint separates, make sure that all the shafts and components stay in the upper half of the case and lift the bottom half away.

Fig. 7.19 A photograph will remind you of the order in which to replace these.

Fig. 7.20 An effective method of separating the top and bottom cases.

Fig. 7.21 A full view of the engine internals.

Everything is now revealed, and can be spun and checked easily. On the subject engine, the crank spun nicely in its bearings and all the big-end bearings were in good condition. It is easy to mount a DTI to check that the crank runs true in its own bearings, and this engine passed the test.

Crankshaft Oil Seals

What you cannot be sure about is the condition of the seals between the cranks for the different cylinders. Plastics become hard and brittle with age. There were signs that the outer seals had become hard; in general, any engine that has been standing for more than five or six years should have its oil seals replaced. If the subject engine were to be put into running order, it would need to have either the crank rebuilt or an exchange crank fitted, with new seals. That is definitely a job for a specialist.

CHECKING THE GEARBOX

One great advantage of the horizontally-split crankcase is that the gearbox can not only be thoroughly examined in situ, but also even run through the gears, by turning the selector drum.

Fig. 7.22   The gearchange detent mechanism.

All the gear teeth and engagement dogs can be checked. In the event that a broken tooth or worn set of dogs is discovered, the gear shaft can simply be lifted out and the defective pinion removed. Do be careful, though, as the gears are held in place by circlips and aligned with thrust washers. The best tip, unless you have a really good exploded diagram to work from, possibly from the official parts list, is to fix a rod into a block of wood and slide each component on to the rod as you

remove it. Then, when you reassemble the shaft, it is just a case of fitting them in the same order and the same way up. There was no visible wear on any of the gearbox components on this engine, so the gear shafts were not disturbed.

REASSEMBLY

Reassembling the Cases

Fig. 7.23   Make sure that the oil feed connections are clear.

Before putting the case halves together, it is always a good idea to make sure that any oil passages are clear. Behind the cylinders are three connections where the oil pipes are attached. These are the only places where oil feeds into the cylinder, so they must be clear. A blast with compressed air is the most effective method.

With the engine upside down, the first item to install is the gear selector drum. It is held in place by the retaining plate and two screws (*see* Fig. 7.22).

DIFFERENT APPROACHES

A comparison between the Yamahas discussed in Chapter 6 and the Kawasaki examined here indicates that Yamaha employed three selector forks on two selector shafts, whereas the Kawasaki had one of the selector forks on the selector drum itself, and only a single selector shaft for the other two. This makes for a rather neater design. Manufacturers tend to stick to their respective designs over a wide range of models.

Line up the gear selector forks in the groves in the selector drum. Everything will go together most easily if the selector is set to the neutral position, that is when the shallower dimple on the detent cam is against the detent roller. The dimple and detent roller can be seen on the far side of the drum in Fig. 7.22.

Next install the two gear shafts. It is often easier to fit the two shafts together and drop them into their bearing housings at the same time, taking great care that the selector forks engage properly with their grooves on the sliding gears. Nothing in this process should require any force at all. If it does not go together easily, there is something wrong.

Fig. 7.24   Here, the shafts can be seen resting on top of the selector forks, and not engaged with them. Replacing the other case half at this stage would cause serious damage. Also visible is the hole for the peg that stops the shaft bearing from turning and the groove on the outer rim of the clutch shaft bearing that prevents sideways movement.

Fig. 7.25   This shows everything as it should be, with all the shaft bearings properly located on their pegs and C-shims.

Fig. 7.26   Hold the end of the kickstart spring down while you fit the top case.

Fig. 7.27   The case halves must fit snugly before they are bolted together.

There is a hole in the shaft bearing that engages with a peg in the top half of the case; the peg prevents the bearing from turning. There is also a groove on the outer rim of the clutch shaft bearing. This prevents the bearing from moving sideways, because there is a C-shim in the upper half of the case.

The only item left to fit is the kickstart mechanism. There are three points to watch:

1. The friction spring must fit into its groove inside the cases (*see* Fig. 7.25).
2. The bearing hole must fit over the peg in the left-side bearing housing.
3. Before the crankcase half can be pushed down, the end of the kickstart spring must be pulled into place. It is held by a groove in the rim of the casing between two studs (*see* Fig. 7.26). The trick is to pull the spring down and hold it in the groove with a screwdriver while you drop the lower case half on to the studs.

Make sure that the mating faces of the crankcase halves fit together perfectly before you bolt the two halves together. If the engine were being assembled in the expectation of starting it straight away, sealant would be used in the joint. As it was, the nuts were only tightened sufficiently to keep things together, not torqued up to the correct value, which would be about 10Nm (7.5lb ft) for the 10mm nuts, and about 20Nm (15lb ft) for the 14mm nuts.

Refitting the Clutch

Before the clutch is put back, remember to refit the bearing cap (labelled 'Japan') that fits across the crankcase joint and closes the end of the other gear shaft. You also need to install the (cleaned and lubricated) gearchange shaft at this stage, engaging the detent claws with the pins on the selector drum.

The 'triangular' thrust washer goes on to the clutch shaft first – the cutaways that make it triangular allow oil to reach the ball race on the shaft (*see* Fig. 7.19).

Fig. 7.28 *Fit the little end cap across the joint.*

Fig. 7.29 *The new clutch basket has all its lugs.*

Fig. 7.30 *Fit the tab washer to the clutch shaft.*

The bearing sleeve goes next, followed by the round thrust washer.

Install the clutch basket on the shaft. In this case, a replacement basket was fitted; conscience would not allow me to refit the basket with the broken tags.

The clutch centre can now be fitted on to the splined part of the shaft, followed by the tab washer. This has a tab that is bent downwards to fit into a hole in the middle of the clutch centre

TEMPORARY FIX

The clutch basket of this Kawasaki engine is typical of a very large number of Japanese bikes, in that it is made of cast aluminium. Not only is it brittle and easily broken if you attempt to remove or tighten the clutch nut without using a proper holding tool, but also it does not have a very hard surface. The result of this is that the tabs of the clutch plates can wear notches in the tabs of the clutch basket.

Fig. 7.31 *Make sure that the top pressure plate fits on to the splines on the centre.*

You can see some marks on the upper face of the tab at the top left of Fig. 7.30. If these became deep, the clutch would become impossible to engage and disengage smoothly – it would be 'snatchy'. If these notches become noticeable, they can be smoothed slightly with a smooth file. Once this has been done, however, the clutch plates will have a little more play in the tabs, which will wear the notches more quickly in the future, so it only postpones the day when the basket will have to be replaced. This is one of the reasons why competition motors sometimes, and at great expense, use 'billet' clutches with baskets machined from solid bar.

Fig. 7.32   Hold the clutch and tighten the nut to the correct torque setting.

(*see* Fig. 7.30). Lock the clutch centre with a holder and tighten the retaining nut to about 30Nm (22lb ft)

One of the corners of the tab washer should be bent up and, using a punch, hammered firmly against one of the flats of the nut.

Put the clutch plates on to the clutch centre, alternating steel and lined plates, a wavy washer being fitted along with each lined plate.

Finally make sure that the long clutch pushrod, the ball bearing and the clutch pushrod mushroom are in the centre of the gear shaft. The push-rod and the bearing can be fitted from the other end of the shaft, but the mushroom must go in this way.

After close scrutiny, I was unable to find any marks to line up to ensure that the pressure plate engaged smoothly over both the spring bosses and the splines on the clutch centre. On many engines, there is only one place where this occurs, and it is indicated when an arrow on the pressure plate lines up with a mark on the centre. In this case, it was a matter of trial and error – five trials and four errors!

Unless the pressure plate fits on to the splines, the clutch will not grip, so make sure that it is tightly in contact with the top lined plate before fitting the springs and tightening the five screws that compress them.

The Clutch Release Mechanism

This is a spiral device that fits into the drive side of the casings, close to the

Fig. 7.33   The mushroom must go into the shaft before the pressure plate is fixed. The tab washer holding the clutch nut is also visible.

Fig. 7.34   Tighten the screws evenly.

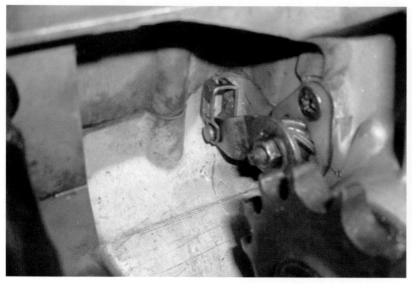

Fig. 7.35   The clutch release lever is next to the drive sprocket.

sprocket. It is retained by two cross-head screws, and has an adjuster screw and locknut in the centre. Once the engine is in the frame, this adjuster will be set so that as the clutch lever is pulled in, the arm into which the cable fits passes through the 90-degree position.

Refitting the Cylinders and Pistons

Install the middle piston first.

Fit the rings, remembering that the ring pins are offset in their grooves, so the rings must be the right way up – with the longer section of the ring gap to the bottom. Check that the piston is the right way round, with the arrow pointing to the front, exhaust side. If you are refitting the original pistons, check that you have the correct piston for the cylinder.

Fit the circlip to the far side of the gudgeon-pin hole. Warm the piston so that the gudgeon pin can be pushed easily into the piston, then push it in so that the end of the pin just protrudes very slightly from the inner edge of the gudgeon-pin boss inside the piston. This should allow you to feel when the pin is in line with the small-end bearing in the small-end eye. Once you can feel that it is centred properly, push it in gently, rocking the piston slightly as you do so. Do not use force; it is very easy to catch the pin on the end of one of the small-end bearing rollers and force it out of its cage. When the pin is right up against the far-side circlip, you can fit the near-side clip. The cylinder studs will be in the way, however, so a pair of narrow-nose pliers with curved tips will prove useful.

Install the other two pistons, in each case fitting the inner circlip first, before assembling the piston to the connecting rod, of course.

The cylinders are fitted in the same order. When you are sure that the piston rings are correctly aligned, with their gaps fitting over the pins, no special measures are needed to persuade the rings into the cylinders. The base chamfer is generous, and the rings are narrow and flexible. A squeeze with the fingers is enough to get them in.

Fitting the Alternator

The alternator on this model is a conventional permanent-magnet type. The H1 and some earlier Kawasaki triples use a 'wound field' electromagnetic rotor, which can easily be recognized by the circular copper tracks and brushes on the front face of the rotor. It must be noted that these models use a completely different regulator/rectifier system, and the two types are not readily interchangeable.

On removal of the alternator, it was found that the crankshaft taper was slightly corroded. It is vital that the rotor fits perfectly on to the taper,

Fig. 7.36   Narrow-nose pliers with bent tips are best for fitting the circlip to the middle piston. Note that this is a mocked-up photograph to illustrate the use of the pliers. In reality, your thumb would obscure the clip.

Fig. 7.37   *The crankshaft taper had to be cleaned up.*

Fig. 7.38   *The ignition points mount on the outside of the stator. The green wire was moved out of the way – that would be a very bad route for it, rubbing against the cam.*

around the 11-o'clock position. It is possible to time the ignition on each of the cylinders using these timing marks, having set the maximum gap to 0.3–0.4mm (0.012–0.015in). Each points assembly can be moved around the circumference of the stator plate, once the fixing screws have been loosened slightly, by using the notches in the rim of the plate. Set the timing so that each set of points is just opening as the timing marks on the rotor line up with the line on the window. A timing light, a continuity tester, an ohm-meter or, more traditionally, a piece of cigarette paper placed between the two contacts, which can be pulled free as soon as the points open, are all ways of determining the exact opening timing of the points.

More Accurate Timing

Whichever method you use, you are relying on the absolute accuracy of the machining of the keyway, the markings themselves and the alignment of the crankshaft discs relative to each other. Timing with a dial gauge overcomes all these problems:

1. Set the crank so that the left-hand cylinder is roughly at Top Dead Centre.
2. Fit the dial gauge to the left-hand spark plug hole.
3. Adjust the dial gauge so that it reads around 5mm.
4. Turn the crank to find the exact TDC.
5. Turn the bezel on the gauge to zero the gauge at 5mm.
6. Turn the crank back by 2.6mm. You can either count the turns, or rotate it until the gauge gives a reading of 2.4mm. (Back in this case means clockwise, as viewed from the generator side.)
7. If the mark in the timing window marked 'L' lines up, be happy. If it does not, make your own scratch mark, and be very glad you have a dial gauge.
8. Set the points for the left cylinder so they are just opening at this setting.
9. Repeat for the other two cylinders.

I have to admit that I did only use the timing marks. The subject engine needed a crank rebuild and new points before it actually went into service, so

since, as with all taper-driven flywheels and rotors, it is the friction between the two tapers that actually takes the force of the drive. The Woodruff key is only supposed to locate the rotor (or flywheel) in the correct position.

The solution was to lap the rotor on to the shaft with a spot of fine grinding paste. This cleaned both the shaft and the hole in the rotor, and ensured a perfect fit. The shaft and the inside of the rotor should look smooth, with a perfectly even grey colour and no high spots.

Fit the Woodruff key, then slide the rotor on to the shaft, making sure that the key stays in its groove.

The next item to install is the ignition cam. There is a peg on the base of the cam that fits into the keyway in the rotor, setting the basic timing for all three cylinders. Both cam and rotor are fixed in place by a long bolt that runs down the centre of the shaft.

Fit the stator assembly, easing the three sets of points over the cam, and tighten the pan-head screws to hold it in place.

Setting the Timing

The stator plate has a little window that allows you to see timing marks on the face of the rotor. This lies at

Fig. 7.39 *The reassembled engine is ready to go back in the frame. The heads were fitted temporarily for the photograph; installing the engine without them is much easier.*

there was no possible reason to set it up accurately at the time.

The Oil System

The oil pump and its pipes should be refitted next. The pump is simply secured with pan-head screws to the drive side of the engine and the three oil pipes connected to it. In fact, it is a good idea to fit the pipes through the hole in the casing of the oil pump cover first, then connect them to the feed holes at the base of each cylinder. That way, it is easy to see which pipe goes to each cylinder. At the oil pump end, this is not so important, since the feeds are the same to each cylinder. There is a little triangular plate that locks all three screws that connect the pipes to the pump. Before you tighten anything, however, note that there is a banjo fitting at each end of the three pipes, and each banjo fitting has a copper or soft aluminium washer on each side of it, so you should have had twelve washers in your bits box before you started

fitting the pipes, and there should be none left now.

The oil pump cannot be bled to get the air out until the engine is fitted in the frame and connected to the oil tank, though you can save a little time by fitting the tank pipe and filling the pump with an oil can at this stage.

MORE PROBLEMS CAUSED BY STANDING

Before refitting the engine to the frame, it is a good idea to check that all the other components that will need to be connected to it are in good condition while you still have easy access to them. The main items are the coils and ignition leads and the carburettors.

As far as the coils and leads were concerned, it proved impossible to test the ignition system. The ignition switch was impossible to turn and the battery was well beyond use, so the job of sorting them out had to be left for the bike's eventual purchaser.

The hornets' nest had been cleared

from around the coils, using a pressure washer.

One of the items missing from this bike was the float bowl. Apparently this is something that is often missing from Kawasaki triples that are imported as projects from the USA, and it is more common for all three to be missing. The float bowl's absence indicated that there might be problems with the carburettors – and there were. In two of the carburettors, the slide would not move and could only be removed by the use of heat. The slides had become stuck fast by a build-up of 'varnish' caused by deterioration of the fuel, as mentioned previously in this chapter.

The slides were cleaned up with a green kitchen scouring pad and paraffin. They were the normal aluminium colour underneath! The choke plungers were given the same treatment, after heating the carburettors with a heat gun, holding them in a cloth and pulling the choke cables very hard to remove them.

It seemed a good idea to remove the other two float bowls to give the jets

Fig. 7.40 *'Varnish' had glued the slide into the carburettor.*

Fig. 7.41 *The float chamber was full of unidentified black stuff!*

a clean. The right-hand one produced one of those 'Well I never…' moments, being coated with something that was black and flaky.

I do not know what the substance was, and I don't really want to, but it came off quite easily, and the air passages were blown clear with compressed air. The jets needed a wire jet cleaner, meant for oxy-acetylene welding tips, to clear them. That is something you are not normally advised to do.

With the carburettors assembled, as far as they could be, they were taped to the top of the frame while the engine was fitted.

FITTING THE ENGINE

With the cylinder heads removed to provide clearance, the fitting of the engine is remarkably easy because of the separate engine plates.

Lift the engine into the frame and shuffle it backwards until it engages between the only fixed engine plates at the bottom of the swinging-arm pivot gussets. The bolt can be fitted to that point and the engine allowed to pivot on it while you use a lever to align the other engine bolts and plates.

Once the engine is in place, the same system of working around the bike to refit all the parts you removed at the beginning, in the reverse order, will ensure that everything goes back on correctly.

There was nothing more that could be done to this bike. This was a zero-budget strip-down to free a seized piston and provide a report on the machine's condition, and the only task left to do was create that report.

CONCLUSION

By comparison with a wide range of other imported project bikes on show at DK Motors, this Kawasaki was one of the rougher examples. While there were bikes in worse condition, the majority were better.

An S2 Kawasaki in showroom condition will be comparable in price with a brand-new middle-weight bike; a good runner will be in the £4,000.00 bracket (mid-2015). It would have been possible to put this bike into service for less than that if you had done the work yourself.

The triples have a lot of fans, so if you buy carefully, an imported project bike could be a good way to set yourself up with a very enjoyable classic two-stroke.

Fig. 7.42 *The rear engine plates are solidly mounted to the frame.*

Fig. 7.43 *The air-cleaner box had been home to a swarm of hornets.*

Fig. 7.44   The engine is reinstalled in the frame.

Fig. 7.45   Kawasaki KH400, successor to the S2.

Fig. 7.46   Kawasaki H1 500.

Fig. 7.47   Kawasaki H2 750 – famously terrifying at the time.

ABOVE LEFT: Fig. 7.48   Suzuki GT750, affectionately called the 'Kettle' in the days when water-cooling was unusual.

ABOVE RIGHT: Fig. 7.49   Suzuki 750 racer, a replica of the TR750s that Barry Sheene raced.

RIGHT: Fig. 7.50   Beyond the threes were the fours. This is an inline 4-cylinder TZ500G.

Fig. 7.51   Suzuki produced a square-four RG500, Honda made a V3 in the NSR400, but this is the Yamaha V4 RD500, labelled with the American RZ500 name.

the last of the (roadster) line?
Aprilia RS125 (Rotax 122)

It has been said that one of the oddities in the development of road-going motorcycles is that almost the only item on a bike that was not originally developed for the racetrack is the electric hooter. Clearly modern machines have far more electrical accessories than was the case in the 1960s, but it is still true that a bike with a solid race pedigree has a great appeal to the market, and that adding extra race features increases that appeal. So it is that the golden years of two-stroke race bikes coincides very closely with the golden era of two-stroke roadsters.

Environmental concerns about the exhaust emissions of two-stroke engines played a political part in the ending of the golden age, particular attention being drawn to the fact that an engine that burns its upper-cylinder lubrication produces visible smoke.

Those in power seem to have ignored the facts that the invisible particulate emissions from diesel engines are not only far greater in volume, because diesel engines are far larger, but also far more damaging to health. The final nail in the coffin was the decision of the FIM, the International Motorcycle Federation, to replace the longstanding Grand Prix engine capacity rules – 500cc, 250cc, 125cc and, for a while, 50cc or 80cc – with three purely four-stroke classes. These were a 250cc single-cylinder bike (currently named Moto3), a 600cc 4-cylinder machine (Moto2) and the prime Moto GP class, which has been based variously on 800cc, 900cc and 1000cc engines over the years. At first, 3-, 4- and 5-cylinder engines were used, but when the formula settled down, 4-cylinder engines became the norm.

Those two changes made it unattractive for the major manufacturers to continue producing two-stroke road bikes. It would no longer be possible to sell them as replicas of the bikes seen in the televised Grand Prix races, and major investment in technical developments would be needed to reach the latest emissions standards.

Along with this came an aging of the motorcycle riding population, at least in the developed world, which made smaller-engined bikes less successful in the market.

APRILIA

However, one manufacturer, by appealing to the youth market, kept the two-stroke flame burning until 2006, and that was Aprilia. Basing their work on Austrian Rotax motors, engi-

Fig. 8.1   The Aprilia RS125.

Fig. 8.2   The Rotax 122 engine. I suspect that it may have been a race engine. The ports had been worked on, while the phrase 'No Oil' written on the flywheel cover was a sign of an experienced mechanic some time in the engine's past.

neers from Aprilia were responsible for not only the last but also the most powerful engines on the international race circuits in the 125 and 250cc two-stroke classes.

The key factor in the choice of machines for this book was the number of people on Internet forums reminiscing about the bikes of their youth.

APRILIA RS125 ENGINE SPECIFICATIONS

No. of cylinders: 1
Capacity: 124.8cc
Bore and stroke: 54 × 54.5mm
Compression ratio: 12.5:1
Cooling: liquid-cooled
Lubrication: separate oil pump
Induction: reed valve
Carburettor: Dell'Orto PHBH 28
Ignition: CDI electronic ignition
Starting: electric
Alternator: 12v, 180w
Max. power: 28bhp at 10,500rpm
Max. torque: 1.9kg m (14.0lb ft) at 9,000rpm
Transmission: gear primary drive, wet multi-plate clutch, 6-speed gearbox, chain final drive

While people dream of NS250 Hondas, Suzuki RG500 Gammas, KR1S Kawasakis and RS250 Aprilias, the bike they remember fondly is their 125cc learner bike, and the greatest of these was the Aprilia RS125 (alias AF1 or Extrema).

DISMANTLING THE ROTAX 122 ENGINE

We will be concerned with a total engine rebuild in this chapter.

Cylinder Head and Barrel

As usual, and because I was eager to see what I had bought, the first stage was to remove the cylinder assembly.

Rotax 125cc engines have a two-part cylinder head, with an outer cover for the cylinder-head water jacket and the

actual cylinder head inside (very similar to the Scott of many years before).

Four screws secure the cover, but the spark plug must be removed before it can be taken off. The cover is sealed with O-rings, one on the spark plug boss and the other in a groove around the rim of the cover.

O-rings are ideal for an engine that is dismantled frequently, for racing, for example. They seal well and, since the head fits 'metal to metal' with the cylinder, they allow the squish clearance to be set accurately. Often they can be reused in the short term. In this particular case, however, they were old and hard, and were thrown away.

Undo the five screws that hold the inner head to the cylinder, remove the head and you will get your first sight of the condition of the cylinder and head.

Fig. 8.3   The inner cylinder head.

Fig. 8.4   There was damage to the squish band.

Fig. 8.7   On this piston, part of the top ring land has broken off. This is the sort of damage that results when the piston hits a broken RAVE valve.

The squish band and the corresponding part of the piston crown were pitted heavily. The damage included sharp-edged pits of varying depth, the edges of the pits being pushed up like the edges of a crater. This was a sign that debris from the failure of some other component had become trapped between the piston crown and the head. Chapter 11 goes into more details of the damage caused by other unfortunate events, but the combination of this damage with what turned out to be a very sick big-end bearing pointed to the remains of the big-end bearing cage providing the debris responsible.

A fortunate aspect of this cylinder-head design is that it is easy to restore in the lathe.

The big-end bearing, of course, is at the bottom of the engine and the head is at the top, which meant that the debris had had to make its way right through the engine via the transfer ports. It would have been too much

to hope that it had not damaged the cylinder on the way through.

The barrel was removed after releasing the four nuts and washers on the cylinder base flange, and close inspection revealed the extent of the damage to the cylinder. One of the larger fragments had gouged a lump out of the cylinder below one of the transfer ports, which was serious damage. Rotax cylinders are aluminium, with the inner running surface plated with a hard metal/ceramic compound. They cannot be rebored in the conventional way, but must be ground clean, have any damage repaired by welding and machining, and then be replated. The cost of restoring this cylinder was likely to be around £175.00 (2015).

The piston had suffered, too, but that was a lesser problem, since it could be replaced by a new one once the bore had been restored to its standard size.

The gudgeon-pin circlips can be removed with a small screwdriver or

with a pair of small narrow-nose pliers, since they are of the tailless type with extraction grooves to the gudgeon-pin hole. If the piston is warmed, the pin can be pushed out of the piston easily.

I mentioned at the beginning of this chapter that the Aprilia had come with two spare Rotax 122 engines. On stripping the other engine to determine whether it was a better example (it was), another of the motor's common failure modes was revealed.

The Rotax uses what is known as a RAVE (Rotax Automatic Variable Exhaust) valve to vary the exhaust timing. This is a sliding blade controlled by a solenoid, and since it lives in the exhaust port, it is subject to high temperatures, violent forces from the pressure pulsations in the exhaust system and dirty conditions. The genuine Aprilia part is made from high-quality steel, hard-plated, and it is expensive. Cheap, lower-quality versions are available, but they can fail, breaking and dropping down into the exhaust port. When the piston hits the broken valve, the engine comes to a very sudden stop. In this case, the piston exhibited damage from just such an event.

Removing the Flywheel and Stator

Remove the flywheel cover after releasing the Allen screws that secure it. You can hold the flywheel with a strap wrench if the ignition pick-up is

Fig. 8.5   The badly-scored cylinder bore.

Fig. 8.6   The piston was damaged, too.

Fig. 8.8   Use a pair of callipers to find the distance between the centres of the holes in the flywheel before drilling.

Fig 8.9   The homemade flywheel holder in use. It was fastened to the flywheel with M6 screws in two of the threaded holes.

removed first, but you will find it useful to make a proper flywheel holder, or buy the correct Aprilia tool.

The flywheel centre has three M6-threaded holes in it, so to make your own, all you need do is drill two 6.5mm holes in a strip of steel or 'angle iron' and file or grind a clearance notch to allow you to fit a socket on the centre nut. Then it can be attached to the flywheel with M6 screws.

Holding the flywheel, undo the centre nut and remove it with the spring washer.

To pull the flywheel off the taper, you need a puller that can be attached using the three M6 holes in the centre. The one I used was part of a kit bought long ago for work on a 1950s Sunbeam S7, and it is commonly used by people who work on car engines. It can be fitted with a handle, allowing you to hold the flywheel while you screw down the extraction screw. With the screw turned down tightly, give it a knock on the top to jar the flywheel off the taper.

Remove the flywheel and unbolt the puller. Take off the Woodruff key and put it somewhere safe. Unfastening the three Allen screws in the centre of the stator plate allows the stator to be removed, after the grommet for the generator wire has been slid out of its notch.

In this case, the screws had been locked with fixing compound, so it was necessary to use an extension tube to increase the leverage on the Allen key.

As always, store the stator inside the flywheel to preserve the magnetism.

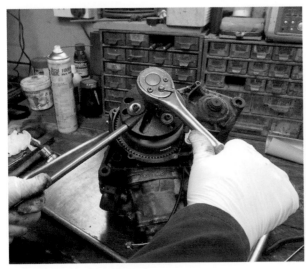

Fig. 8.10   This puller has a handle

Fig. 8.11   A tubular extension is needed on the Allen key.

A WORD OF WARNING

Do not try to use a car-style, three-leg puller that grips the edge of the flywheel rim. This type of tool can distort the flywheel sufficiently to crack the magnets. Modern high-powered magnets are not made of conventional metal; exotic materials are pressed together and baked in a process called sintering. This produces a substance more like a ceramic than a metal, and like a ceramic it cracks easily.

Fig. 8.12 Damage caused by the use of a three-leg puller.

Dismantling the Clutch-Side Components

Undo the Allen screws holding the clutch cover. The chances are that the cover will be stuck, in which case you can tap on the reinforced lugs (*see* Fig. 8.13) to unstick it.

Beneath the cover, you will find the clutch, the balance shaft and its gears, and the gear selection mechanism.

Inside the clutch cover itself, you will find the clutch release mechanism. The ball-and-ramp design of this hardly ever needs any attention, but this is where the clutch cable is eventually attached to the lever arm.

Fig. 8.13 Remove the clutch cover.

Fig. 8.15 The clutch just lifts off.

Removing the clutch is simple – it just lifts out, as a complete, fully assembled unit. There are no nuts or circlips involved. Replacement of the springs and friction plates will be described later.

The Balance Shaft and Gears

All single-cylinder engines vibrate. Weights can be added to the side of the crank webs opposite the crankpin, or removed from the crankpin side to reduce the out-of-balance and cut the vibration caused as the crank spins. Balance shafts are deliberately made out of balance and timed to vibrate in the opposite direction to the crank and piston assembly to cancel out the vibration.

The Rotax balance shaft fits in the casing just behind the cylinder. It is driven from the crankshaft by a pair

Fig. 8.14 The clutch release mechanism inside the cover. The clutch cable attaches to the lever arm just below the thumb in the picture.

Fig. 8.16   *The balance-shaft gears were completely destroyed.*

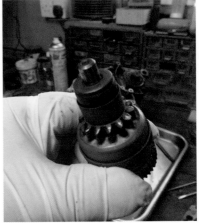

Fig. 8.18   *The Bendix gear assembly.*

With the screws removed, the starter motor can be removed, and then the Bendix gear.

Splitting the Cases

The gearchange shaft can be withdrawn through the casing, disengaging it from the selector drum.

Remove all nine crankcase Allen screws.

Do not use a hammer on the shaft ends to split the cases for fear of damaging them. The crank bearings fit tightly, and you would need to hit them hard.

Fig. 8.19   *You need to use a puller to split the cases.*

of plastic gears. Because the balance shaft is heavy and runs at the same rpm as the crank, it has a lot of momentum when the engine is spinning quickly. If the crank stops suddenly or seizes, the momentum of the balance shaft can destroy the plastic gears. This is intentional; the plastic gears are easily stripped. A more solid connection would transmit very large forces to other, more expensive components, and probably would shatter the cases.

From the two engines dismantled for the purposes of this chapter, only one of the four balance-shaft gears was useable. In two cases, the damage was to the teeth on the outside; in the other, the internal splines had been stripped. All four were replaced by new gears. Earlier remarks about the varying quality of pattern-part replacements are even more relevant here. In 2015, the cheapest price for a pair of genuine Aprilia balance-shaft gears was around £44.00. Pattern parts were available for less than half that price, but their reliability was suspect.

Close inspection showed that the teeth on the water-pump drive gear had also been damaged.

The Starter Motor

The starter motor fits through a hole in the casing, below the clutch. It is held in place by two screws (*see* Fig. 8.17).

Instead you need to use a puller to bear against the crankshaft end and press it out of the bearing. The genuine Aprilia tool is a steel plate with a variety of holes drilled in it. The centre hole is threaded for a puller bolt, while the other holes align with extraction holes in various items inside the engine – in this case with the threaded holes for the case screws. A general-purpose puller should do the job.

Fig. 8.17   *The starter lug is at the bottom of the case.*

Tighten the centre bolt and tap gently on the clutch shaft with a soft mallet. This will split the cases. Try to keep the halves parallel; screwdriver levering points are provided to help with this if necessary.

Dismantling the Gearbox

1. Remove the balance shaft. It will just pull out of its bearing.
2. Pull out the two gearchange fork spindles. Note that the rearmost one is much longer and has a circlip on it.
3. Undo the M6 screw that holds the detent lever and roller that controls the gearchange drum; remove the screw, washer, lever and spring.
4. Lift all three of the gearchange forks out of their grooves in the gearchange drum, then remove the drum.
5. The gear shafts can now be removed together. Tapping on the main shaft will drive both shafts out of their bearings.

Removing and Examining the Crankshaft

The crankshaft will still be held in the other half of the crankcase, and the same procedure with the puller will be the best way of removing it.

At this stage, the two engines on the bench could not have been more different.

In one of them, the big end was clearly completely seized. The shafts were in good condition, however, and the crank was suitable for rebuilding with a new connecting rod and bearing. The other crank carried the words 'Made in Japan', as opposed to the usual 'Made in Austria'. That brings up another point about pattern parts. I had suspected that this had been a race motor, and the label on the crank indicated that the standard version had been replaced by a higher-quality Japanese example, which is a reminder that non-standard parts can sometimes exceed the quality of OEM ones – often at a far higher price, though!

All the bearings and seals were to be replaced in both engines, so the next task was to remove the bearing from the crankshaft. In the other engine, the bearing had remained in the casing.

There was not enough of a gap behind the bearing to allow the three-leg puller to get a grip on the bearing, so after supporting the shaft end securely on a block of wood, a specially sharpened cold chisel was used in the gap between the bearing and the cheek of the crank web. The chisel had been sharpened so that only one side was tapered, and that taper was more gentle than normal. The flat side was placed against the crank web, and a smart blow on the chisel with a hammer caused the chisel to act like a wedge, driving the bearing 3–4mm (0.125in) away from the crank web. The cutting edge of the chisel never reaches the crankshaft, of course! From that point, a puller can be used to extract the bearing.

Clamping the crank in a vice not only holds it in place, but also prevents the jaws of the puller from slipping off the outer race of the bearing. Regardless of the means used to remove the bearing (bearing splitters are readily available from car service tool suppliers), it is not recommended to reuse the bearings.

The good (Japanese) crank was set up between centres in a lathe and checked for truth, run-out and play in the big-end bearing. The distance between the crank webs was also measured. The official Aprilia service manual specifies a distance of between 48.95mm and 49.05mm. That is, it has to be accurate to within

Fig. 8.20 The big end of this crank was completely seized.

Fig. 8.21 This is a high-quality race crank.

Fig. 8.22 A cold chisel is used as a wedge to force off the bearing sleeve.

Fig. 8.23 The bearing puller is held in the vice to prevent it from slipping.

a tenth of a millimetre. Fortunately it was completely within specification in all dimensions.

The factory specifications for the crank are as follows:

- Out of roundness (truth) of the crank webs should be less than 0.03mm.
- Big end up-and-down play should be less than 0.05mm.
- Big end side-to-side play should be less than 1.00mm.
- Small end/gudgeon pin play should be less than 0.03mm.

You should also examine the condition of the threads on the crankshaft ends, the flywheel taper, and the keyways and splines.

CHANGING THE BEARINGS

Using a punch and working from the outside, the crank bearings can easily be driven out of their housings, espe-

Fig. 8.25   Heat the cases to 80°C with a heat gun.

cially if the cases are heated first, but several of the bearings for the gearbox and the balance shaft fit into blind holes, so they cannot be driven out from the far side.

To remove these, you need a specialized bearing puller that fits inside the bearing and has 'fingers' that are expanded by tightening a nut. The puller head is usually connected to a slide hammer – a heavy sleeve that slides up a shaft to hit a block at the top.

Heat the cases thoroughly to around 80°C before you start working with the slide hammer. You will almost certainly need someone else to hold the case down while you do this, and they will need heatproof gloves!

Once all the bearings are out, clean their housings carefully. Penetrating oil makes a very good cleaner.

If you intend having the cases blast cleaned, this is the time to send them off, when they have no bearings installed. Any form of abrasive cleaning will ruin bearings.

Fitting the new bearings is almost a case of just dropping them into their housings, as long as the cases have been heated well.

Fig. 8.24   Using a bearing puller and slide hammer.

Fig. 8.26   Fit the oil seal before the bearing.

Fig. 8.27 The bearing must be flush with the internal surface of the crankcase.

Note that on both sides an oil seal fits up against a shoulder from the inside, so the seal goes in before the bearing. The oil seals will also be easy to install while the cases are hot. However, you might need to tap around the outer race of the bearings with a punch to settle them fully into the cases. The outer race needs to be flush with the casing.

With all the bearings and seals in place, you can begin to assemble everything in the flywheel side of the casings.

REASSEMBLY

Assembling the Gearbox, etc

Starting from the front, the components that need to be fitted in the case are as follows:

Fig. 8.28 The waterpump impeller fits first.

1. The waterpump impeller. This fits into a bearing and seal in the top front part of the casing. Check that the vanes of the impeller are undamaged, and lubricate the shaft before fitting.
2. The crankshaft. If you have had the crank rebuilt, or have changed the crank or bearings, it is important to check that the side-to-side clearance of the crankshaft is correct. The only way to do this is to fit the crank and put the two halves of the casing together, including the gasket that fits between them. You can then measure the clearance with a feeler gauge. It should be between 0.1 and 0.5mm. If it is less than this, there is either a problem with the rebuilt crank or, more likely, because a pattern-part gasket is too thin. The genuine gasket is between 0.41 and 0.45mm thick when compressed. If the clearance is greater, shims must be added to the flywheel side of the shaft to take up the play. This may involve putting the case halves together more than once, so it is best to do this before the gearbox and balance shafts are fitted, which will make the task easier.
3. The balance shaft. The balance shaft can simply be fitted into its bearing at this stage. Timing the shaft comes later.
4. The two gearbox shafts. Install both shafts at the same time. Hold them so that the two sets of gears mesh with each other and fit them into their bearings. It is a good idea also to fit the selector forks into their respective grooves in the sliding gears. The two forks fit on to the output shaft. Push them back to leave room for the selector drum to be fitted on to its spindle.

Fig. 8.29 Fit the selector forks to the grooves in the gear pinions. Note that this only shows the output shaft – I could not find a way of showing everything together in one photograph.

5. The gear selector drum. Fit this on to the boss on the casing. The three selector forks need to be pushed forward and manoeuvred so that the pegs on the forks can engage with the grooves on the selector drum. Line up the selector forks with the holes in the casing.
6. The two selector-fork shafts. The longer shaft, with the circlip, goes to the rear, while the shorter one must be fitted with the chamfered end upward. The shafts should slide in easily, right to the bottom of their holes.

Fig. 8.30   Cut the link in the gasket.

Fig. 8.32   A comparison between a worn standard spring and a new competition item.

Fitting the Cases Together

This engine has a gasket between the case halves; it helps to use a thin smear of sealant on this.

Lubricate all the shafts and bearings, heat the cases to around 50°C and fit the case halves together. Squeeze them together by hand, but if any more force is needed, tap the cases on the engine mounting lugs to settle them fully into place.

The gasket has a bridge across the mouth of the cylinder base. This helps retain the shape of the gasket during fitting, but it must be cut away once the crankcase halves are together. Insert the Allen screws, tightening them gradually and evenly.

Check that the crankshaft turns freely, then complete the assembly of the gearchange mechanism.

Fit the detent lever and spring, with the little wheel engaging with the notches on the selector drum. Do not forget the two washers. The washer with the central boss goes to the inside of the lever. Fit and tighten the Allen screw to 10Nm (7.5lb ft) of torque.

The gearchange-pedal shaft goes in next. The legs of the hairpin spring fit on either side of the long selector shaft, and the claws of the mechanism engage with the pins on the selector drum. The shaft goes right through the cases to the other side.

Renewing Clutch Plates and Springs

The clutch is a separate unit, so it can be worked on by itself, on the bench.

Undo the six 8mm screws in the

Fig. 8.31   Loosen the clutch screws gradually and evenly.

normal manner, gradually and evenly. Take off the upper pressure plates and examine the thrust ball bearing carefully. It is possible for the ball to come loose and drop out, causing a lot of damage. Make sure that it is both free to turn and secure.

Take off the top steel plate and set it aside – it needs to be put back in the

same position. Note that the top friction plate is located with its lugs in the shorter slots in the basket.

Remove the other plates and springs.

The condition of the springs can be checked by measuring their length. The specified minimum length is 31.6mm. Always replace clutch springs as a full set.

The minimum limit for the thickness of the clutch plates is 2.8mm for the lined plates. These days, it is probably simpler to replace all of both types of clutch plate, too, since the better after-market replacement kits include both steel and lined plates.

Check the condition of all the slots in the clutch basket for notching.

Reassembling the clutch is a little complicated, since it is a 'pull from the outside' type.

The two clutch-basket needle-roller bearings go in the centre of the basket. The spider, or spring guide, goes on next.

Fig. 8.33   Assemble the plates on the inner hub.

Fig. 8.34   You can compress the clutch with a bench drill.

Fig. 8.35   Three Allen screws secure the stator.

Fig. 8.36   Align the drive tag and fit the oil pump.

Assemble the plates on the clutch centre, alternating lined and steel, six of each type, wrangling them gently into the basket. Turn the final lined plate so that its lugs fit into the shorter slots in the basket.

Install the springs on the bosses on the spider, then fit the pressure plate, the outer plate and the six 8mm screws.

If you are using competition springs, it helps to compress them a little first (using a bench drill or even a G-cramp). Tighten the screws gradually and evenly. Then the assembly can be fitted on the gearbox shaft.

The Flywheel Generator

The generator stator can now be fitted to the flywheel side of the crankshaft. The wire and its grommet will give an obvious clue to its orientation. It is fixed by the three Allen screws (*see* Fig. 8.35).

At this stage, you must fit the starter Bendix gear into its housing. It will not fit when the flywheel is in place.

Install the Woodruff key in the keyway and fit the flywheel snugly on to the tapered shaft, adding the washer and nut. Lock the flywheel with your holder and tighten the nut to 43–45Nm (31.7–33.2lb ft).

It is not advisable to dismantle the oil pump; fit it into the casing as a complete assembly, taking care that the drive tag engages with the slot in the gear.

The Cylinder and Piston Assembly

As noted, the original cylinder was badly damaged, but another one in good condition was available. Rotax cylinders come in fractionally different sizes because of manufacturing tolerances. The size code is stamped on the

Fig. 8.37   There is a bore-size code on the cylinder base, in this case 'A'.

Fig. 8.38   Size and direction are stamped on the piston crown.

cylinder base; in this case, it was 'A'.

A new, good-quality aftermarket piston kit was bought to suit the 'A' cylinder with a size of 54.97mm. The kit included the piston, gudgeon pin, piston rings, small-end roller bearing and circlips. Fit the piston rings and one circlip, then warm the piston. Install the piston on the small-end bearing, followed by the gudgeon pin and finally the remaining circlip.

Make sure that the arrow on the piston crown points towards the exhaust port.

Coat the inside of the bore with oil, slide the piston into the bore and lower the cylinder on to the cases. Fit the cylinder base nuts and washers, tightening them gradually and evenly to a torque of 10–12 Nm (7.4–8.9lb ft).

Checking the Squish Clearance

Fig. 8.39   Lay a piece of solder on the piston crown to act as a gauge when checking the squish clearance.

Renew the O-ring on the top face of the cylinder and place a length of solder across the piston crown. Fit the inner head and tighten it down. Turn the engine so that the piston passes Top Dead Centre. Then remove the head and measure the thickness of the solder where it has been compressed between the cylinder and the head. This will give the squish clearance. For

a standard engine for road use, the squish clearance should be no more than 1.5mm. For a tuned engine running on high-octane fuel, the squish clearance should never be less than 0.7mm. The reason will be explained in Chapter 11.

You can adjust the clearance easily by adding or removing gaskets at the cylinder base or, more drastically, by machining material from the inner cylinder head on a lathe. When the clearance is correct, fit the inner head and tighten it down to a setting of 20Nm (15lb ft).

Fig. 8.40   An O-ring seals the inner cylinder head to the outer one.

Renew the large O-ring on the base of the outer head and the thicker orange O-ring on the spark-plug boss in the centre of the inner head. It is not a good idea to use gasket sealant with O-rings. If it is difficult to keep an O-ring in its groove, a little grease will do the job.

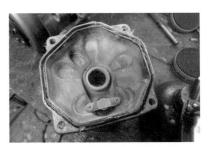

Fig. 8.41   The outer head seals with an O-ring all the way round.

Then fit the outer head and its screws, tightening it down to 10Nm (7.4lb ft).

Fitting the RAVE Valve

The blade of the RAVE valve has a curved chamfer so that, in its down position, it blends with the curve of the top of the exhaust port. So install it with the chamfer pointing downwards.

Fig. 8.42   The blade of the RAVE valve.

Fig. 8.43   The blade fits with the chamfer downwards.

The stem of the valve fits into a housing, which contains a small valve-guide seal and spring. Renew both the seal and spring.

Fig. 8.44   Fit a new seal to the valve guide in the housing.

Install the blade in the housing and fasten the housing to the cylinder with the two Allen screws.

CONTEMPORARIES

Fig. 8.45   The RAVE valve housing is held by two Allen screws.

There are a few similar bikes to the Aprilia, from Gilera, Derbi, Cagiva and others, but they are rare and difficult to find. The Kawasaki AR125, Yamaha TZR125, Honda NSR125 and Suzuki RG125 were the more mainstream entries in this market, and all are beginning to be restored. Their modern replacements are all four-stroke powered.

off the beaten track: MX, trials and trail

Kawasaki KMX125

My personal riding interest and experience are based on road riding and circuit racing, and the closest I have ever come to off-road riding are a few outings on grass-track machinery and one Super-Moto-style event as part of a three-man team in a six-hour event on a Piaggio Typhoon, an automatic scooter!

I do also claim to be a serious contender for the title of the worst trials rider in the district, once scoring a five between sections – by falling off before the start!

However, it is very clear that green-laning, motocross and enduro competitions arouse a fanatical enthusiasm in many people. Internet forums are full of photographs of the trail bikes

people wish they had never sold, and the auction sites indicate the increasing interest in, and rising prices for, bikes like DT Yamahas, TS Suzukis and so on. I live in a semi-rural area and I have noticed that far more young riders start on MX-style machinery than on the sports-bike replicas that would have been my choice if I were starting out now.

The bike chosen for this chapter, the Kawasaki KMX125, is another good example. It also demonstrates another technical advance in two-stroke design, which makes it even more interesting. There is very little difference between the 125 and 200cc versions of this bike, beyond the obvious, and the fact that the 125 version was learner legal under

the earlier capacity-based rules. Apart from the state of tune and a few specialized details, the KIPS series of 'KX' full motocross Kawasakis follow very similar lines to the trail-bike models – although the components are sturdier in critical areas.

POWERVALVES AND THEIR DEVELOPMENT

The interesting aspect of the Kawasaki off-road engines is the Kawasaki Integrated Powervalve System (KIPS) version of the variable exhaust valve concept. This adopts a different approach to the Yamaha rotating powervalve and the guillotine-type RAVE valve in the Aprilia.

Fig. 9.1   Kawasaki trail bike (actually the very similar KDX125).

The intention of the KIPS is to combine the advantages of the variable exhaust timing of the Yamaha and Aprilia systems with the resonant chamber used to vary the timing of the pressure pulses in the exhaust pipe. It employs two vertically-mounted rotating valves actuated by a centrifugal device driven from the crank. These open extra exhaust ports at higher rpm, while at lower engine speeds, one of them opens a resonant chamber on the side of the cylinder.

Honda also had a resonant-chamber system that was used during the 1980s. It was called the Automatic Torque Amplification Chamber (ATAC) system. Suzuki's version was the most complex. The Super AETC version on the last of the RG250 Gamma V-twins had three moveable valves! It combined guillotine power valves with a large resonance chamber above the exhaust port. AETC stands for Automatic Exhaust Timing Control. Marketing people love these acronyms; most people just call all of these systems powervalves.

THE TASK

The subject engine of this chapter, part of a bike that had been completely dismantled, was found on an Internet forum. It is owned by an enthusiastic collector of off-road bikes, Anthony Goodwin. He acquired it in a number of boxes, which contained everything needed to build the complete machine, which dates from around 2000. This is typical of the sort of project that someone putting a bike back on the road (or track) might face.

The boxes containing the engine components were delivered to the workshop, along with new bearings, seals and gaskets. Whenever a machine arrives like this, the one thing you can be sure of is that something will be missing. No matter how carefully you

---

KMX125 ENGINE SPECIFICATIONS

Bore and stroke: 54.0 × 54.4mm
Capacity: 124cc
Compression ratio: 7.8:1
Induction: reed valve
Carburettor: 26mm
Claimed power: learner-legal
    version, 12bhp; unrestricted
    version, 20bhp
Transmission: gear primary drive,
    wet muti-plate clutch, 6-speed
    gearbox, chain final drive

---

check, and regardless of the assurances of the person who supplied it, there is always something. And there was.

DISMANTLING

Because the engine had already been dismantled, the procedure given here is purely theoretical, although the photographs of the assembly process should help. Consequently, the aim of this section is to give some advice on the order of dismantling, along with any hints and tips about key points along the way.

1. Remove the cylinder head. It is retained by five hex-headed screws. They should be loosened gradually and in a diagonal pattern, as usual. The crosshead water-drain screw does not need to be removed and the thermostat housing can be left in place, unless you intend to replace the thermostat – or want to check that it is inside!

2. Remove the cylinder. Assuming that the carburettor is already off, the first step is to take off the cover of the KIPS valve operating mechanism, on the right-hand side of the cylinder, and remove the screw that holds the operating

Fig. 9.2   The contents of the boxes of engine parts.

lever to the shaft. Further dismantling of the KIPS valves can be left until later. Undo the four cylinder base nuts, taking the usual steps to prevent distortion. Both the cylinder base joint and the head joint can be a little sticky, and a gentle tap with a soft mallet may be needed to break the joint.

3. Remove the piston. Wire circlips are used – original Kawasaki pistons have tailless circlips with extraction notches (Hooray!). They are easily removed by inserting a small screwdriver, or some small snipe-nose pliers, in the extraction notch. Either way, make sure that they do not get away, either into the crankcase or into a dark corner of the workshop. Put a rag in the crankcase and keep your thumb over the gudgeon-pin hole while you are removing the circlips. After warming the piston, the pin should push out easily.

4. Take out the small-end bearing.

5. Remove the kickstart pedal, if this has not already been done.

6. Make sure that you really have drained the oil from the engine, then undo the 8mm hex-headed screws that secure the clutch cover; remove the cover and gasket.

7. Undo the four clutch-spring screws; remove the screws, washers and springs. Measure the springs. They should have a free length of 33.2mm for KMX125 and 36.5mm for the 200cc version. If

they are more than 1.5mm shorter that this, they must be replaced.

8. Lift the entire package of steel and lined clutch plates from the clutch basket.

9. The clutch centre of the 125cc model is held in place by a circlip; that of the 200cc version is secured by a nut. For the latter, you will need to find a way of holding the clutch while you undo the centre nut. The official Kawasaki clutch holder is Y-shaped, but a modified steel clutch plate will also work.

10. Lift off the clutch centre. Beneath it there is a wavy washer and a splined thrust washer that rotates and is locked to the gearbox shaft. Remove the washers.

11. Remove the clutch basket. This will provide a clear view of the idler gears that drive the water pump, the oil pump and the balance shaft. The kickstart gears and gearchange mechanism will be visible, too. It is worth taking a photograph of all this to remind you how everything fits into the case.

12. The detent lever (or gear positioning lever) with its spring, and then the cam on the end of the gear change drum must be removed next.

13. If you intend splitting the cases, all of the aforementioned gears must be removed, along with the primary-drive gear on the end of the crankshaft.

14. On the other side of the engine, remove the flywheel cover's five screws and pull off the cover.

15. Hold the flywheel, using your preferred method, but take care not to damage the generator coils inside. Undo the flywheel nut and remove the washer.

16. Use a suitable puller to remove the flywheel from its tapered shaft. The tool requires a 27mm, fine-pitch, left-hand thread, the same as that used for the Yamaha RD and LC.

17. Take out the three crossheaded screws that hold the stator in place. Pull the connector off the neutral-gear switch below the flywheel casing, slide the rubber cable grommet out of its slot and remove the stator.

18. If the sprocket is still attached, undo the two screws that secure the fixing plate, then turn the plate through about 10 degrees so that the splines align with the shaft. You can then pull off the fixing plate and sprocket.

Splitting the Crankcase

The crankcase halves are held together by thirteen screws with 8mm hex heads. Remove them all, but unscrew them in stages to avoid distorting the casing. There are three different lengths of screw: the longest fit at the back of the casing, on either side of the swinging-arm lug; the middle-sized screws fit inside the flywheel housing; the shortest ones go into the small lugs around the outside of the cases.

The manufacturers have provided two places, close to the large lugs at the front and back of the casing, where

Fig. 9.3   A circlip holds the clutch in the KMX125.

CLEVER IDEA

At the risk of sounding like an advert, I have recently acquired a set of round blocks, a little like ice-hockey pucks, called Bench Cookies, which are excellent for supporting an engine on the bench, since they have a grippy rubber surface and stay where they are put. They can also be stacked if you need a higher support.

a screwdriver can be used to break the seal and prise the two halves of the case apart. Split the crankcase carefully. You should find that all the components remain in the drive side of the case. If they do, you will need a couple of blocks of wood on which to rest the engine so that it lies flat and firm while you work on it.

Replacing the Main Bearings and Seals

If the bearings and seals are to be replaced, the first step is to remove the crankshaft. This is a process that is always easier when the crankcase is thoroughly warmed to around 80°C. Never use a steel hammer directly on the ends of any shaft. A copper-faced mallet is a good tool, but if you do not have one, use a flattened piece of copper pipe or a piece of soft aluminium between the hammer and the shaft. Even wood is better than nothing. Hammering on the crankshaft itself will damage its threads and ruin it forever.

While the cases are hot, use a large socket and extension bar to drive the bearings out of the crankcase. The process will damage the seals, but they will be scrap by this stage anyway.

Clean the bearing and seal housings carefully, heat the cases again and fit the new seals. Use a socket of the same size as the outer diameter of the seal to push it into place. The open face goes to the inside. Do not use force except on the outer rim of the seal.

The bearing can be pushed into place with your thumbs if the crankcase is hot. Repeat the process for the other crankcase half.

REASSEMBLY

Assembling the Gearbox

In the subject engine, the gear-shaft bearing fitted tightly to the shaft. To avoid damaging the bearing, it was not removed from the shaft. Instead, the case was heated sufficiently to loosen the fit of the bearing's outer ring in the case, allowing the two gear shafts to be installed in the case together without having to use force.

Fit the selector drum next. The plastic disc on the end contains a contact

Fig. 9.4 You can push the bearing into place by hand.

Fig. 9.5 Fit the gears together.

Fig. 9.6 The black plastic disc operates the neutral light.

Fig. 9.7   The selector shaft fits through all three selector forks.

Assembling the Crankcase Halves

Before putting the crankcase halves together again, the crankshaft and balance shaft must be installed. Setting the correct timing of the balance shaft comes later, but take care not to damage the spiral worm gear on the end of the shaft. When everything is together, it drives the tachometer.

Ensure that the sealing faces of both case halves are clean. There is no gasket, so apply a thin smear of sealant to one joint face, then fit the other case half carefully over the shafts, taking care not to damage the seals in the process. Oiling or greasing the seals beforehand is always a good idea.

You should not need to use force to squeeze the case halves together; hand pressure should be sufficient. However, a few taps with a soft mal-

that touches another on the casing to illuminate the neutral light.

As in many Kawasakis, the KMX has a single gear-selector shaft to carry all three selector forks. The first step is to identify the correct location of the forks. Helpfully, the forks have cast numbers, and they fit into the casing in numerical order.

The first fork engages with the groove above the second-from-lowest gear. The second, much shorter, fork engages with the groove on the sliding gear on the input gear shaft. The third fork engages with the groove below the second-from-top gear. (Note that 'lowest' and 'top' refer to the positions of the gears in the cases, not the gear ratios.)

Fig. 9.9   The crankshaft is fitted next.

Fig. 9.8   Carefully align the selector forks.

Engage the forks with the grooves on the gears, and also their respective grooves in the selector drum, then oil the selector-fork shaft and slide it through the forks until it is fully inserted in the support hole in the casing.

Fig. 9.10   Squeeze the cases together, then tap them down.

let will probably be needed to settle the cases on to the alignment dowels. Tap against the engine mounting lugs, which are strong enough to receive this treatment; this will prevent damage to any sealing surfaces.

Insert the crankcase screws, tightening them gradually, gently and evenly around the case in a diagonal pattern.

The Clutch Side

Let us take a moment to consider all the extras inside the drive-side casing of a modern two-stroke. The drive side of the Villiers engine consists of the primary-drive sprocket – that is all! The subject engine incorporates gears to drive the powervalve, the water pump, the oil pump, the balance shaft and the kickstart, as well as the primary drive and clutch itself.

Connecting the Accessories

1. Fit the Woodruff key to the drive side of the crankshaft.

2. Temporarily fit the centrifugal pulley shaft that operates the KIPS valves. This will allow you to check that it connects properly to the other gears in the case. In fact, it must be installed in the outer case when that is fitted, so that it can be engaged with the shaft that runs up the side of the cylinder and turns the KIPS valves.

3. Install the kickstart shaft assembly, making sure that the end of the spring enters the hole in the casing below the shaft. A curved and (deliberately) bent steel plate is bolted to the two bosses to the upper right of the shaft. This acts as the kickstart stop and creates a ramp to disengage the kickstart ratchet when the pedal is in the up position.

4. Fit the oil-pump drive gear. It is driven by a pin through its shaft. The gear fits over the pin and is held in place by a circlip.

5. Wind up the kickstart shaft and hold it in place. Use the proper pedal if

possible, but failing that, clamp a vice-grip wrench to the shaft. Lean on the pedal or wrench with your body and fit the stop plate. It should point anticlockwise, with the leading edge being its lowest point. Release the spring slowly and you should see the plate lift the ratchet on the kickstart assembly and act as a stop for the kickstart.

6. Install the primary gear, making sure that the Woodruff key remains in place. Add the washer and nut. Lock the engine with a bar through the small-end eye (note the Bench Cookies used to protect the cylinder base joint) and tighten the nut to 58Nm (43lb ft).

7. The first step in setting up the balance-shaft timing is to turn the crank so that the dot on the primary gear aligns with the little arrow on the crankcase.

8. Next, turn the balance shaft itself until its punch mark aligns with the arrow on the casing as well. The large primary-drive gear on

Fig. 9.11   Fit the Woodruff key.

Fig. 9.12   Fit the KIPS actuator and pulley temporarily.

Fig. 9.13   The oil-pump drive and the kickstart plate.

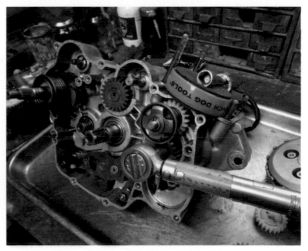

Fig. 9.14   Tighten the primary-gear nut to the correct torque.

the clutch basket forms the idler gear that connects these two gears. Make sure that the dots and arrows are still aligned when the clutch basket is in place.

Fig. 9.15   Align the marks on the balance-shaft gear.

Fig. 9.16   A pin punch settles the circlip into its groove.

Assembling the Clutch

With the clutch basket on its shaft, fit the splined thrust washer to the shaft, then the wavy washer. Next install the clutch centre. As mentioned, the clutch centre of the 125cc KMX is retained by a circlip. If the clip has been distorted at all during the dismantling process, you will need a new one – it is a very critical fitting. Push the centre down and hold it so that you can get the circlip to sit properly in its groove. To be sure, use a small punch to drive the circlip completely into place.

The 200cc KMX has a retaining nut and washer instead of a circlip. In this case, you would need to hold the clutch centre to allow the nut to be tightened.

The clutch centre forms the first of the steel clutch plates, so fit the plates by starting with a lined plate. There are six lined plates and five steel plates, and they are fitted alternately. Like the Aprilia, this is a 'push from the outside' clutch, so the final lined plate must be fitted into the shorter slots in the clutch basket.

It is worth checking the condition of the ball-bearing thrust bearing in the centre of the pressure plate.

There is a little pusher shaft that fits into the gearbox shaft. It has a spring on the lower end, and both the pusher and spring go into the gearbox shaft before the pressure plate is fitted.

Note that the pusher shaft engages with the clutch release mechanism built into the outer case, but it is only free to slide in and out of the release mechanism when the lever is in the withdrawn position. When both removing and replacing the outer cover, you need to move the clutch lever (where the clutch cable attaches) to free the pusher shaft.

Install the pressure plate, clutch springs, washers and screws. Tighten the screws evenly and in a diagonal pattern. The recommended torque setting is 9Nm (6.6lb ft).

Everything should now be in place, allowing you to install the outer cover.

Fitting the Outer Case

Install the centrifugal pulley shaft into the outer casing. Make sure that the

Fig. 9.17   The clutch pushrod is gripped when the lever is released. The photograph shows the pusher shaft held in place in the release mechanism. Note that this was set up for the photograph; you should not see this while you are assembling the motor.

Fig. 9.18   Fit the centrifugal pulley.

pulley on the shaft is engaged with the lever on the shaft that runs up the side of the cylinder.

Check that the sealing faces are clean and fit a new gasket.

Offer up the outer case, taking great care not to let the splines on the kick-start shaft cut grooves in the oil seal. Wrapping insulating tape around the splines will help if you do not have a very steady hand.

You will probably need to look carefully through the gap at the front of the cases and use a small screwdriver to turn the KIPS actuator gear to align it so that it meshes with the primary gear.

Pull back the clutch operating lever to allow the pusher shaft to slip into the release mechanism.

When you are sure that everything is in its correct place, push the case right down, applying a gentle tap with a soft mallet if necessary. Fit the case screws and tighten them evenly.

Fitting the Generator Assembly

Turning to the other side of the engine, install the stator, fixing it in place with the three hex-headed screws. The position of the cable clearly indicates its orientation. In fact, the ignition pick-up is a separate item, so the position of the stator is not as critical as on many other engines.

As it happens, the ignition pick-up was missing from the boxes of components for this engine – there is always something, remember? Ideally, this would go on next, attached to the two bosses outside the diameter of the flywheel, which can be seen in Fig. 9.20.

Check that the Woodruff key is in place on the crankshaft taper and carefully fit the flywheel on to the shaft. Make sure that the key is still in place before adding the washer and nut to the crankshaft. Lock the flywheel and tighten the nut to 60Nm (44lb ft).

The Top End

Before refitting the piston and cylinder, it is always a good idea to have a look at the KIPS valves and the mechanism that moves them.

If you ever read any of the classic two-stroke books from the 1960s or before, you will find lots of advice

Fig. 9.19   *Use a soft mallet to fit the cover.*

Fig. 9.20   *Install the generator stator. The two bosses for the ignition pick-up can be seen at the upper right.*

Fig. 9.21   *Tighten the flywheel nut to the correct torque.*

on how to decarbonize the engine. This process involved using scrapers to remove the carbon from the piston crown and, in particular, from the exhaust port. Even in the 1970s, it was not unusual for the owners of scooters and mopeds to complain of a loss of power, the cause often being a build-up of carbon in the exhaust port, which sometimes reduced its area by a half.

Even with modern oils, and the much smaller amounts of oil permitted, some carbon is produced by the burning of the oil. In the 1930s, fuel was mixed with oil at ratios of between 8:1 and 16:1. Oils were simple mineral oils or the famous castor oil-based Castrol R. Bikes of the 1960s and later employed ratios of about 25:1 to 32:1. Oils of the era often included deter-

gent chemicals, and some synthetic molecules.

Fully synthetic oils, based on long-chain molecules that cling together and provide a strong lubricating film on the engine parts are commonly used in high-performance motors. However, although there is far less carbon now, there is some. Powervalves are wonderful things for performance and rideability, but the exhaust port of a two-stroke is not a benign environment, especially for any moving parts.

The gas coming out of the exhaust port during the exhaust phase of the two-stroke cycle will be at a temperature around 800°C. The melting point of pure aluminium is around 650°C. Clearly this could lead to trouble. Fortunately there are several features that ensure that the average temperature remains within workeable limits while an engine is running. Moreover, the actual cylinders are made from aluminium alloys that are more heat resistant than pure aluminium.

The KIPS Valves

If an engine has any type of power-valve system in the exhaust, any carbon build-up in the exhaust port will cause problems, so the owner has a regular maintenance task – to check and clean the powervalve.

As discussed earlier, the KIPS system is a dual-action arrangement. At high engine speeds, it adds extra port time area during the blowdown phase; it also adds a Helmholtz resonator chamber that virtually elongates the exhaust front pipe at low engine speeds. (If these terms are unfamiliar, they will be

covered more fully in Chapter 11.) The two functions are performed by two rotating drums alongside the main exhaust port.

To remove the two valves, they must be pulled up halfway to disengage them from the rack rod that turns them. Then the rack can be pulled out, passing the narrower sections of the valves between the gear and drum itself. This allows the valves to be taken out fully. You can clean them with a kitchen scouring pad, adding a little washing-up liquid to make it easier. On top of the valves, there are small valve-guide bushes. Their main job is to hold O-rings that seal the shaft spindles.

A small bottlebrush (raid the kitchen cupboard again!) is useful to clean out the holes into which the valves fit. Before putting them back into the cylinder, lubricate the drums with a little two-stroke oil.

Note that the valves are not identical. The valve on the right-hand side of the cylinder, as you look at it while facing the exhaust port, has a groove around it. The process for setting up the timing of the valves is quite simple.

Each gear has a punched dot on the top face. The rack rod has three lines on it. Turn the gears until the dots face the rack – that is facing forward as viewed when the engine is in the frame. Do this while the valves are withdrawn halfway, then insert the rack into its hole. Push it in as far as it will go. At this point, the outer lines on the rack will line up with the dots on the gears. Push the valves fully into their holes to engage with the rack. Operate the rack to check that the auxiliary exhaust

MORE OIL, MORE POWER

There are bikes now (mostly slow-running trials bikes) that require a 100:1 fuel/oil ratio! Some expert engine developers have shown that this is nothing like enough lubrication for the bearings. The suggestion is that minimal oil is used to eliminate the exhaust smoke that would be a problem when the bike is ridden in indoor trials. However, this is at the expense of big-end bearing life, which is measured in only a few hours. Many studies have shown that in all engines that operate at high speed for any length of time, more oil means more power as well as longer life.

Fig. 9.22 *Align the KIPS valves using these marks. The two valves can be seen partly withdrawn from the cylinder, along with the gears and rack rod that turn them. They are black with a thin coat of carbon.*

Fig. 9.23 *The groove marks the differences in the two valves.*

ports open and close properly. Install the small valve-guide bushes, with the stepped part upwards, and fit new O-rings to them.

You will need to have the engine running to check that the complete KIPS system is operating. It should start to move at around 6,500rpm. This will be done much later.

Fitting the Piston and Cylinder

Installation of the piston follows the usual procedure. If it is new, fit the rings. Both rings were the same on this 125cc model. I presume it had an aftermarket piston and ring set, since the original pistons have a tapered Keystone ring in the top groove. In this case, the word 'Top' should be etched on the top face of the top ring. Do check for this. (The KMX200 employs an expander ring on the lower ring.)

If you intend refitting the old rings, place them, one at a time, into the barrel, about halfway between the top of the cylinder and the top of the exhaust port. Use the piston to ensure that they are straight in the bore. Then check the ring gap with a feeler gauge. It should be between 0.15 and 0.35mm (0.006 and 0.015in if you have imperial feelers). Any gap less than this is dangerous, since it is a recipe for a seizure. A larger gap than that specified, oddly, may cause exactly the same problem, as hot gases leaking past the rings can overheat parts of the piston and cause it to expand unevenly.

The remainder of the installation procedure is as follows:

1. Fit the gudgeon-pin circlip that will be on the far side of the piston as you fit it to the connecting rod.

Fig. 9.24   Warm the piston.

2. Fit the small-end bearing into the small-end eye on the rod. Lubricate the bearing and the gudgeon pin.
3. Warm the piston and fit the gudgeon pin into its near-side boss. Make sure that the arrow on top of the piston will point at the exhaust port when the piston is in place.
4. Align the piston on the connecting rod so that you can see right through the pin to the other side and that the pin can slide easily through the small-end bearing. Use a pair of small narrow-nose pliers to hold the pin, rotating it gently to work it through the small-end bearing.
5. Fit the remaining gudgeon-pin circlip.
6. With a new base gasket in place, and a good smear of oil to lubricate the cylinder bore, the cylinder can be fitted.
7. The narrow steel rings will be easy to squeeze in with your fingers, after you have made sure that the ring gaps align with the piston-ring pins. There is a generous chamfer on the bottom of the cylinder, so it should be easy to fit. Do not rotate it more than a few degrees while doing this, as it is easy to catch the end of a ring in a port. This could break the ring or even chip the plating on the cylinder. Either of these will cause serious damage when the engine is run.
8. Slide the cylinder on to the piston as far as the top of the cylinder-flange studs. At this point, you can ensure that as the cylinder is finally seated, the operating lever on the KIPS mechanism engages with the pulley on the end of the rack. Then slide the cylinder right down, and fit the nuts and washers.

Fig. 9.25   Make sure that the ring gaps are aligned.

Fig. 9.26   Make sure that the KIPS rack engages with the lever.

9. Tighten the nuts evenly and gradually, and in a diagonal pattern. You would need a very special torque wrench to ensure that you tightened them finally to the recommended value of 25Nm (18lb ft), so tighten them firmly with a ring spanner.

Fig. 9.27   You need a ring spanner for the base nuts.

Fig. 9.28   The cylinder-head gasket has to fit this way up.

Fig. 9.29   One KIPS cover is plastic (left), the other is aluminium.

10. Fit a new head gasket, then the head itself. It has five retaining bolts, so there is no possibility of getting it the wrong way round, although the head gasket has a right way up and is marked with the word 'Top'. The same procedure of gradual and even tightening should be used for the head bolts as for the cylinder-stud nuts. The same torque settings apply, but these are easy to measure.

11. There are two covers for the two sides of the KIPS system. One is plastic and covers the actuating lever (you will have to take this one off again later when you test the operating speed of the KIPS system). The other is aluminium and acts as the resonance chamber. This should be fitted with a new gasket. Any leakage here will make a lot of mess on the side of the cylinder at the very least. Very hot exhaust gases straight from the cylinder could cause far more problems if there were any serious leakage.

The Drive Sprocket

At this stage, the only parts left in the box were the drive sprocket and fixing plate. The sprocket simply fits on to the splines of the drive shaft. The fixing plate goes over the splines, too, but when it reaches the groove in the shaft, it can be turned by half a spline so that its holes align with the threaded holes in the sprocket. Lock the plate and sprocket together with the two fixing screws.

That completed the assembly, and the engine was ready for collection.

KMX125 ENGINE RECOMMENDED TORQUE SETTINGS

Case screws: 8Nm (6lb ft)
Clutch spring screws: 9Nm (7lb ft)
Cylinder base: 25Nm (18lb ft)
Cylinder head: 25Nm (18lb ft)
Flywheel nut: 60Nm (44lb ft)
Primary gear: 60Nm (44lb ft)
Water pump: 10Nm (7.5lb ft)

Fig. 9.30 The completed engine.

Fig. 9.31 Kawasaki 250 trials bike.

Fig. 9.32 Engine detail of the GasGas trials.

Fig. 9.33 A traditional Bantam trials bike.

ABOVE: *Fig. 9.34   Suzuki RM125 motocrosser.*

LEFT: *Fig. 9.35   Modern GasGas 320 trials bike.*

Fig. 9.36   Yamaha TY175 trials bike.

on track: popular road-race bikes
Honda RS125 & Yamaha TZ350G

With the exception of Scotts, which began winning TTs in 1912, early two-strokes did not have a very illustrious racing history. Prior to the Second World War, the thunderously loud DKW supercharged two-strokes won the TT by eleven minutes in 1937. Apart from that, however, it was four-strokes all the way. Interestingly, both the Scott and the supercharged DKW were excluded from the starting grid by the regulators of the sport, rather than by being beaten on the tracks. This might sound familiar. After the change of classification for Grand Prix racing, is there a justification for the feeling that there is an establishment bias against two-strokes?

Whether there is an anti-two-stroke conspiracy or not, it was the post-1945 work of MZ engineer Walter Kaaden on the design of resonant exhaust systems that really put the screaming two-stroke cat among the four-stroke pigeons.

So with the aforementioned two exceptions, two-stroke racing history really began with the IFA (roughly translated as Vehicle Manufacturing Company) that was set up in the ruins of the old DKW factory in what had become East Germany, under Soviet control. Their political masters demanded a race department, so work began on a competition machine. The initial bike was the DKW RT125, mentioned as the ancestor of many modern two-strokes in Chapter 1, but the piston-port engine was soon replaced by a rotary-valve motor – with an expansion-chamber exhaust. This was the first appearance of what soon became the pioneering MZ two-strokes, which changed the shape of racing for the next fifty years. The full, dramatic story is told in Mat Oxley's book, *Stealing Speed*.

THE HONDA RS125

The subject engine of this chapter is a direct descendent of the little 125 single from those days. It is the Honda RS125 racer. Without seeing the exact figures, I suspect that this was the biggest selling pure race bike ever in the UK. Certainly many of them are still around racing in the Classic classes these days.

When the racing regulations put an end to the multi-cylinder 125s, Honda chose a very simple approach to providing clubman racers with a competitive and affordable bike. They took the engine from their successful Red Rocket CR125 motocrosser and fitted

Fig. 10.1   Honda RS125.

Fig. 10.2   The original Honda Elsinore 125 'Red Rocket'.

it into a simple steel-tube frame. (This engine was very successful when fitted to karts, too.) At first, the engine was air-cooled, the bike being designated MT125. It was soon superseded, however, by the water-cooled RS model. This history means that many engines are painted red to this day.

THE YAMAHA TZ250/350

There is one more candidate for the title of most popular and influential two-stroke pure race bike, however, and it is a machine that cannot be omitted, the TZ Yamaha.

The reason for choosing the Honda RS over the TZ is partly for balance, since there has not been a Honda engine in the book so far. In addition, the TZ was very close in design to the RD motors, certainly until the appearance of the TZ350G in 1980. (There was a TZ350H, but only an expert would know the difference from the G-model, though the H-version did come with sinuous crossover exhaust pipes.)

One of the obvious differences between the TZ350G and the RDLC was the dry clutch, which produced a loud rattle while the bike was warming up in neutral and sometimes would throw out broken friction plates. In the heyday of the TZ, paddocks seemed to be paved with pieces of broken TZ clutch plate! The second major difference was the fact that the TZ was a piston-ported engine instead of a reed-valve unit. Some riders fitted reed-valve cylinders from the later TZ750 4-cylinder bikes to make the machine easier to ride.

In Ireland, very competitive 200cc single-cylinder racers were built from TZ350 cylinder blocks, by sawing them in half.

After the 350 class was dropped from the GPs, development continued on the TZ250, using separate cylinders and a design that, at first, was similar to the TZR road bikes.

WHAT IS IT ABOUT RACE BIKES?

What is it that makes a race-bike engine different from the motor in a road bike? It is not just a matter of one having a harder life than the other – in fact, how would you define a hard life? A race bike is expected to run at peak speed and load for maybe forty-five minutes. After a few hours of running, it will be stripped and anything that is subject to wear or stress will be replaced. A road bike will be expected to start every day, run for thousands of miles without attention, and be happy crawling along in traffic as well as maintaining high speeds on motorways. For those reasons, it is normal for road bike components to be sturdier and heavier than those on an equivalent race bike.

The main point of difference is in the tolerances in fit and finish. Even with the best CNC machining and casting techniques, mass-produced components will have some variation in size and accuracy. On the production line, the workers assembling a twin-cylinder crankshaft will fit the next two connecting rods that lie in the parts hopper. In the race department, the entire parts bin will be examined for a pair of rods that are absolutely identical in length and weight. This is just one example of the meticulous atten-

tion to detail aimed at ensuring that a race engine lasts the full duration of a race meeting without carrying an extra gram of unnecessary weight.

At every stage, everything must be done with a strict adherence to the manufacturer's specifications – unless you know better or are fitting a more modern upgrade. The works manual should be your bible. However, race bikes are rarely completely standard. Very often lighter, upgraded parts will be used to replace the original parts. Lighter components often incorporate higher-specification materials, like carbon fibre and titanium, or rely on special processes, such as forging or machining from a solid billet. This means higher cost, sometimes much higher!

For this reason, the approach of this chapter will be somewhat different. A road-going machine will have service intervals stated in miles or kilometres. Race bikes do not have milometers (or odometers, as they are also called), but do have their service lives specified in miles or kilometres, so meticulous record keeping is essential with such machinery. The topic of record keeping will covered in greater detail in Chapter 11.

EXPENSIVE AT THE TOP

At a college where I used to work, we undertook the care and preparation of a competitive privateer BSB Ducati 999. The official recommendation was that the service life of the crankcase casting was 500km (310 miles) or 20hr. After that, the instruction was that it should be changed, along with the majority of the rest of the engine components. Top-level racing is not cheap, especially with a four-stroke.

LOOKING AFTER THE RS125

Unlike the previous chapters, where engines have been stripped and rebuilt because they are being checked and restored after storage, or assembled from parts to be put back into service, this chapter will deal with work that must be done on a routine basis.

Fig. 10.3   The engine from an early RS125.

Running-In

The running-in period of a race bike has to be quite short. There is no way that you can ride the first 800km (500 miles) around the track at speeds below 65km/h (40mph)! The procedure that I used for my 80cc racer (with modified YZ80 engine) was as follows:

· Run the bike in the workshop, blipping the throttle gently until the water temperature comes up to 60°C.
· Stop the engine and let it cool.
· Do the same again (but not late at night if you have neighbours).
· Repeat the procedure at the track as soon as you are allowed to start the engine.
· Take it gently on the way to the start line, using less than half throttle.
· Short-shift during the first lap of first practice to keep the engine below 9,000rpm.
· Go racing. The engine is now ready to go.

Honda's recommendation is slightly more specific:

The running-in requires about half an hour. During this time the emphasis is in avoiding both high revs and, even more importantly, running it at low revs and large throttle openings. As the manual states, do not let the engine 'lug'. Recommended rev limits are 8,000rpm for the first 15km (9 miles), 9,000rpm for the next 15km and 10,000rpm for the third 15km. That will take about thirty minutes in all.

Fettling the Piston

Even if the utmost care is taken during the running-in process, quite often the engine will suffer minor seizures. That is where the fettling comes in.

If there is evidence from smeared marks on the piston ring that the ring has seized, or if it appears to have stuck in its groove, it is a good idea to form small chamfers on the top and bottom corners of the ring groove, especially in the area where the ring passes over the exhaust port. The ideal tool for this is a very fine-grain slip stone – that is, a triangular or wedge-shaped

Accordingly, we start with a list of the service intervals for the various components inside the engine. The official Honda owner's manual has another list for the cycle parts and frame.

HONDA RS125 ENGINE SPECIFICATIONS (1992 VERSION)

Type: water-cooled single-cylinder
Bore and stroke: 54.0 × 54.4mm
Capacity: 124cc
Compression ratio: 8:1
Induction: reed valve
Carburettor: Keihin PJ38 (38mm power jet)
Starting: push only
Claimed power: 39bhp at 12,000rpm
Transmission: gear primary drive, wet multi-plate clutch, 6-speed gearbox, chain final drive

Service life

Piston: 500km (310 miles)
Piston ring: 500km (310 miles)
Gudgeon pin: 1,000km (620 miles)
Connecting rod: 1,000km (620 miles)
Small end: 500km (310 miles)
Clutch plates: 1,000km (620 miles)
Piston circlip: every time piston is removed
Reed valve: 1,000km (620 miles)
Gearbox oil: 500km (310 miles)

Added to this list are all the rubber mountings and sleeves for the exhaust.

Cylinder O-rings, clutch springs, all the clutch parts, the spark plug and the sprocket are regarded as expendable parts that should be replaced before every race meeting.

In addition, optional gear sets are available, and need to be selected and changed to suit the particular circuit if the bike is to be used at its absolute limit.

The process of dismantling and reassembling the engine is likely to become very familiar to the owner, and in fact it is little different from the procedures for the Kawasaki and Aprilia singles in the previous chapters. The emphasis here will be on working to the exacting specifications needed for a race engine.

Fettling

Previous generations of motorcyclists would have been perfectly content for engine components to come from the factory in a partly unfinished state. These days, we tend to assume that CNC machinery will produce perfection every time, but that is not quite the case. It is near enough for the general run of parts, but race machines demand a higher standard. The traditional word for checking for small inaccuracies and correcting them, and improving the surface finishes of newly produced components is 'fettling'. A race bike will need a little fettling.

Fig. 10.4 Single-ring pistons are often used in race bikes.

often see a trace of aluminium from the piston welded to the cylinder wall. The seizure may even have happened after the finish of the race.

When the piston is out of the cylinder, it is worth spending a little time cleaning up the bore. You need a very fine grade of wet-or-dry abrasive paper, no coarser than 600- or 800-grit. It should be oiled well. Rub the surface of the bore lightly with the oiled paper to remove any smears of aluminium. Be very careful not to use too much pressure, particularly with a plated cylinder – the plating is very thin.

Never use a rotary grinding tool for this.

The other thing that is worth taking time over is chamfering the edges of the ports. This can be done with finger oilstone. A very smooth triangular needle file is an alternative. The chamfer should remove no more than 0.2mm from the edges of the groove, but it will make sticking of the ring far less likely.

It is also a good idea to slightly widen the semi-circular cutaway on the inside of each ring end where it fits over the piston's ring pin. A round needle file is required for this.

As a guideline for any engine, the gap between the square ends of the ring can be calculated by multiplying the bore size by 0.0055. So for a 54mm bore, the ring gap should be at least 0.3mm. If the ring is placed in the bore, levelled accurately with the piston and set around 20mm from the top of the cylinder, the gap will need to be adjusted with a smooth file if it is less than 0.27mm, while the ring should be changed if it is more than 0.45mm.

The correct clearance between the ring and the groove is very important, too. Checked with a feeler gauge, it should measure 0.07mm.

The best advice is to change the ring for every race meeting, and whenever the piston is removed. Fit new circlips as well.

Fettling the Cylinder

If there is a seizure of the piston or piston ring, even if it is so slight that the rider may not have noticed it, you will

---

RISING HEAT

An FS1-E-based 50cc racer, belonging to a youth racing scheme that I was running at the time, had completed six laps of Brands Hatch at a perfectly respectable midfield pace. The bike and rider crossed the finish line in good style, the engine being shut off as the bike entered the paddock. When we came to start it again, it proved to have seized. If fact, if you watch the temperature gauge of a water-cooled bike, you will see that the water temperature often reaches its peak reading after the race. The engine is still very hot, but the water pump has stopped, and there is neither airflow through the radiator nor lubrication from the fuel any more. The FS1-E is air-cooled, and as the bike slowed down, the throttle was closed and the heat continued to build; it seized as it stopped.

Fig. 10.5 Using a 'fettling stick' to chamfer port edges.

Fig. 10.6   The process of boring out the cylinder.

Fig. 10.7   Turning an iron sleeve to make a new cylinder liner.

Fig. 10.8   After modifying the cylinder, cut the ports in the sleeve.

Fig. 10.9   The cylinder is heated, and the sleeve frozen. Once in place, the fit is perfect.

pressure behind the abrasive paper, but it is easier if you use a length of dowel. A piece of around 15mm diameter is about right. Wrap the emery paper around the dowel and secure it with adhesive tape. Holding the dowel at a very shallow angle to the cylinder wall, rub the abrasive gently along the top and bottom edges of all the ports to produce a chamfer around 0.5–0.75mm wide. Obviously you need to work on the bottom edges from the base of the cylinder and the top edges from the top.

While the cylinder is under inspection, it is a good time to check that at room temperature, the cylinder bore, checked 20mm from the TDC position, should measure no more than 54.015mm.

A new cylinder may need more

work. Any casting roughness should be removed from the ports; indeed, Honda suggest that all the transfer ports can be enlarged, at both top and bottom edges, by 0.04mm. The exhaust-port bridge can be reduced to 2mm in width and the top edge lifted by 0.8mm. There is further work to do in the areas, between the pairs of transfer ports. They should be ground to remove the convex curve of the inner wall, providing a straight entry into the cylinder for the new fuel/air mixture.

Much more radical alterations are possible. If complete changes in the port shapes or timings are needed, you could bore out the whole inner wall of the cylinder, rework the port passages, and make and fit a whole new cylinder liner.

Working on the Engine

In the workshop, it is always easier to work on the engine out of the bike, on a stand on the bench. However, even with the best-maintained bikes, there are times when components have to be changed in the paddock – and time will always be of the essence.

When time is short, the following items can be accessed with the engine in the frame:

- The cylinder head, cylinder and piston.
- The clutch.
- The gearchange linkage.
- The water pump.
- The carburettor.
- The generator rotor and stator.

Fig. 10.10 *An engine on a bench stand.*

BROKEN REED

I have personally completed one-and-a-half laps of Oulton Park on a bike that had a broken reed petal. The carbon-fibre item had passed right through the engine without damaging anything. The bottom-end power had completely vanished, and there was a lot of fuel blowback from the carburettor, but if the revs were kept over 10,000 there was no noticeable loss of power at all. In fact, high-speed photography has shown that at high revs, assuming a well-designed exhaust pipe and inlet system, the reeds are open for the full 360 degrees when the engine is running in its power band.

It is very useful to have an engine stand for bench work.

DISMANTLING THE ENGINE

Remove the cylinder head, cylinder and piston.

The head is retained by four studs and nuts; the cylinder base has a thick flange, also secured with four nuts. In standard form, there are gaskets in both top and bottom joints.

The piston is a single-ring item with tailless circlips and clip extraction notches.

Remove the reed block and examine the reed very carefully. Look for splits and cracks at both the tip and the roots of the reed blades. If the reed curves away from the block in its resting position, starting might be difficult if it does not seal properly. Some people say that if the reed is curved, you can refit it the other way up. Any curve is a symptom of stress damage, however, and fitting a new reed is better. Never bend the guard plates behind the reeds. This will encourage them to break at their roots, since that is where they will bend if you just grab them with a pair of pliers.

Special Tools

When you are going to be working on an engine as often as a race bike demands, there is no point in skimping on buying the proper special tools. The holder for the primary gear is a toothed wedge, slightly similar to the sprocket holder for the Villiers 2T discussed in Chapter 2. It has teeth that mesh with both the primary gear and the gear at the back of the clutch, thus locking the two together. On the other hand, I have seen people jam a two-pence piece between the gears. A word of warning, though: since 1992, British 'copper' coins have been made of steel with only a thin layer of copper over the top. Copper is soft enough that it will not damage a steel gear tooth. You cannot be quite so sure with a steel-cored coin.

Working on the Bottom End

To remove the standard flywheel, you need either a Y-shaped universal holder from the Honda special tools

Fig. 10.12 *An aftermarket ignition with the rotor inside the coils.*

Fig. 10.11 *The cylinder and cylinder head.*

Fig. 10.13   *The standard generator has an outside stator.*

inside the inner race of the bearing, in which case the shaft will show signs of excessive heat and galling of the metal surface. A crank damaged in this way can be metal sprayed and reground; otherwise it should not be refitted.

Examine all the bearings thoroughly. Check the selector forks for any indication that they are bent or damaged. It is worth measuring the hardened tips of the selector forks for a thickness of at least 4.8mm, too. Every tooth and dog on the gear pinions should be checked, as should the splines on which the gears slide.

Oil seals on the shafts of a race bike should be regarded as expendable and should be renewed at every strip-down. As usual, a smear of grease around the outside will make installation easier; both bearings and seals can be fitted more easily when the crankcase is warm.

list or a strap wrench, as used for other projects in the book. These days, however, you cannot guarantee that an RS125 will still have its original generator and ignition.

Many upgraded ignition systems involve a smaller-diameter magnetic rotor that runs inside the stator windings, instead of outside like the standard item. Some of these smaller rotors have a hexagon cast into the outer face so that they can be held with a spanner while the nut is removed.

Remove the flywheel/rotor, followed by the clutch.

Ten small hex-headed screws hold the crankcase together. Loosen them gradually and in a diagonal pattern.

The procedure for splitting the crankcases is the same as for the Aprilia engine (*see* Chapter 8). A puller is attached by means of the stator mounting holes, and the cases are split by winding down the centre screw of the puller against the end of the crankshaft. Lightly tapping on the other shaft with a soft mallet will help to separate the case halves.

There is a gasket between the two case halves. Remove the gasket and the locating dowels from the joint.

Pull out the selector-fork shafts and the selector forks.

The two gearbox shafts are best kept together during removal and refitting.

The recommended method for removing the crank from the other crankcase half is to use a press. However, a gentle, but determined mechanic with a copper hammer can do the job, too.

You may need a bearing puller to remove the main bearing from the shaft. If it comes off easily, make a very careful examination of the crank where the bearing was seated. It is possible for the shaft to have been spinning

CHECKING THE CRANK AND BEARINGS

Crankshaft

Set the crank in V-blocks, or between centres, and use a DTI to check run-out on the shafts beyond the bosses where the bearings fit. Note that the run-out is half of the total variation shown on the DTI. The crank must run true, with run-out no greater than 0.02mm.

Fig. 10.14   *Mount the crank in V-blocks to measure the run-out.*

Fig. 10.15   *Check side-float with a feeler gauge.*

Fig. 10.16   *Check for radial play in the big end. This example, which has suffered a seizure, has over 0.5mm.*

Fig. 10.17   *Compare the reading with the previous image.*

End-float on the big end, measured with a feeler gauge, should be less than 0.7mm.

Up-and-down play on the big-end bearing must be no more than 0.03mm, measured with the DTI. A damaged big-end bearing will have far more play.

There should be no detectable play in the small-end bearing, tested by hand.

Main and Gearbox Bearings

There are two checks for these bearings. First, wash them out with penetrating oil and blow them dry with compressed air.

A VERY IMPORTANT WARNING!

Never be tempted to use a blowgun and compressor to spin a bearing on your finger. It can spin up to a very high speed, and when it does so, it possesses an enormous amount of kinetic energy. If the bearing happens to seize, all of that energy will be applied to your finger, and it will be enough to cause serious injury. On the other hand, if the spinning bearing flies off your finger, it will hit the floor or bench top and hurl itself across the workshop like a missile. Whatever it hits will suffer. Under these circumstances, bearings have been known to knock lumps out of a brick wall.

When the bearing is clean and dry, spin it gently (with your finger of course!) and listen. It should sound quiet and smooth.

Second, hold the edge of the bearing between finger and thumb, and roll your finger and thumb back and forth. You should not feel any movement between the inner and outer races.

REASSEMBLY

Before reassembly, clean all the components, including the crankcases, and give them each a light coat of oil.

Fig. 10.18   *Listen for any roughness.*

Fig. 10.19   *Use the hand movement that often means 'money'!*

Fig. 10.20   *The selector drum in place.*

Fig. 10.21   *The selector forks and their shafts are added.*

1. Install the selector drum.
2. Add the selector forks. They are marked 'L' (left), 'C' (centre) and 'R' (right).
3. Install the two gearbox shafts together in the right-hand side of the crankcase.
4. Work the selector forks into their grooves and insert the selector-fork shafts.
5. Fit the crank into its bearing and seal. The correct tool for this task is a tubular puller that fits against the inner race of the bearing and engages with the thread on the end of the crank. It has a thread that pulls the crank into the bearing. On the other hand, if you warm the bearing and chill the crank, it can be tapped into place with a copper hammer. Grease the lip of the oil seal before you fit the crank.
6. With the crank in place in the right-hand side of the case, and all the gear shafts installed, fit the case gasket, fixing it with a very light smear of sealant.
7. Fit the locating dowels into the joint face and tap them into place.

Fig. 10.22   *The assembled gearbox.*

8. Put the case halves together and fit the ten screws, tightening them gradually and evenly in a diagonal pattern. The final torque setting is 10Nm (7.4lb ft).
9. Make sure that the crank turns easily. If it does not, something needs attention before you go any further. In particular, check that the

Oil seal has not caught on the shaft and been turned inside out.
10. Fit the gearchange spindle and engage the gearchange mechanism. Install the retaining plate.
11. Fit the collar to the drive end of the shaft and add the primary gear. Fit the washer and nut, tightening it to 45Nm (33lb ft).

Fig. 10.23   *Install the gearchange shaft mechanism.*

Fig. 10.24   *Fit the drive collar and primary gear.*

12. Install the clutch basket and centre, tightening the clutch nut to 45Nm (33lb ft).
13. Fit the plates, the clutch pushrod mushroom (Honda call this part the 'clutch lifter') and then the springs and pressure plate.
14. Insert the five screws in the clutch, tightening them gradually and evenly to 10Nm (7.4 lb ft).
15. Fit the water pump, making sure that its drive gears engage properly.

Fig. 10.25   Tighten the cylinder-head nuts.

A LITTLE HISTORY

The water pump is at the back of the engine on this bike, requiring an external pipe to carry the coolant forward to the cylinder. The reason for this is that the original engine in the MT125 was air-cooled, and the first of the water-cooled versions was supplied with an air-cooled cylinder installed, but with the water-cooling kit included separately. To enable use of the same crankcase casting, the water pump was fitted where originally the kick-start had been located.

Install the stator and rotor of the generator, tightening the nut to 55Nm (41lb ft).

Assembling the Top End

1. Fit the reed valve and carburettor rubber.
2. Put a new gasket on the cylinder base, oil and fit the small-end roller bearing, then fit the piston after warming it first. Always use new circlips.
3. Align the piston ring on the pin, squeeze the ring with your fingers and fit the oiled cylinder, taking care not to twist it as it slides down on to the studs.
4. Fit the four washers and nuts, tightening them gradually and evenly to 23Nm (17lb ft).
5. Use a little grease to hold the cylinder O-ring in its groove and fit the cylinder head. Install the four washers and nuts, tightening them gradually and evenly, in a diagonal pattern, to 23Nm (17lb ft).

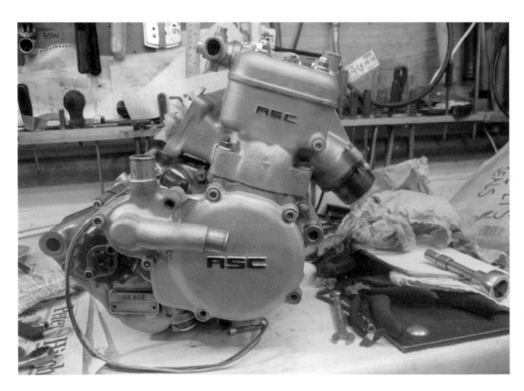

Fig. 10.26   The later RSC version of the engine.

Fig. 10.27   Another example of the RS125.

Fig. 10.28   An alloy-framed RSW125, successor to the steel-framed version in Fig. 10.27.

Fig. 10.29   The engine installation of the RSW.

Yamaha TZ Gallery:

TOP LEFT: *Fig. 10.30   A typical TZ350G in the workshop.*

TOP RIGHT: *Fig. 10.31   The last of the parallel-twin TZs had reversed cylinders.*

LEFT: *Fig. 10.32   Many TZs were installed in special frames to improve handling.*

Fig. 10.33   TZ350G at Oulton Park. It is equipped with Two-Cycle Development's pipes.

ABOVE: *Fig. 10.34   A TZ350 crankshaft. (Compare with the RDLC in Chapter 6.)*

Fig. 10.35   Inside the TZ350.

more power: modern approaches to two-stroke tuning

One of the delights of two-stroke engines has always been the way in which the owner, at relatively low cost, has been able to extract more power. It is quite possible that many bikes that have been through the hands of several previous owners will have benefited – or suffered – from attempts to 'tune them up'.

This chapter will consider performance enhancement for two-stroke engines and describe some of the most recent developments in the art. I should just mention that I shall concentrate on competition and, in particular, road-racing machinery. There will be no mention of 'stage one', 'two'

and 'three' or even 'fast road tune'. This is about racing and the best that can be achieved from an engine.

It is also important to admit that there is no way that a single chapter can provide a step-by-step guide to tuning every two-stroke from Joseph Day's original engine to the latest motors in the current two-stroke championships. The best I can do is give a brief description of what is being done today and why.

THE ABSOLUTE BASICS

The chart in Fig. 11.1 shows a typical printout of the readings from a

dynamometer, that is a series of power curves, but what do they all mean? We must start from the very beginning, and nobody can afford to skip this stage. We are talking about power. Basic physics says that power is the rate of doing work. So far, so good; more power does the same work faster. It is easy to understand that if the 'work' consists of getting the bike and rider from the starting grid to the chequered flag, then more power will get them there sooner.

The definition of work is not quite so easy to grasp, since the word 'work' is used in a number of different ways in day-to-day speech. In an

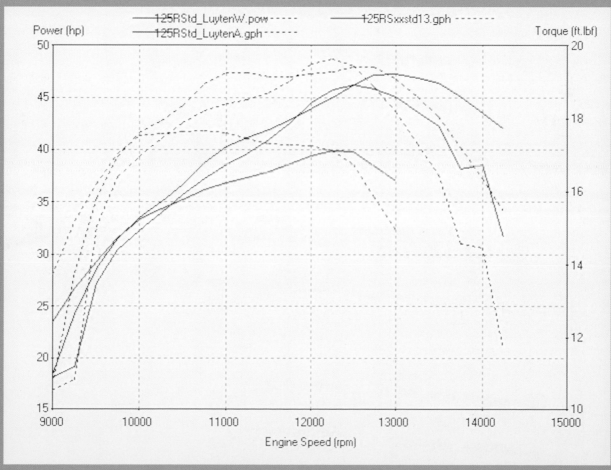

Fig. 11.1   A typical dynamometer chart.

engineering context, work is done when a force moves something through a distance, and it is measured by multiplying the force by the distance. In imperial units, it is specified in foot pounds. Note that it is pounds of force, not pounds of mass. In metric units, the work is measured in Joules. It is not what common sense would tell you, but, according to the definition, if you hold a kilogram (2lb) weight at arm's length, although you are exerting a force with your muscles to oppose the force of gravity on the weight, you are not doing any work. If you raise your arm by 10cm (4in), you have done work. A shelf does no work, but in lifting the tailgate, a car's tailgate strut does.

Horse Power

The most usual measurement of the power of an engine has the rather odd name of 'horse power'. The apparent origin of comparing the power output of an engine with that of a horse goes back to the need for engineers to be able to explain the advantages of powering factories by installing steam engines during the nineteenth century. James Watt calculated the amount of work a horse could perform in a four-hour shift, by turning a horse gin or lifting weights with a rope and pulley. He came up with an average figure

that has become the standard. Naturally, Watt used imperial units, so that figure, 33,000 foot pounds per minute, became defined as one imperial horse power, or hp(I).

That corresponds, in metric units, to 745.7 watts (W). Metric horsepower, calculated the same way, but using 75 kilogram metres per second as a definition of the standard, comes out a little less at 735.5W.

Metric horsepower is abbreviated as hp(m). When reading engine specifications, you may also see ps, cv, hk, pk, ks or ch. All of these represent the same measurement, one horsepower, although the same engine, producing the same power, may have different stated power outputs in each different ratings system. This will be explained later.

Following the establishment of this standard definition of horse power, a Victorian mill owner could be sold a 10hp steam engine on the basis that it would cost him less to run than maintaining a stable of ten horses, but that it would do the same work.

As an aside, you will see that the suspicions that 'foreign' bikes have their power measured by using smaller horses are actually valid, to the extent of 10W per horsepower ('horse' and 'power' have long since been combined).

In the same way that James Watt could calculate the power of a horse from the weight that it could pull, the distance over which it moved and the time taken, we can calculate the power of an engine from the force on the piston, the length of the crank throw and the rpm. Measuring the last two is easy; measuring the first is certainly not.

Brake Mean Effective Pressure (BMEP)

Back in the days of steam, it was possible to measure the pressure inside the cylinder with a device called an indicator. This would record the cylinder pressure on a moving drum of paper to produce an engine indicator diagram. The drum rotated at the same speed as the crank, so the resulting diagram showed how the cylinder pressure changed as the piston moved.

For a petrol engine, a pressure diagram produces a sort of banana-shaped trace (*see* Fig. 11.2).

The indicator employed on steam engines was a useful device in many ways, and engine indicator diagrams are becoming useful again now that electronic sensors and processors are capable of coping with the far higher speeds of modern internal-combustion engines. One thing that you can discover from an engine indicator

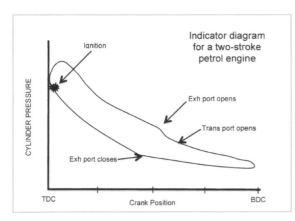

ABOVE: Fig. 11.2   An engine indicator diagram for a two-stroke petrol engine. Note that this is a simplified composite of many traces to give a typical curve, not a trace from one particular engine run.

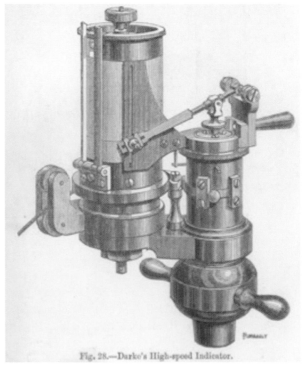

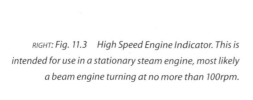

RIGHT: Fig. 11.3   High Speed Engine Indicator. This is intended for use in a stationary steam engine, most likely a beam engine turning at no more than 100rpm.

diagram is the average pressure on the piston during one entire working cycle, that is 360 degrees of crank rotation for a two-stroke and 720 degrees for a four-stroke. Using the word 'mean' as the more mathematically correct term for 'average', that is the mean effective pressure (mep). As mentioned, it is possible to calculate horsepower from mean effective pressure; in practice, we do the opposite.

It is far easier to measure the power output of an engine using a dynamometer, a machine that measures the turning force that an engine can produce at a certain rpm by testing it against an adjustable load, or brake. The brake can be an actual friction brake, a very heavy flywheel, an electrical generator or a water pump. The force that the engine applies to the brake, the length of the lever arm attaching the brake to the measuring device and the time taken for one revolution of the engine give you the three factors needed to calculate power, namely force, distance and time. Engine power measured in this way is 'brake horsepower', and from this you can calculate the mean pressure in the cylinder, which now becomes 'brake mean effective pressure' (bmep). Expect more discussion of bmep as this chapter progresses.

So, given that it is the cylinder pressure that is transferred to the crankshaft by the connecting rod that generates the turning force, or torque, that eventually produces the force that propels the bike, it is clear that to Increase performance, a good method is to increase the bmep, but before any of that…

What Work Does An Engine Do?

Let us consider what work, in the technical sense, an engine has to do. Most obviously, it has to accelerate the bike. Once again, some of the basic laws of physics need to be explained. Newton's laws of motion state that an object in 'uniform motion in a straight line' has no forces acting upon it. This was hard to grasp in Newton's day, though in the modern world, where we are used to the ideas of weightlessness and the vacuum of space, it is easier to see that out in space, an object such as the deep space probe *Voyager* can continue in a straight line forever, once it has been given the initial push of its launch. A force applied to an object moving in space in this way will tend to accelerate it.

However, 'accelerate' is another word that scientists use in a slightly different way from the normal meaning of 'speed up'. If the force is applied in the direction in which the object is moving, it will indeed speed up. If the force is applied in the opposite direction, it slows down or, as a scientist might say, it has an acceleration measured in minus numbers, a deceleration in other words. A force at right angles to the direction of motion will cause the object to move in a curve, adding a sideways acceleration to its forward motion. Thus an object turning in a circle, changing its direction every fraction of a degree, is constant every fraction of a degree, is constant ly accelerating to the side, and to keep doing that, it has to have a sideways force constantly applied to it.

Meanwhile, back on two wheels, a motorcycle and the engine that powers it operate in a gravitational field that provides a force that would cause a free falling object to accelerate towards the centre of the earth at a little over 9.8m per second per second (in imperial units that is 32ft per second squared). We call that force weight! We also live in an atmosphere, which is useful, since it is vital for both bike and rider, but it does behave as a fluid and resists objects moving through it, or trying to move it from one place to another. Then there is friction, the force that resists the motion of one substance moving against another. Friction converts movement energy into heat, which adds to the problems it causes.

From this brief outline, it should be clear that even within the engine alone, there are forces that the combustion energy has to overcome. The piston has to be accelerated from a dead stop to its maximum speed, and then stopped again as it goes from Bottom Dead Centre to Top Dead Centre and vice versa, and this must be done twice in every stroke. The top part of the connecting rod, including the small-end bearing and gudgeon pin, adds to the reciprocating mass, increasing the force required to perform this stop-start process. At a mere 6,000rpm, that process is carried out a hundred times per second. The energies required to overcome these

---

AVOID WASTING POWER

One of the best pieces of advice I ever had was from a very experienced BSA Bantam racer. He had been preparing Bantam motors for the track for many years, and when I asked him how he had managed to get so much speed from such a basic motor, his reply went like this:

Him: 'Have you read all the books? Do you know about truing the crank and checking that the rod is straight? Getting the piston-ring gaps right, bearing clearances and all that?'

Me: 'Yes.'

Him: 'Well, you have to do it.'

There is a well-known phrase popular in my native Yorkshire: 'A penny saved is a penny earned.' It is the same with horsepower. Find and remove the things that are costing your motor power, and there will be more power to knock those critical tenths off your lap times. First, you have to do it!

forces are taken from the total output of the engine and are described as 'inertial losses'.

Gases have to be accelerated through narrow ports, where skin friction between the gas and the port wall and turbulence add to the force required to overcome the resistance. The fuel/air mixture is compressed on the up-stroke and naturally resists compression; this too absorbs energy. These factors are the causes of 'pumping losses'.

The piston, if it is to survive, should be kept from rubbing directly on the cylinder bore by a thin film of oil, which should also protect the bearing and sealing surfaces of the crank assembly. While this does reduce friction, it

does not eliminate it. Thus there are 'frictional losses' to add to the load on the engine.

There is one final set of loads on the engine, and they cause what are sometimes called 'parasitic losses'. They are the loads caused by extra items that the engine has to move, such as ignition systems, generators, balance shafts, the clutch, and the primary and secondary gears – and all that is before we have managed to get any useful work out of the engine.

To return to the question of why different claimed power figures can be given for the same engine, these losses are responsible for some of the variations in stated brake horsepower. Some testing systems allow engines to

be run with none of the items attached. In other cases, everything normally attached must be included. Sometimes the entire bike is tested, so that losses caused by friction in the final drive and the flexing of the tyre are also taken into account. In many ways, this rear wheel brake horsepower is the most useful measurement of all.

CUTTING YOUR LOSSES – BLUEPRINTING

The first step in any process of tuning an engine is to make sure that all of these sources of power loss are reduced to the absolute practical minimum. The method used is known as 'blueprinting'. This involves setting all the fits and clearances to their ideal measurements.

For example, according to the Aprilia RS125 workshop manual, the specification for the crank is as follows: 'Out of roundness (truth) of the crank webs should be less than 0.03mm.' In a blueprinted engine, no more than 0.01mm would be acceptable.

Everything must be set up to the highest degree of accuracy, especially in respect of crankshaft alignment, straightness of the connecting rods, bearing clearances and the alignment of the crankcase halves. The alignment and mesh of any drive gears or chains and sprockets must be optimized, too.

Any opportunity to reduce the weight (technically the mass) of any of the moving parts is an opportunity to save power, provided the reduction of mass does not critically reduce the strength of the parts. Anything that revolves absorbs power to accelerate it whenever engine revs increase, but everything that moves up and down, or backwards and forwards, costs power to accelerate and decelerate it at every revolution.

Saving weight on the piston, the rings, the small-end bearing and the connecting rod is always beneficial. In almost every case, lighter, higher-performance – and much more expensive – replacements are available.

No detail must be neglected, including ensuring that the lubrication system operates at maximum efficiency.

The process takes its name from the engineering drawings that were created by an early copying process.

Fig. 11.4   The components of a flywheel set up in a jig for pressing together.

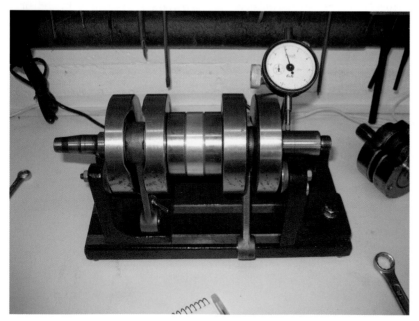

Fig. 11.5   The flywheel must be absolutely true.

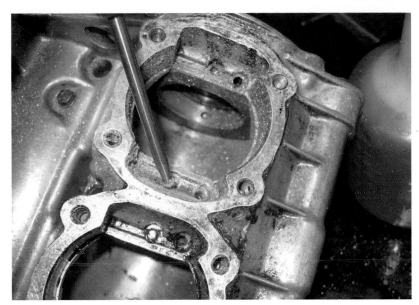

Fig. 11.6   A burr cutter being used to improve the oil supply to the main bearings of a Yamaha TZ – typical of the detailed work that must be done when blueprinting an engine, and emphasizing the importance of lubrication. Also shown is the typical blue engineer's marker, which had been used earlier to ensure the absolute flatness of the cylinder-joint face.

This produced 'negative image' copies of drawings on which the detail was white against a blue background, hence 'blueprints'.

When the blueprinting has been completed, all the ink and metal swarf have been thoroughly cleaned out of the casings, and all the bearings and seals have been renewed, it is time to look at the methods by which the engine can create more power.

CARBURETION

Whether your engine is fed by a carburettor or by a fuel injection system, the job it does is extremely difficult. In both cases, it is required to take in air and mix it thoroughly with exactly enough fuel so that there are two atoms of oxygen for every atom of carbon in the petrol. An ideal carburettor would be capable of counting atoms at the rate of millions per second. Clearly there is nothing that could do that. What our fuel systems actually do is based on a reasonably accurate estimate of how many atoms there are in a gram of air and in a gram of fuel. It works out that you need around 15 grams of air for each gram of fuel. Unfortunately, weighing fuel and air is not easy either, so we have to make do by estimating how much mass of fuel or air there is in a certain volume. Carburettors do this well, but there are some serious issues.

First, air is compressible. You need to know both temperature and pressure before you can work out how much a given volume of air weighs. Second, and this may come as a big shock to some readers, there is no such thing as petrol.

What we know as petrol has to meet a legal specification for viscosity, calorific content, anti-knock (octane) rating, flash point and several other aspects. There are no regulations, however, to specify its actual constituents, although the maximum amount of ethanol, the most usual form of alcohol incorporated, is regulated.

The chemical constituents that come out of the refining process are things like pentane, hexane, heptane and the more famous octane. If you are familiar with classical languages, you will spot that those names appear to be derived from the numbers five, six, seven and eight in ancient Greek. The reason is that the names refer to the number of carbon atoms in the compounds: octane, for example, has the chemical formula C_8H_{18}. That is a compound of eight carbon atoms and eighteen hydrogen atoms. These various compounds are blended, in the most economical way for the oil company, and boosted back to the required specification by the addition of aromatic (easily evaporated) chemicals and alcohols, and frequently detergents.

Perfection is out of reach, but there are important things that can be done. The manual for the Honda RS250 gives different recommendations for jetting sizes for Avgas (high-octane aviation petrol) and unleaded race fuel. They include 175–180 for the main jet on Avgas, and 185–188 main jet for unleaded, for example.

In addition, they recommend an increase in main jet of one size for every drop in temperature of 4–5° from the standard of 15°C. A corresponding reduction is recommended if the temperature goes up. Equally, you should go to one size larger main jet with every 20 per cent drop in humidity, and the opposite when humidity increases by 20 per cent. You will need a barometer in your tool kit, too, since

Fig. 11.7   The carburettors from a TZ350G.

each drop in atmospheric pressure of 33 millibars (mb) from the standard setting of 1,000mb requires one size smaller main jet.

Honda's final piece of advice on the subject is that, after all of this has been taken into consideration, any circuit with a long straight needs a main jet that is one more size larger. This applies especially with powerjet-style carburettors. They give a temporary rich mixture as the throttle is opened, but when this mixture boost has been exhausted at the end of a long straight, the motor can be running lean and may seize.

One thing that is vital when a competition engine is being prepared is that you need to keep full and accurate records. These should include weather data such as humidity and temperature, air pressure and the settings that you have found to work in these conditions. If you are tuning a road bike, this is just not feasible. A road bike must be set up conservatively. Its main aim is to get you where you are going and back home again. A wild, fun ride can be really spoiled by a 30km (20-mile) push home across the moors with a broken bike.

FUEL INJECTION

In the second decade of the twenty-first century, electronic fuel injection (EFI) is just becoming a viable alternative to carburettors. Until recently, though, it was a slight disappointment. The very promising Bimota V Due, a 500cc V-twin two-stroke, was compromised by problems with the fuelling from its EFI. However, digital electronics are at last becoming fast, reliable and cheap enough to be able to cope with a reasonably low-revving two-stroke. Many modern trials bikes and some small scooters feature EFI, but until the abandonment of two-strokes in racing, electronically controlled carburettors were still the state of the art.

Who knows where we would be if MotoGP were still two-stroke? Certainly the current four-strokes are utterly reliant on their electronics. As it is, it seems that EFI has been chosen with the intention of improving fuel consumption and reducing emissions rather than as a route to higher performance.

COMPRESSION RATIO

It was not too long ago that the first thing a tuner would do would be to look for ways of raising the compression. This would range from simply removing the head gasket to turning or milling material from the head or cylinder face. The only limits to compression were the ratio at which the fuel would detonate and the point at which the piston would hit the head. Current thinking is much more complex. At the very basic level, more compression does not always mean more power. There is a point at which more compression reduces maximum revs and costs power. In practice, the optimum compression ratio will be around 11:1–12:1 for a race engine running on petrol. But what does that mean?

For a start, compression is normally measured by dividing the swept volume of the cylinder plus the combustion-chamber volume by the combustion-chamber volume alone. This is called the 'geometric compression ratio', but that is not much use to us here.

In a two-stroke, the cylinder swept volume is only measured from the point at which the exhaust port closes. This means that the actual compression ratio will be around half the geometric one, depending on the exhaust-port timing. Even this is not entirely accurate, since the cylinder pressure starts to rise immediately after BDC, and before the exhaust port closes (*see* Fig. 11.2). Back pressure from the exhaust accounts for this, whether from restrictions in the pipe or returning pressure waves in an expansion chamber. As a result, if the compression ratio is set to a reasonable value on the bench, the effective compression will adjust itself to a suitably higher value when the engine is running hard.

To find and set the compression

Fig. 11.8 Measuring the combustion-chamber volume.

is surrounded by a flat band cut at an angle and matched to that of the piston crown. The purpose of this is to allow the piston to approach very closely to the head at TDC, and for the fuel/air mixture to be forcibly squeezed, or 'squished', out of this outer band and towards the spark plug in the centre. This creates violent turbulence in the combustion chamber, which is intended to speed up the growth of the 'flame kernel' created between the plug electrodes by the spark.

It has been shown in both theory and practice, however, that if the squished gases are travelling too fast when they arrive at the plug, they can, in ordinary language, blow out the flame. A good general guideline is that the squish band should represent about 50 per cent of the total cross-sectional area of the head. In a 54mm bore, 125cc cylinder, a 50 per cent squish band would be 7.91mm wide.

A squish band with a width of 50 per cent of the bore is a good guideline. However, there is an even more

Fig. 11.9 Measuring the volume in the cylinder head.

ratio, you need to find the combustion-chamber volume. Honda's race manual defines combustion chamber volume as 'The volume of a fully assembled cylinder with the piston at TDC up to the top face of the plug hole.'

This definition takes account of the fact that in some engines there is a gap, called deck clearance, between the piston crown and the top face of the engine, and that in some engines, the piston actually stands a little proud of the head face at TDC.

Sometimes it is suggested that the head volume can be measured using the head alone, by laying a clear plastic sheet across the head face and filling the combustion chamber through a small hole in the plastic.

This method is best used when modifying the head, since it provides a means of measuring the amount that has been added to or removed from the head volume without having to assemble the engine every time. It does not necessarily tell you the com-

bustion-chamber volume in an assembled engine.

The first step is to ensure that the cylinder-head volume is correct for the compression ratio required. The second vital aspect is the squish band.

SQUISH

In a typical squish/dome head (*see* Fig. 11.10), the combustion chamber takes a half-dome shape, which minimizes the surface area for heat efficiency. It

Fig. 11.10 A typical squish/dome head.

CALCULATING THE SQUISH BAND SIZE

The full calculation for determining the squish band size is given here:

- The area of a circle is πr^2 (3.1417 multiplied by the square of the radius).
- The radius of the bore is $\frac{d}{2}$ = 27mm.
- So the area of the head is $27^2 \times \pi$ = 2,290mm^2.
- 50 per cent of 2,290 = 1,145. The squish band should have an area of 1,145mm^2.
- Therefore, the dome part of the head also has an area of 1,145mm^2.
- The radius of the dome part, r, $= \sqrt{\frac{1,145}{\pi}}$ = 19.09mm. Its diameter, therefore, is 38.18mm.
- The diameter of the bore is 54mm by definition. Subtract 38.18 from 54, and the difference in diameters is 15.82mm. The squish band is shared equally between two sides, so the width of the squish band is half of this, 7.91mm.

important measurement, the squish clearance.

Squish Clearance

The squish clearance is the distance between the piston crown and the squish band of the cylinder head when the piston is at TDC. For the squish effect to work, the squish clearance needs to be 1.5mm or less. However, there is a very strict limit on how small the clearance can be. It would be disastrous for the piston to hit the head, and there is always a little play in the main bearings, the big end and the small end. The crank can flex slightly, too, and there is even some stretch in the connecting rod. These tiny amounts of movement can all add up to nearly half a millimetre, even in an engine in good condition. If things are becoming worn, you can imagine the result!

A squish clearance of less than 0.55mm is dangerous, except on tiny model engines. For engines with cylinders up to 125cc, 0.80mm is a good basis for development. That would need to increase to 1.00–1.20mm for a 250cc cylinder and even more for 400 and 500cc cylinders.

Some tuners argue that the fuel that remains in the gap between the squish band of the head and the edge of the piston crown is cooled, or 'quenched', by the closeness of the cooler metal of the piston and head, forming trapped 'end gases' that waste fuel and thus power. Various gas-dynamic and chemical effects can cause end gases to explode instantaneously in the phenomenon called 'detonation', which creates shock waves that are powerful enough to knock specks of metal out of the piston and head. This is not unlike the damage caused by debris from a broken ring, except that the metal appears to have been eaten away, rather than battered to death.

Where detonation does occur, however, it is not the squish clearance itself that is the main problem. The source is always some other factor that raises the temperature in the engine. Typical culprits are too much restriction in the exhaust tailpipe, incorrect ignition timing and poor fuel quality.

MODIFYING THE CYLINDER HEAD

Previous chapters have mentioned the advantages of using an O-ring to seal the head face instead of the more common gasket. A useful modification to an older-style head is to have it converted to accept an O-ring. This is not a job that can be done with hand tools. On a round head, such as that used on the Aprilia (*see* Fig.11.11), the groove can be cut in a lathe, using a specially ground cutter. For the rectangular groove around the outside of a Yamaha TZ cylinder head, however, you would need a vertical milling machine with a very small-diameter end mill.

The ideal O-ring groove should have a square section, and be only 15 per cent shallower and slightly wider than the thickness of the rubber cord from which the ring is made. There are

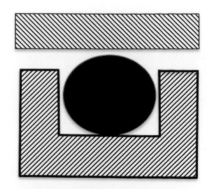

Fig. 11.12   O-ring in correctly-sized groove.

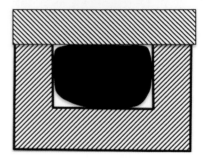

Fig. 11.13   O-ring when the joint is assembled correctly.

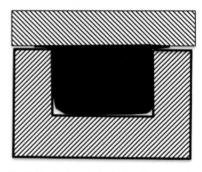

Fig. 11.14   O-ring pinched when the groove is too small.

tables of groove sizes to suit the different cord diameters available from the manufacturers, but those are the general guidelines. The worst thing that can happen is that the groove is too small and the rubber is squeezed out, becoming trapped in the sealing surface. The diagrams show how a properly fitted O-ring works and the problems caused if the groove is too small or too shallow, or if a sealant has been put into the groove first.

Changing Compression Ratio

Honda's handbook for their RS series of racers makes it clear that for the optimum performance, the combustion-chamber volume must be varied according to the air temperature and barometric pressure. In hot or low-

Fig. 11.11   Damage to the squish band – not caused by detonation.

pressure environments, the combustion chamber must be 0.3cc smaller and the ignition timing advanced by 1 degree. The clear implication is that there needs to be an easy way of changing the compression. Some of the old GP two-stroke 500 racers actually did have hydraulically variable compression, but it is more usual for competition engines to have changeable inserts that form the combustion chamber itself.

The Rotax engines are made that way, but there is a lot to be said for converting earlier engines to this style of cylinder head. (Not necessarily earlier, the first one that I saw with that design, not counting the Scott, was a Bultaco 125 racer from the 1970s.)

Insert-type cylinder heads are available for some models as aftermarket items, the Yamaha RDLC twins, for example. If you are spending time and effort in converting a head in this way, it is logical to add O-rings at the same time.

PORTING

It was not too long ago that there was a great deal of secrecy and mystique about porting. Each tuner had his secrets, and they were closely guarded – and just as widely copied. Tuning was often described as a 'black art'; in fact, it was the product of a lot of practical experience and a dash of inspiration. Very few people outside the universities and the works development teams carried out any basic research and development. These works engineers would present their research papers to professional bodies, such as the Society of Automotive Engineers. Mostly, the papers were too specialized and technical to have much influence outside academia. In 1971, however, two Yamaha race engineers, H. Naitoh and K. Nomura, described a method of quantifying the effectiveness of the ports of a two-stroke. In a paper titled *Some New Development Aspects of 2-Stroke Cycle Motorcycles*, they described the concept of 'specific time area'. This term is a measure that describes how wide, and for how long, a port opens relative to the cylinder size. It also takes account of the fact that a port is only fully open for part of the time. That line of thinking was

popularized by Gordon Jennings in his book, *The Two Stroke Tuner's Handbook*, first published in 1973. The book was the basis of a more scientific approach to port tuning.

Fig. 11.15   Honda RS125 head converted to a removable dome. Note the O-rings around the stud holes.

For the first time, you could work out the port area and timing that the inlet, transfer and exhaust ports needed to have to achieve the rpm that you were aiming for – or, conversely, the best

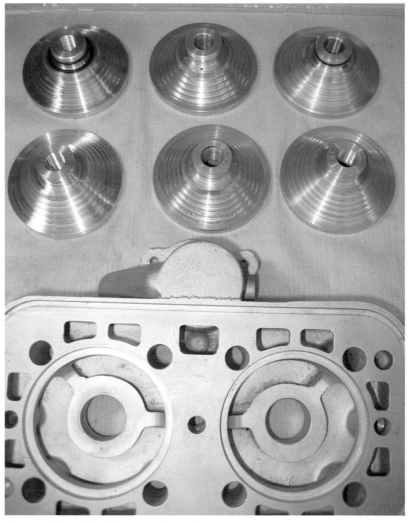

Fig. 11.16   A TZ350G head in process of conversion to insert type.

rpm that could be obtained with the ports in their current state. When this ability was combined with the availability of home computers, tuning started to become scientific.

The big step forward occurred at Queen's University in Belfast, where Professor Gordon Blair was working on what would become his world-changing book, *The Design and Simulation of Two Stroke Engines*. Before this, engine development had been built upon mechanical development and improvements in materials technology. Electronics had started to appear with the adoption of capacitor discharge ignitions (CDI), but now the focus shifted to computers and the speed at which they could perform calculations. Mathematical formulas to describe the flow of fluids, gas or liquid, had been devised and used since the 1920s, mostly by aircraft designers working on wing sections. The equations were complex, repetitive and restricted to analysis in two dimensions. By the 1960s, university computers were being used to do the calculations. The development of computers has allowed the investigation of fluid dynamics in three dimensions, giving rise to the current name for the topic, computational fluid dynamics (CFD). To cut a long story short, Professor Blair developed ways to adapt the complex equations of CFD to every stage of the gas flow through a two-stroke engine – from air filter to tailpipe. That meant that with full details of all the ports, spaces and passages inside an engine, a mathematical model of the engine could be generated in the computer. Having done that, the simulated engine could be run and the results printed out. Alterations in port size, timing or angle and compression or pipe design could be tried in the simulation, and the results assessed before anyone needed to cut any metal.

The number of calculations involved can be imagined by considering that the process begins by dividing the whole flow system into short cells, the 'mesh'. The physical geometry of each cell is defined, and from this the behaviour of the gas in the cell is calculated using three-dimensional equations. The output from the first cell then becomes the input for the next and so on, right through all the stages of the

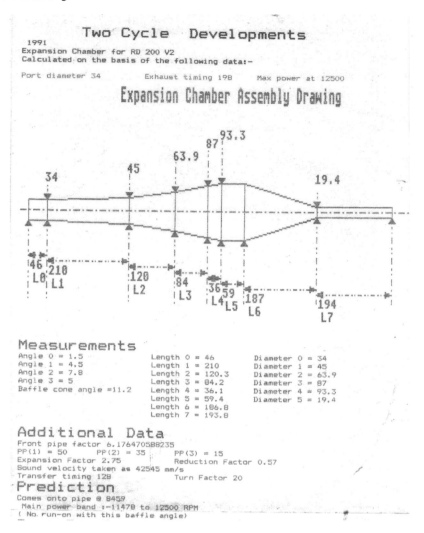

Fig. 11.17 Printout from pipe design program (note prediction).

flow during one revolution. The whole process is repeated several times, since, in a running engine, what happens in one revolution can affect what happens in the next, or in several subsequent revolutions for that matter, as a gas flow builds momentum, for example.

When this approach was first used, it required the computing resources of a major university. Nowadays, a decent desktop computer, or a modern laptop, will cope readily.

In fact, there were computer programs designed for optimizing a two-stroke before this. I wrote one myself in the late 1980s, and it was developed from an expansion chamber design program that had been devised originally for a Sinclair programmable calculator. More and more elaborate versions were run on a series of early home computers, and the final version, on an Atari ST 1040, included Jennings-inspired time area calculations and

power band prediction. It would also produce full-size plots of the pipe sections required to make up the curved front pipe.

Similar commercial programs are still available, *Dynomotion* being one example. It is also possible to obtain versions of Blair's own software to accompany his book; the development team behind the Aprilia RSW race bikes had their own advanced version of CFD software. Key team members still have it in retirement!

The software used by the majority of serious two-stroke developers these days comes from a South African expert who goes by the name of Vannik. The program is *EngMod2T*; there is an *EngMod4T* as well for the four-stroke community. It is not cheap, at around £270.00 in early 2015, but the cost is in line with that of the professional software used in other fields of work, such as CAD, accounting or music production.

Fig. 11.18 *New-style and older port shapes compared. The modified one has had the port built up with weld and then cleaned up. It will need an adaptor to blend the oval to round before the pipe itself.*

Exhaust Ports

The great value of using CFD engine-simulator programs is that ideas that may be completely counter-intuitive can be tested and may turn out to be very effective.

For example, in the 1980s, like most tuners, I would open out exhaust passages as far as practically possible. However, simulators show that in fact the exhaust passage should form a nozzle, with the outlet where it joins the exhaust front pipe being round with an area equal to 70 per cent of that of the total exhaust port(s). Having discovered this fact on the computer, I found that it worked on the

Fig. 11.20 *Triple port in standard Rotax 122.*

dynamometer and on the track, too. An extra refinement is based on the need to blend the auxiliary ports very gradually into the main exhaust duct – even if this means making an adaptor to allow the transition to the round profile at the pipe joint.

Small details of porting – such as the entry angle of the transfer ports, whether all ports should open to-gether or whether the two ports next to the exhaust port should open slightly earlier – can all be tried and the best combination incorporated into a port map. This can be used to create a laser-cut steel cylinder, which can be employed as a template to mark out the cylinder itself.

Another major discovery was the vital role played by the blowdown phase of the cycle. Blowdown is the period when the exhaust port is open, but the transfers are still closed. It lasts only around 15 degrees of crank rotation, or at 6,000rpm, under 0.4millisec.

At this time the pressure in the cylinder falls rapidly, but quicker is better, so instead of the oval or rectangular ports that we used to create in the 1980s, exhaust ports are a trapezium shape, much wider at the top. Sometimes the top of the exhaust port is widened so much that it becomes a T-shape, overlapping the transfer ports on either side.

Better still, there is a triple port, with an auxiliary port on either side of the upper part of the main port. A standard Aprilia 125 has triple ports; the race version has far bigger auxiliary ports.

It is generally accepted that the widest exhaust port that can support the

Fig. 11.21 *Bridged exhaust port.*

Fig. 11.22 *Trapezoid port overlaps transfers.*

Fig. 11.19 *Template made from port map.*

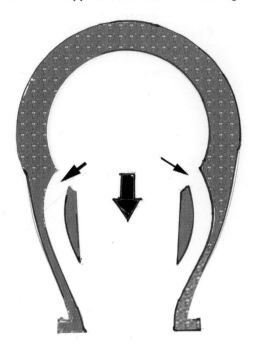

ABOVE: *Fig. 11.24   Boyeson ports in the reed cage.*

LEFT: *Fig. 11.23   Auxiliary ports should be radial.*

piston well enough to avoid having the piston ring bulging out and jamming against the top and bottom of the port is equal in width to 70 per cent of the bore. If the STA figures required show the need for a wider port than this, the port must have a bridge (*see* Fig. 11.21).

Of course, the bridge must then be 'relieved', ground back a little. This gives a little more clearance between the bridge and the piston, to cope with the fact that a bridge in the exhaust port becomes very hot and would otherwise bulge out into the cylinder and cause a seizure. Once again, the triple-port layout avoids that problem.

There is a further refinement with a triple-port layout. It is perfectly logical that as the hot exhaust gases expand to leave the cylinder through the exhaust ports, they will try to expand outwards from the centre of the cylinder, that is radially. The ideal exhaust port should allow the gases to follow their natural route, so in an ideal triple-port exhaust, the three port passages should follow a radial pattern, blending as gradually as possible into a single round port at the joint with the exhaust pipe.

Transfer ports

In Chapter 2, I introduced the idea that transfer ports needed to be in symmetrical pairs and perfectly matched. In those days, there were only two of them. As early as the 1950s, tuners would grind grooves into the cylinder wall to act as extra transfer ports. It was also common at the time to reduce the crankcase volume as much as possible to increase the crankcase compression to force as much fuel/air mixture as possible up the limited transfer ports. This was necessary because the trick of using the expansion chamber as a way of generating a wave of low pressure to 'pull' the mixture into the cylinder was not known.

Modern engine developers take the opposite approach, adding case volume by fitting spacers under the reed valve. Often they will open the transfer ports directly into the inlet port in what are called Boyeson ports. The exhaust's suction is good enough

TRANSFER PORTS

Honda's port map for an RS250 with a five-transfer arrangement is shown here (*see* Fig. 11.25). Note that the transfers adjacent to the exhaust port open earlier than the others. This is to start the fresh, cool, unburned mixture moving away from the exhaust port before the other ports join in. When transfer ports come this close to the exhaust, there is a danger of 'short circuiting' as the new mixture from the transfers just loops around and goes straight out of the exhaust. Sometimes this pair of ports is angled upwards by about 15 degrees. Sometimes the engine gives more power when they are not! Often it is the port opposite the exhaust that is angled upwards. The simulation program can predict the best approach for a particular engine – provided all the data on the engine layout are input accurately.

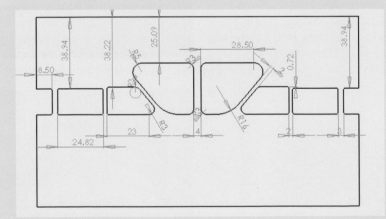

Fig. 11.25   The official port map for a Honda RS250.

to draw mixture directly from the inlet port, up through the transfers into the cylinder. It is also enough to keep the reed valve open for up to a full 360 degrees of crank rotation. These days, there are quite likely to be five, six or seven transfer ports.

THE EXHAUST PIPE

It would be easy to make this section as long as the rest of the book put together, but I shall try to keep it to the minimum. If you are interested in the origins of expansion-chamber exhausts again I refer you to *Stealing Speed* by Mat Oxley. If you want to see a graphic representation of an expansion chamber in action, there are many examples of animations online – try searching for 'expansion chamber GIF'.

The main thing that you need to understand is that each section of the exhaust pipe has its own function (*see* Fig. 11.26).

It is well known now that it is possible to design the exhaust pipe so that the pressure wave, which is launched along the pipe as the exhaust port opens, is reflected from the converging baffle cone. The length of the pipe is calculated so that the wave arrives back in time to force the excess unburned fuel/air mixture back into the cylinder just before the exhaust port closes. The animated diagrams on the Internet make this far clearer than a thousand words in print.

That is a very simplified version of what actually happens in an engine. For it to work well, there are other things to consider.

When you start to calculate the dimensions of a tuned pipe, the first thing to work out is the 'tuned length'. This is the distance that the pressure wave must travel between the time that the exhaust port opens and the

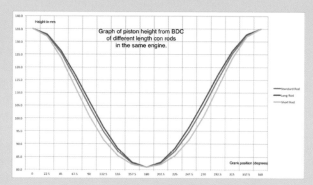

THE EFFECT OF CONNECTING ROD LENGTH

Fig. 11.27 Graph of the effect of connecting rod length on port timing.

The spreadsheet chart in Fig. 11.27 compares the distance from the piston height of a typical 54 × 54mm bore-and-stroke cylinder at every 22.5 degrees around one revolution of the crank. The blue line shows the piston height of an engine with a typical connecting-rod length of twice the stroke – 108mm. The red line represents the same engine with a much longer connecting rod; the green line assumes an unfeasibly short rod. All of these lines have been corrected so that they appear on the same scale, as if you had jacked-up or shortened the cylinder to suit the rod length. From the chart, you can see, for example, that at around 90 degrees after TDC, the piston following the green line is significantly further down the cylinder than the blue, and that the red, long-rod version is much higher still. In fact, the longer the rod, the later the exhaust and transfer ports open, relative to crank position – and the shorter the time they spend open. However, the long-rod version not only has a longer power stroke before the ports open, but also exerts a more direct push on the crank, so it increases the torque by reducing the side force on the moving parts.

All of this means that calculating the length of time that the ports are open must be based on the actual dimensions of the engine, including rod length.

time just before it closes. To find it, you need to know how long the exhaust port is open at the rpm when you want to get the most boost from the pipe, and how fast the pressure wave travels along a pipe.

Calculating Actual Port Open Duration

How long is the exhaust port open? It would be easy to imagine that while the engine is running, it turns regularly at a constant speed, and that the piston moves evenly up and down, but they do not. For a start, the crank clearly must accelerate during the power

stroke and slow down as the mixture is compressed. It is only the rotating mass of the crank wheels and the flywheel that keeps the engine turning during the compression stroke, and the lighter the rotating parts, the more the speed will vary during a single revolution of the crank.

Second, the piston is linked to the crank by the connecting rod. At TDC and BDC, the vertical distance between the gudgeon pin and the crank pin is equal to the length of the connecting rod. At every crank angle between TDC and BDC, however, the connecting rod is at an angle. If you remember your school geometry, the connecting rod then becomes the hypotenuse of a right-angled triangle, where the two other sides are the horizontal distance of the crank pin from the centre line of the cylinder, and the vertical distance between the crank pin and the gudgeon pin. That is Pythagoras' theorem. To find the vertical height of the piston above the crankshaft, you need to square the connecting rod length, subtract the square of the horizontal offset

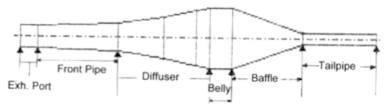

Expansion Chamber Assembly Drawing

Front Pipe — Diffuser — Belly — Baffle — Tailpipe
Exh. Port

Fig. 11.26   Naming of parts for expansion chamber.

of the crank pin at that crank angle (the sine of the crank angle in radians multiplied by half the stroke will give you that), and then calculate the square root of the result.

Complicated? Nevertheless, a machine can do it easily!

Calculating the Tuned Length

Once you know how long the exhaust port is open, you need to discover how far the pressure wave will travel in that time. The speed of sound in air is taken as 343.59m (1,127ft) per second. In fact, that is the speed of sound in air at 20°C at sea level. It is not constant, however, varying with pressure, temperature and the density of the material through which the sound is passing. In water, the speed of sound is nearly 1,500m/s (4,900ft/s); in solid brass, it is 4,700m/s (15,420ft/s)! Exhaust gas is denser than air, and hotter, so the average figure that was taken as a basis for exhaust pipe calculations was 425.45m/s (1,395.83ft/s), or 42,545cm/s. It is a basis only; the exhaust-gas temperature varies according to ignition timing, carburettor settings and of course, rpm. Fortunately, this is a good thing, because it allows the pipe to adjust itself over a reasonable range of conditions to give a broader power band than might be expected. Assuming the pressure wave travels at 42,545mm in one second, and that an engine with its exhaust port that opens for 180 degrees is running at 6,000rpm, the exhaust port is open for 0.005sec (5millisec). In that time, an exhaust pressure wave will travel 2,127.75cm (42,545 × 0.005).

The pressure wave must travel from the piston face to the reflection point in the baffle cone and back, so the 'tuned length' of the pipe is 1,063.6mm.

If you think about it, though, that length represents the pipe that, at 6,000rpm, would return the pressure wave just as the exhaust port closes. A little earlier would actually be better. Later would be useless.

The Front Pipe

The front pipe performs two functions. First, it positions the diffuser at the right distance from the port to set the timing of the negative pressure wave correctly. Second, it provides a confined and controlled space for the unburned mixture that enters the pipe at the later stages of the exhaust stroke. This unburned mixture must be kept together and not allowed to mix with the burned gases. Confining it in a relatively narrow pipe achieves this. It is important to understand that two things are happening at the same time: there is a physical flow of a large amount of exhaust gas along it (called the mass flow); and there are pressure waves that pass along the gas as it flows through the pipe.

Anything that restricts the mass flow will create backpressure, making it more difficult to get new mixture into the cylinder. Keeping the first 100mm (4in) or so of the pipe straight and designing the front pipe with a gentle taper, to allow the gas to expand gently, help with this. Its overall length needs to be enough to contain the over-scavenged, unburned fuel/air mix so that the returning positive pressure wave can push it back into the cylinder.

The Diffuser

Anywhere that the bore of the exhaust changes in size significantly there will be a drop in pressure, and where there is a change of pressure, that change will diffuse along the pipe in both directions. It occurs because gases are effectively springy. The pressure in the pipe behaves like a spring that is loaded with a mass. Lift the mass and drop it, and the spring does not just return to its resting length; it stretches further, then bounces back up, rebounding past the neutral point again. It will continue to bounce, or oscillate, several times. This means that when the pressure drops as the pipe becomes suddenly wider, it drops too far. Gas then flows into the low-pressure area, lowering the pressure in the regions on either side. Thus the low-pressure wave moves along the pipe.

Old-fashioned horn gramophones and musical wind instruments rely on the phenomenon of the 'exponential horn': a tube that becomes wider at an increasing rate along its length can actually increase the volume of a sound wave passing through it. This can be exploited in the design of the diffuser.

Fig. 11.28   Chart showing an exponential horn curve.

In a three stage diffuser (*see* Fig. 11.26), the front pipe expands at an angle of 1.5 degrees, the first stage expands at 4.5 degrees and the second at 8 degrees. This approximates an exponential horn and amplifies the pressure wave. The third stage is only 5 degrees, since there was a limit in the diameter of the pipe that could be fitted to the bike, an RD200 twin. At some stage, as the pressure wave created by the exhaust port opening passes through the diffuser, it will reach a place where its pressure has dropped below the backpressure in the pipe. At this point, a negative, low-pressure, wave will be generated, and as described, this low-pressure wave will diffuse backwards towards the open exhaust port. If this negative wave arrives just after BDC, it will drop the pressure in the cylinder and draw new mixture up through the transfers.

The Belly

The main purpose of the belly it to set the baffle at the right distance from the piston to give the correct tuned length. However, the volume of the entire chamber has a large effect on the backpressure. This is the origin of the common saying, 'You always know when you have got the exhaust pipe design right when it is too big to fit on the bike.'

The Baffle Cone

If the baffle cone were replaced by a flat plate with a hole, the pressure wave would bounce back when it hit the plate. With a cone, the wave comes up against the point at which its pressure is exceeded by the backpressure and turns back. If the cone has a shallow taper, as the amount of exhaust gas increases as the engine runs harder and faster, this pressure point moves forwards into the larger part of the cone. Effectively the pipe becomes shorter – just what is needed as the revs rise. The steeper the cone angle, the less movement of the pressure point. Accordingly, a shallow-angle cone, 8 or 9 degrees, will continue to work at over the designed rpm; it allows the engine to over-rev. A steeper angle, over 10 degrees, will produce a stronger return wave, but there will be very little over-rev.

The Tailpipe

US practice is to call this the 'stinger'. Its main job is to regulate the backpressure. Too small, especially when it is also too long, increases backpressure and pipe temperature to the extent that it is a common cause of melted pistons. Too large, and the pipe does not work efficiently. The modern approach is to fit a venturi, or nozzle, to the point at which the tailpipe joins the baffle. This sets the critical size for the diameter and allows the rest of the pipe to be big enough to be safe. This is important when the tailpipe is long to allow the use of a high-level silencer. It is even possible to have a set of replaceable graduated nozzles so that the backpressure can be tailored to atmospheric conditions.

The Silencer

Silencers are a requirement in the modern world. Unless the silencer is to be considered as part of the tailpipe, it should have in internal bore size that is big enough to fit over the outer diameter of the tailpipe.

THE IGNITION

Half of the bikes in this book were sparked by fixed timing systems using mechanical contact points, but since the 1980s, self-energizing CDI ignitions have become standard. A CDI is a circuit containing a large capacitor that stores an electrical charge drawn from the stator coils of the generator. An extra trigger coil, which senses the position of a boss on the flywheel, sends a signal to an electronic switch that directs the charge, all in one burst, to the ignition coil. The coil steps up the voltage and fires the plug.

Since the electronic switch is triggered by a set voltage level, and since the voltage generated by the trigger coil is proportional to rpm, a CDI gives a slight natural advance curve. In other words, the ignition occurs sooner when the engine is running faster. This is better than a fixed system, but it is not what is really needed.

The speed at which the flame spreads from the spark between the electrodes of the plug depends on the pressure of the gases in the combustion chamber. The combustion-chamber pressure is highest at the rpm at which the engine is producing the most torque, so ideally the ignition should retard a little at this speed. It is possible to insert speed-sensitive delay circuits into the trigger mechanism, such as a resistor or an extra trigger coil. Sometimes it is useful to retard the ignition when the engine is running below its peak rpm on wide throttle openings, or to increase exhaust-gas temperature to bring the pipe into tune sooner. The same response is useful if the engine starts to detonate the mixture.

To do all this, the ignition system needs to be designed with more data inputs, not just rpm, but also throttle position, exhaust temperature, detonation sensors and more. It may also need other outputs, to control a powervalve, for example, run a traction control device or record engine data. This is going too far for an analogue system, so now the CDI box has been replaced by a digital engine control unit (ECU). Digital ignition allows the tuner to program the ignition curve and the outputs.

A STEP-BY-STEP GUIDE?

A detailed step-by-step tuning guide, even for the handful of bikes described in previous chapters, would need a book many times the size of this one. As I type this, much of the bookshelf behind me is taken up by books on two-stroke tuning. None of those books was written about the procedures of the computer age, however, and in the twenty-first century the method for seriously enhancing the performance of an engine is quite different.

THE IDEAL POWER CURVE

Many a young rider has 'tuned' his engine according to teenage folklore – bigger main jets, removing exhaust baffles and air cleaner, fitting a 'hot' plug and such. The engine may then demonstrate an exciting power band, in that when it reaches a certain rpm, it will accelerate rapidly. In fact, what they have produced is a hole in the mid-rpm range. It might be excitingly difficult to ride, but a more linear power curve would be faster and result in fewer visits to the A&E department.

Fig. 11.29   Chart comparing power curves.

A much simplified (and synthesized) dynamometer sheet in shown in Fig. 11.29. The blue line is the torque curve. It is a graph of the actual turning force produced by each firing stroke. You will notice that at high rpm, the force of each stroke falls, although power still increases. This indicates that the engine is starting to reach the speed at which the ports are unable to flow any more gas. The force is less, but it is occurring more often, so the engine still produces more power, up to the point at which the gas flow, and thus the torque, is not sufficient to turn the engine any faster.

The red line is an exaggerated version of a 'teen tuned' power curve. It might be an engine with the powervalve jammed open. The black line is an ideal power curve. The engine will feel milder, more controllable, but you will note that at any useable speed, it is actually showing more power than the red line.

This is the time to experiment with ignition curves, powervalve opening and closing speeds, reed-valve specifications and carburettor size.

Fig. 11.30   CAD drawing of port shapes in 3D.

If you intend doing this sort of work at a level beyond that of a small-scale hobbyist, you should obtain and learn to use CFD software. You will almost certainly need to get in contact with fellow users on the Internet forums. The best of these are closed forums, but many of the users are also on Facebook, LinkedIn, etc. If you can establish your credentials as a serious tuner, you will be invited to join the forums where the other serious tuners hang out. You will find that many of the engines that are most likely to be tuned have already been fully analysed, and that forum members will be willing to share the data packs. If your project is a one-off, the best advice would be to look for someone who does use the software to do the analysis for you.

Practice 'tuning' the simulated engines in the software. Watch and carefully analyse the pressure graphs and power and torque curves of your experimental 'engines'. The interpretation of power curves needs some thought.

When you have reached the design you need, you are nearly halfway there. The next step is to learn computer drafting. A CAD program will allow you to design and see on screen the actual ports that your engine will need. Simi-

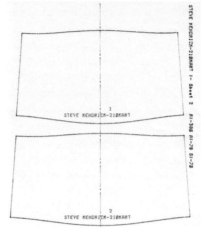

Fig. 11.31   This is a CAD printout of templates for a curved and tapered pipe.

lar programs will turn a drawing of an exhaust pipe into flat sections for rolling and welding up.

Now is the time to get out your tools. Milling and turning, filing and grinding, all the old skills will be needed and all with the aim of making your engine exactly like the ideal example on the computer.

If you are serious about this, quite recently manufacturing has begun to be democratized, too. It is now possible for a CAD design to be input to a 3D printer that will produce the cores and moulds for a new cast cylinder. CNC machinery will bore it to size, do any other machining and plate the bore, and you will be ready to go.

A friend recently made an enquiry about exactly this service for three cylinders. The quantity was based on experience of ordering similar conventionally cast cylinders and the budget to which they were working. The new company responded, 'Why three? We can do twenty-four at a time and the price is the same for twenty-four.'

In the near future, it may be possible to produce entire engines by 3D printing.

In the twenty-first century, you start your tuning on the computer.

Fig. 11.32   A 2015 125cc racer ridden in the British Superbike series.

caring for your two-stroke

In the previous chapters we have looked at the process of stripping and rebuilding typical examples of two-strokes from different eras, but even when you own a race bike, that is not something you need to do every day – or even every week.

So this is an attempt to draw some general conclusions on the routine of maintenance and diagnosis that a two-stroke owner needs to be aware of.

LUBRICATION

The two-stroke cycle, with combustion occurring every 360 degrees, places a lot of heat stress on the cylinder and piston assembly: without adequate lubrication it would not survive for long. The big end, the small end and the main bearings also rely on oil that arrives in the engine along with the fuel. So the top priority on the maintenance list is to make sure that there is enough oil getting to the engine.

PRE-MIX

Early two-strokes were mostly lubricated by mixing oil with the petrol. Chapter 10 illustrates the fact that competition machines still tend to rely on pre-mix petroil mixture, on the basis that it is reliable – nothing can go break or go wrong. There is a lot of mythology about the ratio of oil to petrol in the mix.

Luckily there is a lot of science too, so the myths can be dismissed. The first scientific fact is that lubricating oil is also a fuel. When the engine is warmed up and running under load, the oil burns along with the petrol. Castor-based two-stroke oil actually has an energy content rather higher than petrol, and as it decomposes in the combustion chamber it even releases oxygen into the reaction too. Even synthetic oils add energy. Older riders will remember the spiralling plumes of smoke from the back of Ariel Arrows or

Leaders as they accelerated away from a start. The smoke was unburned oil. If you had seen the bike a few miles up the road, the engine would have been warm and the exhaust would be clear. You never saw smoke from the exhaust of any of the two-stroke 500cc Grand Prix bikes. So you do not get more power by cutting the fuel/oil mix. Tests on the dynamometer show repeatedly and conclusively that up until the point at which there is so much oil that the spark will not ignite the mixture, the more oil you add, the more power you get.

The other common myth is that you have to change the jetting every

time you change the fuel/oil ratio. The calculations for the viscosity of a mixture of liquids of different viscosities are complex, but common sense should tell you that unless you are going to make a really radical change to the ratio, from 100:1 to 12:1 for a very unlikely example, you would not change the overall viscosity enough to need re-jetting. There has been discussion on internet forums suggesting that if the bike is running on 50:1, and you increase the oil to give you a 32:1 ratio, the 'reduced amount of fuel' will mean that the engine will run weak and seize. This makes no sense. It contradicts existing research, ignores the

Fig 12.1   Pre-mix.

Fig. 12.2   Autolube pump.

fact that oil is fuel, and discounts that fact that the difference is very small. For example, using round numbers, 4.5ltr (1 gallon) of fuel needs 90ml of oil to give a ratio of 50:1. To change that to 32:1, you would need to add another 40ml of oil. That's just over two table-spoons in a gallon. The difference in viscosity would be too small to measure outside a laboratory.

The type of oil is important, too. Mineral oils, vegetable oils and synthetic oils are all available, and many two-stroke oils on the market are blends of two or more of those.

The general rule is that the more high-revving an engine is, and the longer time it spends on full throttle, the more oil it needs. For example a single cylinder 500cc motocross bike will be fine and provide good power with a 50:1 ratio, because of the slower rpm. A much higher-rpm 125cc motocross motor will need a 32:1 ratio to provide the best power and protection for the engine. However, a 125cc engine used in a go-kart or road racer will require from 20:1 to 24:1. A 125cc trials bike would work fine with a 100:1, providing a high quality two-stroke was used. The brand or type of oil, or the fact that there is smoke or black stuff dribbling

out of the exhaust pipe, has very little or nothing to do with the fuel/oil ratio that should be used.

Incidentally, the days when every petrol station had a two-stroke pump on the forecourt are long gone, so it was good to see at a recent show that it is possible to buy a plastic sachet containing 100ml of two-stroke oil. That makes it easy to carry enough oil with you in case you need to refuel while away from home. My own 350 YPVS hybrid, which runs on premix, carries a bottle under the seat that holds 250ml of oil, which is enough for eight litres of petrol at the 32:1 ratio that I prefer.

AUTOLUBE

From the very beginning (around 1913!), but more significantly in recent years, designers have tried to free owners from the oily chore of pre-mix by adding an oil tank and pump to force a measured amount of oil into the engine. I don't remember whether it was Suzuki's or Yamaha's marketing team who first labelled it 'Autolube'.

The engine drives the pump, so the speed of the pump depends on engine revs. The stroke of the pump varies according the throttle opening,

so that the amount of oil delivered by each stroke of the pump is greater when the throttle is open. That is why there is always a set-up procedure to ensure that the position of the pump corresponds exactly with that of the throttle. The one disadvantage of the autolube system is that if any part of it fails, whether the drive gear, the cable or the pipework, the engine is starved of oil. That is why you need to check that everything is as it should be regularly.

However, that is not the main way that an autolube system can wreck an engine – that requires the co-operation of the rider. You must always check that there is oil in the tank. A mechanic friend told me of a young rider who had seized his Aprilia 125 three times, requiring a new cylinder and piston each time. This occurred because when the oil level warning light came on the first time, he claimed he did not know what it meant. The second and third times he ignored it because he assumed it was stuck on.

A final thought on the topic of engine lubrication. Whether you are using pre-mix or autolube, just consider that when the throttle is closed, there is very little lubrication getting to the engine. Taking the time to free the clutch and give a blip of the throttle every now and then if you are riding down a long descent is a good idea.

After that, don't forget the gearbox. If your experience is of four strokes, you are used to engines where there is just one place where the oil goes. Most modern engine units share the same oil between the primary drive, the clutch and the gearbox. Also, there are some oils that contain friction reduction additives such as molybdenum disulphide, which are not compatible with motorcycle clutches that operate in a bath of oil. You can find details of the recommended brands on Internet forums.

IGNITION

It is well known that if an engine stops on a run, or will not start, the first thing to do is to check for a spark. Take out the spark plug, fit it back to the HT lead, and rest it on a clean (preferably unpainted) metallic part of the engine. Turn the engine over and look to see if there is a spark between the electrodes of the plug. You may not see the spark in bright sunlight, so don't give up yet if it does not seem to be sparking. If there is no spark, the next simplest step is to try a different plug. If you do not have one available, unscrew the plug cap from the lead and hold the end of the lead – holding it more than an inch (25mm) away from the end – about 5mm from the engine and see if you get a spark from the end of the lead. If this works, the most likely suspects are the plug itself or the plug cap.

Spark Plugs

Often, a plug can be fouled with oil from unburned fuel, and impurities in the deposits are conductive. This allows the HT current to track down the spark plug insulator to earth instead of jumping the plug gap, so no spark. It is worth trying to clean the insulator with a stiff brush. Traditionally a wire brush is used, but in fact, that can leave traces of the wire on the insulator, spoiling it for good. It has always seemed to me that once a plug has fouled badly, it never works properly again. The other point to consider is that many twin-cylinder engines connect the spark

plugs in series, so that they both spark at the same time, every time. You can tell if this is the case if the coil has HT leads coming from each end. It does mean that the plugs spark at BDC as well at TDC, which is why it's called an 'idle spark' system. It also means that if one plug fails, producing an open circuit, the other one will not spark either. It has a more subtle effect too. In one plug the spark jumps from the centre electrode to the side one. In the other plug the spark jumps from the side electrode to the centre. The reason this is important is because, as the spark jumps, it takes a few molecules of the electrode with it. The side electrode is thinner and hotter and so it gets eroded away more quickly.

Check the spark gaps regularly, and examine the electrodes (a magnifying glass is helpful). You are looking for clean metal and sharp edges. Sharp edges concentrate the electrical potential and allow the spark to jump more easily.

If there is no spark from the wire, the next step is to trace the HT lead back to the coil. There is no simple way to test whether a coil is functioning in the field, but manufacturer's data should contain resistance values for the primary and secondary windings. Typically, the primary coil, the low-tension side, will have a resistance of around 3.5Ω (Ohms), if it's a 12V system, or 1.5Ω if it's a 6V system. The secondary windings, measured between the HT lead and earth will be around $14,000\Omega$, often stated as $14k\Omega$. Remember that many plug caps incorporate resistors to cut down radio interference, so if you are measuring the resistance including the plug cap, the reading will be approximately $5k\Omega$ greater.

Fig. 12.3   Identification numbers on a BR9HS plug.

Fig. 12.4   Plug with a standard 2.5mm electrode.

The other thing to note is that with some plugs, there is a resistor built into the plug itself. NGK plugs that incorporate the resistor add an 'R' to the plug identification number. For example, an NGK B8ES is a non-resistor type, the same plug with a resistor is coded BR8ES. The B indicates a 14mm thread; the number is the heat range. The E indicates the 'reach' – the length of the threaded portion. In motorcycle terms E means 19mm or long reach. A short reach, 12mm, plug uses a letter H after the number to indicate the fact.

The S shows that the plug has a standard 2.5mm centre electrode. If the plug is marked G, or VG, that indicates a thinner, gold/palladium centre electrode.

There seems to be a lot of misunderstanding on the role of heat range. The correct heat range for an engine and riding style combination is found by avoiding the two extremes. In order to reduce the confusion, I always talk of 'soft' plugs, with a low number, and 'hard' plugs meaning those with a high heat range number. The actual number refers to the length of the heat path from the plug electrodes to the cooler engine block. The extremes are having a hard plug that runs too cool and fouls with oil and unburned fuel, and at the other extreme, having a soft plug that gets so hot that the transferred heat burns away the crown of the piston. The correct plug for your bike and the way you ride lies between the extremes. So you don't make an engine more powerful by fitting a higher heat range (harder) plug. All you do is make it more likely that the plug will oil up and refuse to start the bike. A 10 heat range plug will not improve a 50cc scooter. Nor will the

Fig. 12.5   *EGV plug with fine gold-palladium electrode.*

Electronic Ignition

The great thing about electronic ignition is the fact that it requires very little maintenance. Even on very high-mileage bikes, the only real maintenance tasks that occur more than once or are to clean the multi-way connectors that connect the various components. If there is a failure, it is nearly always an entire unit that has failed, and the only remedy is replacement. There are some components, however, that are standard electronic components. A zener diode is a zener diode not a BSA or Greeves one, a bridge rectifier is a bridge rectifier, and I have been successful using a single phase Honda regulator rectifier allowing a two-stroke Mercury outboard motor to charge a boat battery.

CARBURETTOR JETTING

As explained in an earlier chapter, the job of the carburettor is to mix fuel with air in the correct ratio. This is called the stoichiometric mixture. The measuring and mixing is done by metering air and fuel through carefully designed jets and passages. It is therefore vital to keep all these clean and clear. The main way of achieving this is to blow through the jets and airways. A compressor and blowgun is ideal for the job, if you have one. Blowing by mouth works, but far better is to use a can of 'canned air'. It is mostly sold to clean computers and electronic devices.

piston last very long if you fit a 6 heat range plug to a 125 race bike.

Ignition Contact Points

On older machines with points ignition, the condition of the points themselves is a matter to be placed on the checking a maintenance list. Just as the spark at the plug transfers metal from one electrode to the other, the same thing happens to the contact points. When the points are closed, an electric current flows between them and through the primary windings of the coil. When the points open, the collapse of the magnetic field generated by the coil not only induces the high tension that the spark plug needs in the secondary windings, but also generates a voltage in the primary coil. This voltage is enough to cause a spark at the contact points. The job of the capacitor (this used to be called a condenser) is to absorb this generated voltage. If there is a problem with the capacitor, there will be big sparks at the contact points and the points themselves will quickly form a hollow in one contact and a peak on the other, as one side erodes away and the other builds up. This will make the opening and closing time of the points very uncertain and variable. It is vital that the points open and rapidly to create a rapid collapse of the magnetic field in the coil, and generate the

maximum spark. They must also close quickly and fully to give the magnetic field the maximum time to build up first.

The faces of the contact points need to be flat, perfectly aligned and parallel. A fine file will dress the points if they are slightly worn, but replacement is a regular chore.

It is important to keep in mind that the contact point gap does effect the ignition timing, especially in engines where there is no other way to set it to the correct value. Details of ignition timing are described in the individual chapters.

Fig. 12.6   *RG500 GP carb, showing the main jet.*

The process of setting the jetting these days tends to be done using exhaust gas temperature testers, oxygen sensors, detonation sensors and a dynamometer. The old-fashioned way is to start by doing a plug chop, and it still works. To do a plug chop, you need somewhere where the bike can be run, or the engine can be run under load, flat out for more than about twenty seconds. At the end of that time, cut the ignition and shut the throttle. Remove the plug (it will be hot!) and examine it carefully. The basic information comes from the colour of the ceramic insulation. An engine running lean, with the main jet too small, will give an insulator colour that is white. If the engine is running rich, the main jet is too big and the insulator will be black, or very dark. The correct size

Fig. 12.8   The back of the needle jet is cut away here.

main jet produces an insulator colour similar to that of a digestive biscuit – darker than a custard cream, lighter than a bourbon cream.

Have a closer look with a magnifying glass. If you can see light-coloured specks on the insulator, this is bad news: it indicates that detonation is eroding the piston crown. If you are familiar with the phenomenon of detonation, you have my sympathy, but you should have noticed and recognized a harshness and metallic quality to the engine note during the run. Previous chapters mention various approaches to solving the problem of detonation.

A plug chop will allow you to get a good estimation of the correct size for the main jet, which is a start. To set the mid-throttle jetting, the tapered needle that passes through the throttle slide allows you to adjust the mixture at part throttle by raising to the needle to enrich it or lowering it to lean the mixture out. On an old Villiers carb, you can do this by a handlebar lever while you ride, while on the later one there is a screw inside the slide. Most carbs have a series of notches in the top of the needle with a moveable clip. With

the clip in the lowest notch, the part throttle mixture is at its richest, and vice versa. Sometimes there is a need for more radical changes, and in this case both the needle can be changed for one with a different taper, as can the needle jet that it fits into.

An engine that blubbers and four-strokes at part throttle, but will clear if the throttle is opened further, is a sign that the jet is supplying too rich a mixture. A needle setting that is too lean will give the feeling that the engine is hesitating, as if running out of fuel, when the throttle is part open.

The final stage of carb setting is to set both the tickover speed and tickover mixture with the adjusters for the throttle stop and air screw, respectively. It is worth pointing out that on some carbs the tickover mixture screw controls the flow of air while on others it controls the flow of fuel. Without checking the specifications, you cannot guarantee as you turn the screw whether you are enriching or leaning out the tickover mixture. Either way, the general advice is to set the mixture screw at two and a half turns out from fully screwed in.

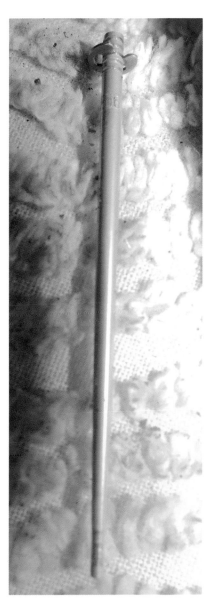

Fig. 12.7   The clip in the middle groove is usual.

Fig. 12.9   *The mixture screw controls the air passage here.*

RECOGNIZING SIGNS OF TROUBLE

Throughout the previous chapters of this book, there have been references to the signs and symptoms that indicate wear, or damage to the components inside. In an ideal world it would be wonderful to include sound clips, video clips, smells, and physical feedback samples in a book. That way it would be possible to share a long experience of what an engine suffering from small end damage sounds and feels like. It would be easy to learn how to know the difference between 'piston slap', pre-ignition and detonation, for example. Current technology will not cope with this, and description of multi-sensory phenomena are not really adequate, so until virtual reality publishing becomes a reality, a novice in the two-stroke world needs to rely on the help of a group of experienced and well-informed friends and acquaintances. Be choosy about the Internet forums you use and even choosier about whom you believe. Are the members worth trusting? Are they actually working in development? What have they done and who have they worked with or learned from? With a few precautions, the Internet gives you access to shared information that previous generations could only have dreamed of.

The truth is out there, amongst the nonsense!

afterword

Throughout this book, there has been a sense that we are at the end of an era, that A.M. Low's two-stroke future has been and gone. More recently, however, I have begun to feel that this is not so. People are developing two-strokes again. The Freetech 50 racing movement is allowing people to build and race machines once more without the restrictions that the Dorna organization has imposed on the GP series.

There is a 'Keep Two-strokes Alive' series for 250 and 350 bikes. All the successful trials bike manufacturers use advanced two-strokes, and in motocross the four-stroke takeover is by no means complete. Some excellent and very powerful single-cylinder engines are being produced in Spain and Italy for use in karting.

The news that, finally, it has been recognized that diesel-engine vehicles are more polluting than governments were led to believe may just revive the chances of the compact and clean running two-stroke power units that have been proposed in the last twenty years.

Perhaps the two-stroke is still 'the coming form of the internal-combustion engine' after all.

Let's hope so.

Many TZs were installed in special frames to improve handling.

RELATED TITLES FROM CROWOOD

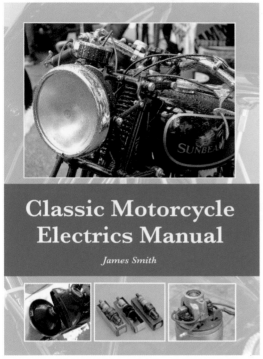

Classic Motorcycle Electrics Manual
JAMES SMITH
ISBN 978 1 84797 995 7
272pp, 590 illustrations

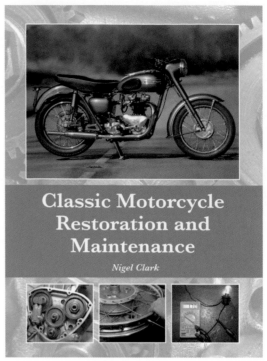

Classic Motorcycle Restoration
and Maintenance
NIGEL CLARK
ISBN 978 1 84797 881 3
272pp, 820 illustrations

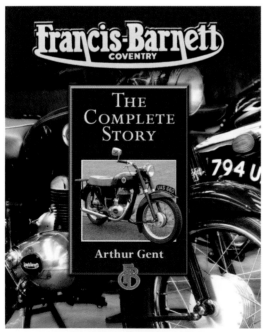

Francis-Barnett – The Complete Story
ARTHUR GENT
ISBN 978 1 84797 426 0
208pp, 240 illustrations

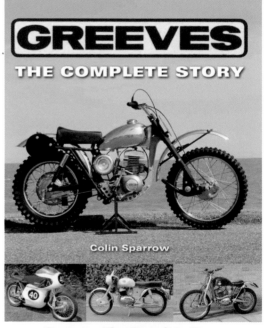

Greeves – The Complete Story
COLIN SPARROW
ISBN 978 1 84797 741 0
224pp, 300 illustrations

In case of difficulty ordering, please contact the Sales Office:

The Crowood Press, Ramsbury, Wiltshire SN8 2HR UK

Tel: 44 (0) 1672 520320   enquiries@crowood.com   www.crowood.com